HOW AMERICA GOT IT RIGHT

★ ★ ★

HOW AMERICA GOT IT RIGHT

THE U.S. MARCH TO MILITARY AND POLITICAL SUPREMACY

★ ★ ★

BEVIN ALEXANDER

CROWN
FORUM
NEW YORK

Published in the United States by Crown Forum,
an imprint of the Crown Publishing Group,
a division of Random House, Inc., New York
www.crownpublishing.com

Crown Forum and the Crown Forum colophon are trademarks
of Random House, Inc.

Library of Congress Cataloging-in-Publication Data

Alexander, Bevin.
How America got it right : the U.S. march to military and
political supremacy / Bevin Alexander.—1st ed.
p.   cm.
Includes bibliographical references and index.
1. United States—Foreign relations.   2. United States—Military policy.   3. United
States—Territorial expansion.   4. National characteristics, American.   I. Title.
E183.7.A44 2005   327.73′009—dc22   2005003662
ISBN 1-4000-5288-2

Printed in the United States of America

Design by Joseph Rutt

10 9 8 7 6 5 4 3 2 1

First Edition

In loving memory of Peggy Bailey Alexander (1928–2004),
who shared a boundless love for our three sons,
and who never ceased from mental fight
to build a better world

CONTENTS

HOW AMERICA GOT IT RIGHT

★ ★ ★

INTRODUCTION

★ ★ ★

GETTING IT RIGHT

The easiest way to get a handle on the worldview of Americans is to realize that we think of ourselves as inhabiting an island. We saw in our earliest days that the Western Hemisphere sat isolated in the midst of two vast oceans, and that these oceans both separated us from the rest of the world and protected us from the rest of the world.

We have consistently sought *not* to share this island with competing world powers. Americans have been resolute to prevent in the Western Hemisphere a replication of the eternally warring and competing great powers of Europe.

The concept of America as an island explains virtually all of American history. It explains why we turned our back on Europe for the first century and a quarter of our independence in order to conquer and populate the most important and favored part of this island, and to eliminate any threat to it from the north or the south. It explains why—although weak, newly independent, and lightly populated—we laid out the Monroe Doctrine in 1823 to close off colonization or interference in the Western Hemisphere, thereby preventing any world power from challenging us on our island. It explains why, at times when we were disillusioned with or distrustful of Europe, we isolated ourselves behind our oceanic moat—as we did after World War I when, in despair at Europe's greed and bickering, we refused to join the League of Nations, and as we did briefly in 1940 when France fell and we feared

Britain was going to fall to Nazi Germany. It explains why, after we were attacked at Pearl Harbor on December 7, 1941, we developed overwhelming military power and, over the following years, went across our oceans and methodically destroyed the enemies threatening our island. It explains why we were willing to risk nuclear war in 1962 when the Soviet Union placed missiles in Cuba and jeopardized not only the United States but also the safety of the hemisphere. It also explains why, after suffering a direct attack on our island on September 11, 2001, we are today repeating the process of World War II, going wherever we have to in the world to destroy those who threaten our island.

The steadfast resolve to protect our island lies at the heart of all our dreams and aspirations as a people and defines everything the United States has been, is, and hopes to be.

We saw early in our colonial history that—because of our isolation from Europe, and because of the immense wealth and bounty of our land—we had the opportunity to build the greatest, freest, and most prosperous nation ever to arise on earth. We spent the first century and a quarter of our independent existence in creating this great nation. But to protect this treasure, we found that we needed to establish the world's paramount military structure and become the world's preeminent political power. This book is the story of America's march to economic, military, and political supremacy, and the ideals that have guided us along the way.

As will be seen, we have made the right decisions in the vast majority of cases throughout our history, choosing democracy over plutocracy, equality over privilege, liberty over oppression, and the prosperity of the many over the greed of the few.

We have not always been consistent. For a while early in our history we listened to Alexander Hamilton, who tried to sacrifice the interests of ordinary people to the avarice of the wealthy.[1] We had a huge blind spot about slavery and allowed that iniquity to continue and to throw us into a bitter fraternal conflict. We withdrew into isolationism between the two world wars and allowed dictators to attack innocent peoples. We fought against what we thought was the spread of Communism in Vietnam when we were actually taking sides in a civil war.

We have made other mistakes. But our lapses have been infrequent, and our intentions have almost always been good.

This inclination to do right has been virtually unique among the nations of the world, and for this reason we have been often misunderstood. How could a country so rich and successful be so unselfish and caring? We *must* have darker motives, critics say. We *must* be seeking to create an empire, to dominate everyone else, to grab the oil or the trade or whatever else for our own selfish purposes. People from more grasping, less-idealistic societies find it impossible to accept that we honestly believe that giving everyone opportunity is the recipe for abundance and happiness everywhere, not merely in the favored reaches of the United States of America. We honestly believe that securing other people's freedom is the best guarantee that we can keep our own. We do not *want* to dominate the world. We want to live our lives in peace, and we hope other peoples will do the same. We go out into the world to redress errors, to stop unacceptable behavior, to challenge threats to our island and our liberty. When we have settled the problem, we want to go home, not stay and build an empire.

From the outset of our history, Americans have focused on creating a great nation in North America, not on conquering other peoples. For more than a century after the Revolution, Americans were preoccupied with establishing the economic and political foundations of this nation. During the entire period we took advantage of the fact that we were largely insulated by a great ocean from the quarreling, avaricious societies of Europe. The British Royal Navy, more to protect Canada and its trade with Latin America than to guard the United States, largely kept other navies at a distance. We saw no need to interfere with European empires, so long as they stayed away from our hemisphere. Therefore, the United States played only a minor role on the world stage, and—despite establishing splendid records in wars on land and sea—created no world-class navy and allowed its army to atrophy after every conflict.

Around the turn of the twentieth century, Americans realized that the protection we enjoyed behind the Atlantic and the Pacific could not endure. An American strategist, Alfred Thayer Mahan, proved in his 1890 work, *The Influence of Sea Power upon History,* that there can be no partial control of the sea because the sea is indivisible. A superior fleet can move over the whole sea, sweeping all lesser navies from it. This was the means by which the Royal Navy had dominated the oceans for the previous two and a half centuries, and the reason why Britain had been able to accumulate the largest empire in the history of the world.

In the first decade of the twentieth century, Germany began to challenge the naval power of Britain, and by implication Britain's world domination. It was this threat, above all else, that caused World War I of 1914–18. This war brought calamity to Britain, France, Germany, and much of the rest of Europe. At war's end a gravely weakened, almost bankrupt Britain no longer could afford the world's largest navy. The United States saw that protection of the Western Hemisphere now rested on its own shoulders. Far more significant, we saw that we could not wait until an aggressive power had built enough strength to invade our hemisphere, but that we must go out to the aggressor, wherever he was, and smash him there. In short, we must take over the world hegemonic role that Britain had exercised since 1660.

This meant that the United States was obliged to build the largest and most powerful navy in the world—a task it took on at the Washington Naval Conference in 1922. The public saw only that Britain accepted naval parity with the United States, the first time it had done so with any country. But leaders of both nations knew the treaty actually signified that the Royal Navy would decline in the decades ahead while the United States Navy would grow.

It took the United States until 1940 to undertake fully the task of creating the world's greatest military power. The spark came with the disastrous collapse of France and the ascendance of Nazi Germany, and in the next five years, the United States developed a military able to defeat any provocation anywhere on earth. We have never relinquished our place since. Indeed, the superiority of the U.S. military has grown exponentially since the end of World War II. Its power now exceeds that of all the rest of the world combined. Along with this power has grown American political strength.

Throughout the cold war, the United States held back the spread of

Communism, and promoted democracy, the rule of law, market economies, and free trade everywhere. After the Soviet Union collapsed in 1991, no nation was able to match the United States. Some countries feared we would use our power to dominate the world. To prevent this from happening, they tried to tie down the United States by means of international bodies like the United Nations and the World Trade Organization.

Since the United States saw no insurmountable dangers on the horizon, it was more or less willing to work within an international context. Then the terrorists attacked the World Trade Center and the Pentagon on September 11, 2001. For Americans, the world changed in an instant. The terrorists had struck directly at our island, at what we hold most precious—at the very treasures we built our overwhelming military and political power to protect in the first place. The attacks transformed our nation from a benign hegemon into a ferocious avenger.

This was another right decision of the United States, and a most vital one. For terrorism and dictatorial rogue nations pose as great a danger to the peace of the world as ever Adolf Hitler or Joseph Stalin did. We saw this with absolute clarity on that horrible day of death and tragedy. And we resolved that *this* we would *not* allow to endure.

As *New York Times* columnist Thomas L. Friedman wrote, most other peoples have not yet comprehended that our primary intention is to preserve and keep our own land with all its liberty and all its prosperity, and that we will do *anything* and go *anywhere* to make this happen. Most people in other countries were unprepared for our resolution after 9/11 to proceed door-to-door in the very heart of the Arab-Muslim world, to make clear we were ready to kill and to die to stop our society from being undermined, and to say, gun in hand, to the people and to the governments who permit terrorists to exist, "What is it that you don't understand about leaving our country alone?"[2]

Misconceptions about American motives and aspirations are not limited to lands that harbor terrorists. In the spring of 2003, France, Germany, Russia, and China refused to sanction America's overthrow of the Iraqi dictatorship. We didn't actually expect the vastly different and more repressive societies of Russia and China to fathom the injustice perpetrated on our people and institutions, but we *did* expect such sensitivity from Western Europe, fellow democratic societies that supposedly stood for the same values we hold dear. Americans were compelled to confront a bitter truth: we were dead wrong in our conviction, held for the last half of the twentieth century, that the United States and Western Europe share a common resolve to preserve and advance freedom throughout the world. We have been forced to accept, as Robert Kagan has written, that Europe "is moving beyond power into a self-contained world of laws and rules and transnational negotiation and cooperation."[3] A century ago, when the world's powers were not facing up to the threat posed by a rising Germany, Winston Churchill warned that "we live in an age of great events and little men." Europe once more is living in an age of great events and little men. Americans believe that Western Europeans bury their heads in the sand when difficult decisions must be made, abstain on issues where they should display moral leadership, and take positions only when their own interests are directly at stake.

This has led Americans to conclude that ours is the only nation that will actually go into the world and strike down evil. We were encouraged when Britain and Australia especially, but also some Continental nations, lined up with us. But we know that they would do little without the active determination of the United States. For these reasons, we *must* dominate the political life of this planet, and we *must* keep an invincible military as an ever-present deterrence.

This book is the story of how we got it right in the past and how we intend to get it right in the future.

ONE

★ ★ ★

THE ILLIMITABLE
FRONTIER

I magine, if you will, the sense of awe that seized the first settlers at
Jamestown in Virginia in 1607, at Plymouth in Massachusetts in
1620, and at the other landings along the coast of North America in
the early decades of the seventeenth century. Here were little English
communities hacking out perch sites on the very edge of an unknown
land. These pioneers thought they would find in America something
resembling the tame, limited, surmountable horizons of England. But
they discovered that this new world was absolutely different. The scale
was vaster than anything they had encountered before. An immense,
almost unbroken forest extended into distances beyond their compre-
hension. Rivers, greater, wilder, and more magnificent than the grand-
est stream in Britain, poured out of the continent—the Connecticut,
the Hudson, the Delaware, the Susquehanna, the Potomac, the James,
the Roanoke, the Cape Fear, the Savannah, and many others. The settlers saw that the land drained by these rivers must be vast, that half a
dozen Englands could easily be fitted in along the coast. As the decades
went by, they ventured up the rivers to find the headwaters, confident
that the highlands where the rivers arose would mark the limit of this
new land, and only the huge South Sea lay beyond. But when they finally reached the great chain of mountains called the Appalachians and

gazed out from its heights, they were utterly confounded—before them an even more boundless, more astonishing land stretched out to seeming infinity toward the setting sun.

This was the moment when the American character was formed. Whatever limits of class and status that the settlers had brought with them from Britain would fall away to insignificance in this prodigious land. When astute individuals looked toward the limitless frontier that they now knew would beckon continuously on the western horizon, they realized that no king, no aristocracy, however selfish, could crush them. At any time they could cross this frontier and put all of Europe's restraints behind them. This had immense and overwhelming effects throughout the colonies. Americans, whether they crossed the frontier or not, were destined to be forever free.

A sense of democracy and equality spread among the people. The seeds of a future republic were sown. Long before Thomas Jefferson articulated it in the Declaration of Independence, Americans recognized their right to life, liberty, and the pursuit of happiness.

But something *else* came along with the discovery of the illimitable frontier. Americans began to see that they had the opportunity to create a country of a wholly different order of magnitude and of a wholly different concept from even the richest countries of Europe. This new land could not only span an entire continent but could also achieve unbelievable wealth and strength. A new aspiration formed—to build on this marvelous, rich, fortunate continent the greatest and most powerful nation on earth, and to people this nation with men and women who were not only prosperous but also free and happy.

It was a vision unparalleled in history. It was not an ambition for empire. It was not a scheme to subdue other peoples. It was rather a desire for a single people sharing alike in the wealth and blessings of the land, and in the freedom of a society without classes and castes.[1] As the colonies grew and more and more people flooded into it, this dream took on a reality and a certitude that led straight to the American Revolution and beyond.[2]

As the frontier advanced inland, the pioneers became less and less

European and "more and more American," as Frederick Jackson Turner, the great historian of the westward thrust, points out.[3] This American not only was independent, but he took as his birthright the authority to travel wherever he wished into the west and to build there a prosperous future with his own hands.

From this immense social movement two ultra-American principles emerged. The first was a deep resolve to gain freedom, democracy, and prosperity, and then to *keep* them. The second was a related resolve to challenge anybody, whether British overlords or other European powers, who might threaten American security or independence. This determination was brandished in the "Don't Tread on Me!" rattlesnake flag of the American Revolution. Only the older settled towns along the coast expressed much interest in integrating Americans into a global economy. And there was virtually no interest in extending American ideals throughout the world. Americans were focused on their own land and their own freedoms, and they were going to brook no interference from anyone in getting them.

★   ★   ★

A NATION THAT restricts its leadership to a narrow aristocracy deprives itself of most of its brainpower. Britain crippled itself in this fashion at the time of the American Revolution, with devastating consequences. Britain's leadership, almost entirely drawn from the privileged classes, was so incompetent that it ignored every opportunity to deflect colonial discontent before revolt started, selected generals incapable of conducting effective military operations, and appointed politicians who wrecked every prospect for negotiated peace.

Adam Smith, the great Scottish philosopher who laid the foundations of classical free-market economic theory, understood the disastrous path Britain was following and offered a solution in his monumental work *The Wealth of Nations*. He called for the consolidation of Britain and its American colonies into a single federated nation, with all its parts having equal representation in a unified parliament.[4] But by the time Smith's book came out in 1776, it was too late. The colonies declared their independence on July 4 that year, and Britain's leaders were determined to bring the colonies back under their heel by military force, not compromise.

But regaining America by military force was a hopeless task so long as the Americans remained defiant. Britain was unable to bring its greatest strength, the Royal Navy, to bear against the thirteen colonies, because they were a land power, not a naval power. Though militarily weak, the colonies covered so vast an area that Britain could not possibly control more than a fraction of it at any time. The moment British forces departed a region, it would become free again. If the Americans were unwilling to return to British rule, Britain could never conquer them.

Adam Smith and other Britons appreciated this fact, but they did not have the authority to change national policy. Smith recognized that the ruling elite's unwillingness to face reality would result in calamity and would ruin Britain's last chance to have a major role in the development of a great new world power. He predicted that, in about a century, America would outstrip Britain in wealth, population, and strength, and that the disparity between the two would accelerate in the years beyond. If Britain could work out a union with America, its importance would be enhanced for a significant epoch to come. But, whether part of a union or not, Britain was destined in the end to become merely an appendage to the greater whole, because the English-speaking world's population and power were going to be centered in America, not England.

The first great success of the American patriots came on October 17, 1777, when a British army under John Burgoyne surrendered at Saratoga on the Hudson River in upstate New York. Burgoyne had gotten into an impossible position because of abominable leadership. British general William Howe, instead of moving his large army up the Hudson from New York City to assist Burgoyne, took it instead to capture Philadelphia. Burgoyne, cut off from all help, had no choice but to capitulate.

The surrender created a sensation in Britain. Belatedly, the leaders realized they were on the wrong track. In March 1778 Parliament repealed all legislation offensive to Americans (the infamous Sugar Act, the Tea Act, the order closing the port of Boston, the law mandating quartering of troops in colonial homes, and so forth), and in April the government sent a commission headed by the Earl of Carlisle to offer the Continental Congress what amounted to complete independence, with the only proviso that the Americans recognize the British sovereign. This was, in effect, what came to be called "dominion status," which London later granted to Canada, Australia, New Zealand, and South Africa. If this offer had been made any time *before* the surrender at Saratoga, the thirteen states most likely would have accepted it, and they would have become the first British dominion.

But the overture came not only after the Americans had realized Britain's incapacity to reconquer them, but also after they had seen the great advantages that would accrue if they no longer were tied to British apron strings. The radical Thomas Paine in his pamphlet *Common Sense,* published in Philadelphia in January 1776, had pointed to one great benefit of total freedom—Britain could not drag the Americans into European wars in which they had no concern. Already, then, Americans were wary of the "entangling alliances" that Thomas Jefferson would later warn against in his first inaugural address.[5] These alliances, they saw, would limit American sovereignty and would divert attention and resources away from the main task they already recognized, that of conquering the North American continent.

Besides, the Americans had the alliance that absolutely guaranteed our independence. The French had been waiting for the opportunity to strike down Britain. They had been humiliated by the British in the Seven Years War (1756–63), had lost Canada and most of their other colonies, and wanted revenge. The colonists' victory at Saratoga showed the French that by allying with the Americans they would be on the winning side. On December 17, 1777, they informed the American diplomat Benjamin Franklin that they would recognize the independence of the United States. On February 6, 1778, the French signed treaties of amity and commerce and of alliance. These made it certain that Britain and France would go to war.

Another European power, Spain, joined the fight on April 12, 1779.

The Spanish refused to acknowledge American independence, hoping only to recover the territories it had lost to the British: Gibraltar, seized in 1704, and Florida, lost in 1763. After declaring war, Spain played a spoiling game—seizing West Florida (then running from Natchez on the northwest to Pensacola on the southeast), trying to arrange a truce between the British and the Americans, and searching for any way to keep the Americans from reaching the Mississippi River. France was no help to the Americans. In 1780, the foreign minister, the comte de Vergennes, pushed for a truce proposed by Czarina Catherine II of Russia and Emperor Joseph II of Austria. The plan would not recognize American independence and would leave the British in control of Maine, the northern frontier, New York City and Long Island, and the major seaports south of Virginia.

Fortunately the British rejected the proposal and were powerless when a French fleet under the comte de Grasse turned back a British fleet under Thomas Graves just off the Virginia Capes on September 5, 1781. This action blocked any relief of a British army under Lord Cornwallis at Yorktown, Virginia, forcing him to surrender to George Washington and a French force under the comte de Rochambeau on October 19, 1781.

This disaster at last convinced the leaders of Britain that they could not resurrect the thirteen colonies, and in February 1782 Parliament resolved that the war must be ended. In March, the ministry of Lord North resigned. Its erroneous policies had brought on the war and it had conducted the unsuccessful campaigns in America. The Marquis of Rockingham formed a new government and appointed the Earl of Shelburne to initiate peace talks. When Rockingham died in July, Shelburne became prime minister but continued to guide negotiations with the United States. Shelburne's appointment was a fortuitous accident for the Americans. He wanted a generous peace to entice the United States into some sort of federation, since he hoped to recapture most American trade for Britain.

The principal American peace commissioners—Benjamin Franklin, John Jay, and John Adams—hoped, along with many other Americans, to secure the whole of British North America in the peace treaty. This, of course, was not going to happen. Britain felt obligated to give back Florida to Spain, and Canada was largely inhabited by descendants of French settlers, who had little interest in joining an English-speaking union, and by Loyalists, who had left the colonies because they did not support the Revolution. Nevertheless, the hope to join Canada with the United States was a will-o'-the-wisp that American leaders pursued for decades after the war. It was a solid indication that the Americans intended, from the very beginning, to dominate North America. Indeed, the Articles of Confederation, under which the thirteen states united after independence, reserved a place for Canada as the fourteenth state.[6]

What the United States Congress *did* lay claim to as a matter of right was the entire region from the Appalachians to the Mississippi River. These claims were based on royal charters that defined the territories of certain colonies as running "from sea to sea." In 1763 Britain had renounced any claims beyond the Mississippi, ending arguments that the colonies reached the Pacific Ocean, but colonial leaders insisted that they *did* extend to the Mississippi. The British government had taken little notice of these claims, forbidding settlement west of the mountains in 1763, and extending Quebec to the Ohio and Mississippi rivers in 1764, thus incorporating into Canada all the Northwest region that was to become Ohio, Indiana, Illinois, Michigan, and Wisconsin.

American negotiators ignored the settlement line of 1763 and the transfer of the Northwest to Canada. They insisted on gaining the entire region that Britain possessed in the West. In the very first decision relating to the boundaries of the new nation, American leaders got it right. They knew pioneers were bounding over the Appalachians every day, and they were determined to guarantee them and the generations to come the immense expanse between the mountains and the great river.

To the south, the Spanish—who claimed all territory west of the Mississippi—had driven British garrisons out of their posts east of the river and had occupied the east bank as far north as Natchez. Not only that, but the Spanish, strongly backed by the French, pressed the British to draw the frontier of the thirteen states as close to the Appalachians as possible. Under no circumstances did they want Americans on the

Mississippi, demanding free passage on the river and expecting New Orleans to be a free port for their exports and imports.

Jay and Franklin, who opened negotiations with the British in Paris, simply disregarded the Spanish and French boundary proposal. In October 1782, Lord Shelburne, after learning that a French and Spanish assault on Gibraltar had failed, took a hard line with the Americans. He demanded that the entire Northwest remain under British sovereignty and that it be settled with Loyalists. Jay and Franklin absolutely refused to accept this; they agreed only to pay claims of Loyalists who had been deprived of their property by the patriots and also accepted a northern frontier essentially running through the Great Lakes to the Lake of the Woods between present-day Minnesota and Ontario.

Thus, in the preliminary treaty signed between the United States and Britain on November 30, 1782, the Americans got all the territory east of the Mississippi to the thirty-first parallel, leaving West and East Florida under Spanish sovereignty. They, as well as British subjects, also got "free and open" navigation of the Mississippi. It is fortunate that the Earl of Shelburne was a typical English aristocrat with only the vaguest concept of the lands he was signing away. To him, all the territory west of the Appalachians, including the Northwest, was of little value to Britain. It seemed to him a small price to pay for possible reconciliation with the Americans.

When the final treaty was signed between all the belligerents on September 3, 1783, Spain did not consider itself bound to grant free access to the Mississippi, nor to respect the thirty-first parallel as the southern boundary of the United States. Also, since Shelburne's government soon fell and wiser heads realized how foolish he had been to give so much away, British leaders made it plain that they had no intention of actually abiding by the terms of the treaty. They expected to retain or at least control all of the Northwest, and to "rectify" the frontier along the Great Lakes and the St. Lawrence River in favor of Britain. Consequently, from the moment of American independence, the United States faced severe problems settling with the colonial powers that blocked its expansion—not only west, but also south into Florida, and north to the Great Lakes.

TWO

★ ★ ★

NAPOLEON ON THE MISSISSIPPI

For years after the treaty of 1783, the United States had to overcome one barrier after another in establishing its sovereignty in the west against the efforts of Spain and Britain to thwart it. These problems had just been surmounted when the nation encountered an entirely new danger from the rising superpower of France.[1] In October 1800 France concluded a secret deal with Spain to take over the entire colony of Louisiana—a region west of the Mississippi the size of the United States east of it. The United States was on the verge of swapping on its crucial western frontier a weak and tottering Spain for a vibrant and growing France led by a bona fide military genius and proven conqueror, Napoleon Bonaparte.

France had owned Louisiana until 1762 and had founded the city of New Orleans in 1718, making this port city near the mouth of the Mississippi its capital. France had ceded the territory to Spain only because it faced the prospect of losing it to Britain as spoils of the Seven Years War. In this war, Britain had seized Quebec as well as France's outposts in India and had driven the French navy from the seas. The French advertised the cession of Louisiana as compensation to their ally Spain for its impending loss of Florida.

The leaders of France, including Bonaparte, were like the leaders of

Britain in their ignorance of North America's significance and potential for growth. The Americans did not suffer from this misapprehension. While only 25,000 Americans had been west of the Appalachians at the time of peace in 1783, by the census of 1800 some half a million had moved beyond the mountains, and the number was growing every day. Americans knew full well that economic possibilities in the west were virtually unlimited, and they were intent on exploiting them. But France's economic interest in Louisiana was primarily to secure food and lumber for the French "sugar islands" in the Caribbean, especially Santo Domingo (present-day Haiti and the Dominican Republic), where both sugar and coffee were lucrative crops.

France presented a different argument to Spain to get it to agree to "retrocede" Louisiana, as well as to give up Florida. Spain, French diplomats told the government in Madrid, could not hope to hold the two colonies against the aggressions of the Americans, who were "devoured by pride, ambition, and cupidity." By ceding Louisiana and Florida to France, the French would be forming "a wall of brass forever impenetrable to the combined efforts of England and America."[2] In this fashion, the French maintained, Spain's possession of Mexico and California would be secure.

The Spanish court agreed with this reasoning, especially since Louisiana cost the Spanish government more than it produced in revenue. But it refused to cede Florida, which was a traditional Spanish territory. The negotiations revealed the petty, myopic thinking of the Spanish court. The only payment that Spain exacted for a region extending to nearly a million square miles was a small kingdom in Italy, Etruria, for a nephew of the Spanish king, the Prince of Parma. Bonaparte also promised that he would always keep Louisiana as a French possession or else return it to Spain. On October 15, 1802, Madrid finally issued orders to transfer Louisiana to France.

The new American president, Thomas Jefferson, had learned of the Louisiana agreement in a message from Rufus King, the U.S. minister in London, on November 20, 1801. The news came as a profound shock. The United States had worked out satisfactory relations with

Spain, which had abandoned the idea that it controlled the Mississippi, and which had granted deposit rights for American goods at New Orleans. Since flatboats floating down the Ohio and Mississippi rivers were the primary means westerners had for getting their products to market, a friendly New Orleans was vital to American interests.

Commerce at this city was already predominately American, and U.S. influence was growing steadily. Jefferson, as well as other American leaders, had concluded that the Spanish Empire was doomed, and they believed that when the empire fell, little would be required to grab Louisiana and Florida, and other territories that blocked U.S. access to the Pacific.

Jefferson could guess that Napoleon wanted more than the food and lumber that Louisiana could provide. Economic considerations alone must not be guiding Napoleon Bonaparte, one of the most gifted military leaders in history. He most assuredly was looking at the huge strategic advantage he would gain by possessing the very heart of North America.

Many American leaders grasped Bonaparte's aim, but didn't think it through. They suspected that he recognized the United States as a potential ally of Britain, that he possessed some intimation of the future economic and military power of the United States, and that he had decided to seize the opportunity to block the expansion of both America and Britain by installing a military cordon along the banks of the Mississippi. This is what Bonaparte told the Spanish king, that France would form an impenetrable barrier between the English-speaking world and the Spanish empire.

Jefferson saw that this argument did not have the slightest possibility of becoming reality because the leaders of the United States would never allow it to happen. France could never set up a military position in Louisiana for the simple reason that the British navy could block all movements of troops and supplies to the region; in other words, to occupy Louisiana the French would need to get reinforcements and supplies through the United States, and the U.S. government would never agree to such an outrageous proposition. A French empire along the Mississippi would stop American expansion in its tracks. Only a leader with no more brains than the king of Spain would fall for such a ploy.

Napoleon Bonaparte was a most arrogant and ambitious man, and perhaps he actually believed that the Americans would allow their considerable anti-British feeling to blind them to their own national interests. Jefferson took immediate steps to quash any illusions Bonaparte might have on this score. In April 1802 he sent an unsealed letter to Robert R. Livingston, the U.S. minister in Paris, by the hand of his old friend, Pierre-Samuel Du Pont de Nemours. He invited Du Pont to read the letter and to convey its contents to people around Bonaparte.

The letter stated that three-eighths of all American produce was now passing through the market of New Orleans, and that before long half of the American population would be living west of the Appalachians and would be dependent on New Orleans to send out their goods and bring in their imports. "France placing herself at that door assumes to us the attitude of defiance," Jefferson wrote. "The day that France takes possession of New Orleans fixes the sentence which is to restrain her forever within her low-water mark [on the French shoreline]. It seals the union of two countries who in conjunction can maintain exclusive possession of the ocean. From that moment we must marry ourselves to the British fleet and nation."[3]

There could be no more direct threat than that: if France took over Louisiana, the United States would form an alliance with Britain. The Royal Navy would blockade French ports and Americans would seize New Orleans and Louisiana. Du Pont didn't want to convey this challenge through the toadies clustering around Bonaparte's court. But there is no question that the message got through to Bonaparte.

Instead of war, Jefferson proposed *buying* New Orleans. On January 11, 1803, he appointed James Monroe as a special minister to assist in negotiations with Paris. Monroe's instructions were to offer up to 10 million dollars for New Orleans, but if Paris refused and meditated hostilities against the United States, he was to cross the English Channel and invite Britain to form an alliance.

Bonaparte had already decided to sell not only New Orleans but the entire colony of Louisiana, however. His reasons were never made public, but it was evident that he had seen what Jefferson had seen, that he could not set up a new empire in the heart of America. Either the Americans or the British, or both, would demolish it in short order, and he could never prevent their actions. Instead, he decided to get as much money as possible for his next war with Britain.

The French foreign minister, Charles-Maurice de Talleyrand-Périgord, approached Livingston on April 11, 1803, the day before Monroe arrived, and inquired whether the United States would care to buy all of Louisiana. Livingston deferred an answer until he could talk with Monroe, but when he did both men jumped at the chance. By May 2, the thrifty Americans had negotiated Talleyrand's asking price down from nearly 20 million dollars to 15 million dollars—a little more than two cents an acre. It was the greatest real-estate deal in history. The United States had instantly doubled its territory and opened the door to the Pacific.

Monroe and Livingston promised to incorporate the 15,000 Spanish and French inhabitants of Louisiana into the Union with all the rights of existing citizens, and they promised that the United States would protect their liberty, property, and religion. These promises revealed with great clarity the democratic, anti-imperial mind-set of Americans. It never occurred to the American representatives that the people of Louisiana could be aliens. They were to become Americans at once, with the same rights as other Americans.

Here, at the first instance of American expansion, the idea was accepted as a given that the United States was to consist of a single people and was to constitute a single nation. The United States of America had been doubled in size at the stroke of a pen, but everyone was to share equally in its bounty. There was going to be no American empire. *E Pluribus Unum*—out of many, one—was not only the motto of this nation but also its guiding spirit. Here two Americans, acting alone and without benefit of advice from their government at home, made the right decision as a matter of course. It was the first of a great series of right decisions that were to come, based on the simple premise shared by the vast majority of Americans that the interests of the United States could best be served by equity, fair dealing, and democracy.[4]

Despite the fantastic bargain Monroe and Livingston had struck, President Jefferson realized that the Constitution did not specifically authorize what they had done. The Constitution did not empower the president or Congress to buy new territory or promise its incorporation into the Union on equal terms with all other elements. At first Jefferson thought he ought to call for an amendment to the Constitution to make it all legal. But when Livingston and Monroe warned him that the French might renege, he decided to go on with an apparently unconstitutional act, believing that "the good sense of the country" would make up for any errors or deficits.

He called in Congress six weeks early and on October 17, 1803, submitted the treaty to the Senate. Three days later the Senate approved it, while Congress as a whole passed a bill setting up a territorial government in the region and another authorizing "stock" (really government bonds) to pay France its price. The only members who opposed the measures were Federalists, representing traders and bankers, now confined mostly to New England, New York, and Delaware, who got most of their income from overseas trade. The Federalists feared doom for their party if the nation expanded beyond the Mississippi.

Here was one of the preeminent instances when Americans were compelled to decide between building a great, expansive nation or choosing, as Europeans had historically done, to follow special regional interests. The vast majority of Americans opted for the widest conception of the nation, not the narrowest. The parochial, minority view lost. The bill authorizing bonds to pay France passed the House by a vote of 90 to 25, the Senate by 26 to 5.

At a ceremony in New Orleans on November 30, 1803, the Spanish flag was lowered and the French tricolor raised. It flew for twenty days. On December 20, 1803, the French prefect surrendered the province to the commissioners of the United States.

The question arose at once: just how far did Louisiana extend? The old maps showed a region of close to a million square miles, but nothing had been surveyed, most of the territory had not been explored, and the edges of it were as uncertain as everything else. The treaty granting Louisiana to the United States defined it as having "the same extent that it now has in the hands of Spain, and that it had when France possessed it." When Monroe and Livingston asked what that meant, Talleyrand answered, "I can give you no direction. You have made a noble bargain for yourselves, and I suppose you will make the most of it."

It became evident that much of West Florida—that is, the region east of the Mississippi and south of the thirty-first parallel—might be part of Louisiana and it might not. This was going to cause trouble, but mostly for Spain, which had no hopes of holding either West Florida or East Florida (the main peninsula) against any determined American bid to take it.

Poor Spain had been betrayed. France had promised an eternal "wall of brass" protecting Spain's colonies from the United States. Moreover, Bonaparte had promised to keep the territory or return it to Spain. Now, even before France took actual possession, he was selling it to the very power Spain feared most.

★   ★   ★

ALTHOUGH THOMAS JEFFERSON did not mention that he had been president of the United States on the epitaph he composed for himself on his gravestone,[5] he was a very great leader of this nation. Born in 1743 in Albemarle County, Virginia, then quite close to the frontier, Jefferson was acutely aware of the transforming character of the westward thrust on the American people. He possessed the same dream other Americans held to expand the United States to its natural limit, the ocean on the west.

Jefferson had long since marked out Louisiana for annexation, although he thought the United States would wrest it from a tottering Spain, not buy it from a French dictator seeking funds for another war with Britain. But Jefferson's aim did not stop at the Continental Divide, the northwestern boundary of the Spanish colony of Louisiana.

Beyond the mountains on the northwest lay the Oregon Country, claimed by both Spain and Britain but actually occupied by neither. To the south Spain held California. This southern region might or might not fall as spoils to the United States when the Spanish Empire collapsed. Time would tell. At the moment the only seemingly feasible way the United States might reach the Pacific was to acquire Oregon.

That Jefferson was thinking of all this *before* the United States bought Louisiana is indicated by the timing of the first great exploration in American history. In January 1803—that is, the very month he appointed James Monroe to go to Paris to attempt to buy New Orleans, and before he had any inkling that Bonaparte wished to sell the whole territory—he asked Congress to authorize an expedition *across* Louisiana into the Pacific Northwest. In other words, this exploration was to be wholly outside the boundaries of the United States. Although advertised as a journey to reveal the region's geographic secrets, study its fauna and flora, and report on possibilities for trade, the actual intent can be inferred quite easily: it was to mark out as clearly as possible *what* obstacles lay in the way of an American conquest of all the land between the Mississippi River and the Pacific Ocean.

Congress granted Jefferson's request. Before the expedition could be launched, in the spring of 1804, Louisiana had been annexed, and the expedition marched through American territory to the Continental Divide. But the moment it crossed the mountains and moved to the ocean, the United States was staking a claim to Oregon, in defiance of both colonial empires.

Jefferson placed the expedition under the command of Meriwether Lewis, his private secretary, and William Clark, the brother of George Rogers Clark, who had led a successful campaign against the Indians and the British into Illinois and Indiana during the Revolution. Lewis and Clark were directed to ascend the Missouri River to its source, cross over the Continental Divide, and descend the Columbia River to its mouth and the Pacific Ocean. The party of forty-five, mostly soldiers, started from St. Louis on May 14, 1804. It took six months for the expedition to reach the Mandan Indian villages near present-day Washburn, North Dakota. The group spent five months with the Mandan, then commenced a seven-month trek to the mouth of the Columbia, where the party spent the winter of 1805–06. The explorers retraced their steps, arriving in St. Louis in September 1806. It was one of the great journeys of exploration in history, an undertaking clearly revealing America's early interest in westward expansion.

THREE

★ ★ ★

'CROSS THE WIDE MISSOURI

In the traditional song "Shenandoah," the lyricist expresses nostalgic longing for the lovely Shenandoah River of Virginia that he has forsaken, while he is bound away to a new land "'cross the wide Missouri." Probably no other song so poignantly conveys the mixed emotions of the pioneer, both his or her hope for a brighter future and the sadness at the loss of cherished people and places left behind.

This was the reality of American life for much of the nineteenth century, and it shaped the nation. The frontier affected everyone. Every pioneer gained in vaster opportunities and wider experiences, and every pioneer lost in abandonment of ancestral homes, giving up the places where childhood memories were made, and leaving only to reminiscence and the occasional letter from the friends and families who stayed at home. The people who did not become pioneers also gained and lost in much the same way. They shared vicariously in the adventures their friends or relatives experienced on the frontier, they gained as the nation's economy burgeoned, and they, too, lost the companionship of those who were bound away across the Missouri and the other broad reaches of the West.

The lure of the frontier was irresistible. The French historian Alexis de Tocqueville, who visited the United States in 1831, wrote that the most extraordinary thing about Americans "is the soil that supports them." The land, Tocqueville wrote, "presents, as in the first days of the Creation, rivers whose source does not dry up, green and moist solitudes, boundless fields that the plowshare of the laborer has not yet turned. At the moment I am speaking, thirteen million civilized Europeans are quietly spreading into the fertile wilderness whose resources and extent they themselves still do not know exactly."[1]

In this rush to the frontier, Tocqueville discovered, the eastern states were being constantly depopulated. Connecticut's population, for example, had grown only a quarter in forty years, whereas England's in the same period had increased by a third. This immense exodus cemented the entire nation into a single whole, for the people from north, south, and east mingled on the frontier, created a common idiom, and shared similar experiences, challenges, and adventures. From all this arose a unified culture, and a collective national experience.

The War of 1812 was a decisive turning point. Americans went into it still thinking of themselves as appendages of the nations of Europe; they came out with a new recognition of themselves as uniquely American. The United States of America became a nation apart. Tocqueville saw that Americans were unique. He coined the term "American exceptionalism" to describe America's profound differences from other nations. "Around every man a fatal circle is traced, beyond which he cannot pass," Tocqueville wrote, "but within the wide verge of that circle he is powerful and free."[2] Most Americans were acutely aware of this circle of freedom and insisted on keeping it. It was this sense of personal independence that defined American exceptionalism.[3] One of the effects of liberty was a tremendous rise in optimism. Americans saw opportunities everywhere and felt everyone who hustled and worked hard could prosper. European visitors noted that Americans were always in a hurry and were angry at anything or anyone that brooked delay. The "quick lunch" was already an American institution.

Frederick Jackson Turner, the great historian of the American frontier, saw another aspect of America. "Nothing works for nationalism like intercourse within the nation," he wrote. "Mobility of population is death to localism, and the western frontier worked irresistibly in unsettling population."[4] After the War of 1812, this process played out in a dramatic, sustained program to conquer the continent. From that point until almost the beginning of the twentieth century, American attention turned inward and away from Europe. Memories of separate European heritages of various immigrant strains diminished in the great melting pot the nation had become, and Americans forged a common patriotism.

Internal improvements stimulated this western migration. In 1811 construction began on the Cumberland Road, or the National Road (now U.S. Route 40); by 1818 the road extended from Cumberland, Maryland, to Wheeling, on the Ohio River, and it connected to Baltimore via a state road. Another project that vastly speeded settlement was the Erie Canal, four feet deep, running 363 miles from Troy on the Hudson to Buffalo on Lake Erie, completed in 1825. From Buffalo, steamboats provided cheap, all-water routes to the shores of Lake Huron and Lake Michigan, opening the Northwest to a flood of settlers. The volume of trade produced by the Erie Canal caused the population of New York City to grow from 125,000 in 1820 to 200,000 ten years later. The first steamboat on the "western waters" was the *New Orleans,* launched from Pittsburgh in 1811. It reached its namesake but was too weak to return against the current. In 1816, however, the *Enterprise* steamed from New Orleans to Louisville in twenty-five days. Within a few years scores of steamboats were plying the Mississippi and its tributaries.

★   ★   ★

THE WAR OF 1812 marked a new conflict with the nation from which the United States had won its independence. Britain sparked a toxic dispute with the Americans when the Royal Navy began seizing sailors off American ships to fill out its crews and interdicting American shipping to France and its allies during the wars that engulfed Europe after Napoleon Bonaparte seized power in 1799. The British, fighting for their lives against Napoleon, never apologized for or abandoned the practice of impressing American seamen, but as much as the practice outraged Americans, it would not have led to war had Britain not interfered with America's westward expansion.

Britain tried to halt the advance of the United States into the Northwest (present-day Ohio, Indiana, Illinois, Michigan, and Wisconsin) by inciting the Indians to resist and by giving them weapons to do so. Britain interfered in part to help Canadian fur traders who were buying pelts from the Indians; once Americans settled the region, the Indians and the game would depart. But the principal reason for British interference was to gain Indian allies in the event strained relations with the United States over ocean commerce led to war.

Here was another example of British incomprehension of what motivated Americans. During the talks leading to the end of the Revolutionary War, American negotiators—fully aware of the surge of people over the Appalachians—had insisted on the Mississippi as the western frontier. The British had agreed, but they continued to occupy the Northwest until 1796, inhibiting the advance of the frontier and arousing enmity. Now they were doing the same thing again. The British were tone deaf to the social and political modulations of the American thrust westward. They could not have chosen an issue more certain to ignite the most aggressive elements against them. They intensified this anger by allying themselves with a great Indian leader, Tecumseh, a Shawnee who had united the Indians of the Northwest to stop the advance of the white settlers. Since frontiersmen held as an article of faith that Indian and white communities could not exist side by side, an Indian alliance was seen as a pact with savages against civilization.

The American belief that Western civilization and Indian culture were incompatible lay at the heart of national policy—carried out for the whole of the nineteenth century with great conviction and force—either to convert the Native American tribes to Western ways or to eliminate or at least neutralize them. This attitude was reflected in the Declaration of Independence, which charges that King George III of Britain "has endeavored to bring on the inhabitants of our frontiers the merciless Indian Savages, whose known rule of warfare is an undistinguished destruction of all ages, sexes, and conditions." Faced with intransigence from Indian warrior bands, especially on the Plains, Americans urgently—and cruelly—took action. In the final stages, Americans deliberately shot down all but a few thousand of the bison, vast herds of which provided the Plains Indians with their main source of sustenance, and, hence, their independence.

None of this reflects credit on the government or the pioneers, but from the start they were determined to reproduce in the western terri-tories the civilization they had inherited from Britain and had accli-mated to America. They were obdurate in their resolve to permit only a *single* culture to exist from Atlantic to Pacific. They succeeded. A few isolated alien groups survived in the West, mostly Indian but also a scattering of Spanish-American pockets, especially in New Mexico and southern California. But none was strong enough to compete with the dynamic American culture. The American melting pot encompassed virtually the entire nation.[5]

The conviction grew throughout the West that the frontier could enjoy security only by expelling the British from Canada and annexing the entire region to the United States. The westerners did not greatly covet Canadian land, but they were convinced Canada would remain a source of trouble with Indians so long as it remained in British hands.

The declaration of war, voted by Congress on June 17, 1812, revealed deep fissures and inadequacies within the country. New England and other commercial parts of the East opposed it because of damage it could do to trade. President James Madison's administration managed the war badly. The army was grossly incompetent. The regular army of only 7,000 men was spread over the country, and the government re-lied on state militias, which were largely useless. Whole detachments refused to fight outside their state. Other detachments ran in panic at the first shots. The generals in command were uniformly incompetent. Attempts to invade Canada collapsed in chaos and cowardice. The navy performed well, but it possessed only sixteen warships, none of them of the first class. By the spring of 1813, the Royal Navy had driven all American ships into port and set up an iron blockade of the Ameri-can coast.

The Americans did have some success on Lake Erie. There, Captain

Oliver Hazard Perry's small fleet found a British squadron at Put-in-Bay on September 10, 1813, and forced its surrender. Perry's report after the battle has gone down in American legend: "We have met the enemy and they are ours." But the success on Lake Erie amounted to little because Americans could not gain control of Lake Ontario, and the entire effort to conquer Canada collapsed.

By the spring of 1814, the war in Europe finally coming to an end, the British planned an ambitious series of offensives against the United States, angered that the Americans had attacked them while they were standing almost alone against Napoleonic tyranny. The first serious strike was to go down Lake Champlain through New York, with the aim of cutting off New England and reannexing it. Sir George Prevost had 11,000 troops, five times more than the American force at Platts-burg, but success depended on eliminating a small American flotilla on the lake, and the British squadron was unequal to the task. In the Battle of Plattsburg Bay, superior American seamanship won the day. Though American losses were heavy, the U.S. flotilla either sank or forced the surrender of every British ship. Prevost, in dismay, led his army back to Canada. Meanwhile, two competent American generals, Jacob Brown and Winfield Scott, took charge at Niagara, where Britain had launched another offensive, and the British attack there went nowhere.

British general Robert Ross landed 4,000 troops under navy escort on the west bank of the Patuxent River, Maryland, and marched within five miles of the capital, Washington. The American militia, well sup-ported with artillery and in superior numbers, waited. President Madi-son and some of the cabinet came out to witness a telling victory, but instead they saw the American forces, commanded by the inept William Henry Winder, run at the first shots. The British marched into Wash-ington on August 24, 1814, and ate the dinner prepared for the presi-dent and his wife, Dolley, in the White House. They burned all the public buildings, delivering a great blow to American pride.

Britain's attack on Baltimore did not go so well. A naval demonstra-tion was futile, and in the first skirmish on land, General Ross lost his life. Discouraged, the British gave up and sailed off to join the cam-paign against New Orleans. The British had designed these attacks to punish the Americans, but now weariness with war had both sides hunting for peace.

The British commander at New Orleans was Sir Edward Pakenham, an experienced officer and brother-in-law of the Duke of Wellington, the British chief in the war against Napoleon. Pakenham had 10,000 men, all experienced British regulars, and he attacked headlong, assuming that the Americans would collapse in panic at the first sight of British bayonets, as they'd done at Washington and other places. But the commander of the Americans at New Orleans, Andrew Jackson, was a leader of a different stripe. A frontiersman who already had acquired a fearsome reputation as an aggressive fighter, General Jackson inspired his men to valor and lined them up behind hastily improvised barricades, including cotton bales. When the attack came on January 8, 1815, the British were stopped in their tracks, lost more than 2,000 men in minutes, including Pakenham, and retreated in panic. The Americans suffered just thirteen casualties.

Everyone ignored the fact that the Americans and the British had already signed a peace at Ghent on December 24, 1814, on terms of status quo ante bellum. To Americans, General Jackson had won the war with a single spectacular victory. The British had been defeated. America had triumphed. From the victory at New Orleans arose a myth of American military invincibility and a surge of patriotism. This sense of success was especially high on the frontier, because Tecumseh had been killed in 1813 and the Indian menace had dissolved, opening the way to an unprecedented advance of the frontier. The "war hawks" quickly forgot they had failed to conquer Canada.

Economically, the war was a great boon. The blockade kept British imports from arriving, giving incentive to American manufacturers and accelerating industrial liberation from England. With swift-flowing streams and numerous waterfalls to produce waterpower, New England took the lead in manufactures, especially in textiles, but also paper, leather goods, and products made of wood. In Pennsylvania, New York, and New Jersey, accessible ore led to many iron industries, while coal could be obtained cheaply to supplement waterpower.

In the South, a more sinister event took place, leading to the greatest tragedy in American history: in 1793 Eli Whitney invented the cotton gin. The gin easily separated cottonseeds from cotton fibers and made it feasible to grow short-staple upland cotton throughout the South. Until this happened, slavery had been dying out because slaves could not compete economically with free farmers in raising grain and other field crops. The gin reversed this equation. All at once the impetus toward emancipation stopped, and planters began planting thousands of acres of cotton. In 1791 cotton exports from the South totaled 2 million pounds; by 1811 the figure had risen to 80 million pounds and was growing every year. Slavery was entrenched, supported by planters who exploited the unpaid labor of slaves to make themselves wealthy. From this point on, human avarice blocked the South, and for a long while the nation, from making the correct moral choice. Here was one of the cases where America did not get it right, and it suffered immeasurably from the error.

American leaders allowed the mistake to be established as national policy in 1820 when Missouri was admitted as a slave state and Maine came in as a free state. The "Missouri Compromise" set into law that henceforth slavery would not be permitted north of 36 degrees 30 minutes north latitude in the territories—but that it *would* be permitted south of that line.

The issue of slavery became more and more controversial as time went on, distracted and divided the nation, and finally brought on a devastating Civil War. Nevertheless, American destiny could not be thwarted by this dispute. Despite its size as an issue and despite its moral implications, slavery was peripheral to the might of the westward thrust. But it did deflect and distort the dream for a time, and its consequences created wholly unnecessary animosity between sections of the country that had no reason to harbor it.

Slavery was a self-inflicted wound on the American dream. It was an irrefutable contradiction to the Declaration of Independence, which declared that all men are created equal. To many doubters, its existence appeared to be a potentially fatal flaw in the moral and ethical foundation of the nation. To them, this inconsistency might split the American people in two or more squabbling countries, no better than the eternally bickering kingdoms of Europe. Yet there was little or no chance of that happening. Most Americans believed that the paradox of slavery in a free land would somehow be resolved. Given a choice between holding human beings in bondage and creating a new nation that extended from Atlantic to Pacific, the vast majority would choose the united nation over slaves without hesitation.

The great Civil War that came would seem to prove a lie to this idea. Yet southerners fought so bitterly not because of some great love for slavery but because the North invaded their homes. Had the South actually won this war, it is inconceivable that the Southern people would have struck out on some separate path of their own. A victorious South would have patched up a reunion with the North in short order—because the southerners shared the dream of a single great continental nation as much as the northerners. Besides, long before the end of the war, the South had decided it wanted nothing more to do with slavery. On April 10, 1865, the day after the Confederate surrender at Appomattox, Virginia, Southern commander Robert E. Lee told Union commander Ulysses S. Grant that the South was as opposed to human bondage as the North.[6] This removed the *only* fundamental issue dividing North and South, and southerners—though still angry at the North for invading—rushed back into the Union with all the enthusiasm and patriotism that had marked the South before the war.

The single greatest mistake after independence was that the leaders did not seize on the great unity of the American people and on their common resolve to conquer the West—and bring slavery to an end. Thomas Jefferson proposed to Congress in 1784 that slavery be prohibited after 1800 in lands west of the Appalachians. His proposal was only barely defeated and was incorporated into the Northwest Ordinance of 1787, which defined government for the region north and west of the Ohio River.

If the issue had been addressed solidly, it could have been solved for the whole country then—or at any time thereafter. The answer was for the U.S. government to *buy* the slaves and set them free. Since the Constitution, which went into effect in 1789, established slaves as legitimate property, the government could not have emancipated the slaves by fiat. To be sure, the slave owners would have fought any attempt to end slavery, but it is critical to recognize that these slave owners represented only a tiny minority of southerners. In 1860 just 10 percent of white southerners owned *any* slaves, and only 4 percent owned ten or more slaves. No aristocracy anywhere has ever given up its privileges willingly. The French nobility's refusal to renounce its exalted status brought on the French Revolution in 1789, and the Southern aristocracy also wanted to keep its ill-gotten gains. But the South was a democracy, not a plutocracy like France, and the vast majority of southerners who did not own slaves would have recognized the arguments of the aristocrats as being motivated solely by greed.

Freeing the slaves in this fashion would have avoided the conflicts and animosities that were to come. As industrialization got underway, ambitious people turned their resources toward factories and commerce because they produced the most returns on their money. Southern cash crops—which continued to be raised largely by hand labor—were nowhere near as profitable. In 1830, for example, a Southern planter had to invest $7.50 to produce the same revenue that a factory owner gained by investing a dollar. This disparity became all the greater with the extension of the railroads in the 1840s. If slavery had been voted out, plantation owners would have diverted their resources from agriculture to industry, the South would have industrialized at the same pace as the North, and the Southern aristocracy would have disappeared as a class in short order.[7]

Instead of reaching an equitable solution, American leaders stepped away from their duty and tried to paper over the difficulties, hoping the next generation would solve the problem. It was irresponsible, a terrible mistake, and left lasting damage. Thus the society persisted with two completely discordant concepts. The most fundamental ideal it extolled was liberty and building the greatest nation on earth. But beneath this ideal it tolerated human bondage.

After the War of 1812 the democracy of the frontier extended to the entire nation, and the egalitarian doctrine of the Declaration of Independence came close to being the correct description of American society, except, of course, in the case of slaves and of women, who were denied the vote. The actual device that produced democracy was the constitutions of the western states, which, without exception, adopted universal manhood suffrage. To still-disenfranchised (mostly propertyless) groups in the older states, this made eminent good sense, and by pressure and demonstrations they forced democracy in these states as well.[8]

The French historian Tocqueville discovered an essential element about American democracy: Americans believed firmly, he wrote, that "it is not the elected magistrate who makes American democracy prosper, but it prospers because the magistrate is elective." In other words, Americans realized that the *institution* of regular elections was a priceless treasure that guaranteed democracy, not the person who actually occupied the elective office. The incumbent might be honest and fair, or he might be a liar and a rogue. It didn't matter. The fact that elections were certain and frequent ensured that the honest man could be returned to office, the rogue kicked out. Democracy remained.

Tocqueville also found that individualism was rampant in America and put his finger on the cause: democracy. "As conditions [among people] are equalized," he observed, "one finds a great number of individuals who have acquired or preserved enough enlightenment and goods to be able to be self-sufficient. These owe nothing to anyone, they expect so to speak nothing from anyone." In this fashion Americans tended to fancy that their whole destiny lay in their own hands, and thus they felt they were fully equal to every other person, however exalted his status.

This democracy was sometimes difficult for European aristocrats to accept. Fanny Trollope, mother of the English novelist Anthony Trollope, was forced to live in the United States from 1827 to 1829 because of her husband's debts; she found equality perfectly proper to discuss with other members of the English gentry over dinner in an upperclass dining room, but "less palatable when it presents itself in the shape of a hard, greasy paw, and is claimed in accents that breathe less of freedom than of onions and whiskey. Strong, indeed, must be the love of equality in an English breast if it can survive a tour through the Union."[9]

Irrespective of Fanny Trollope's misgivings, equality was deeply rooted in the American breast. The New England essayist Ralph Waldo Emerson (1803–82) held firmly that "a man has a right to be employed, to be trusted, to be loved, to be revered."

To combat the isolation that individualism brought about, Tocqueville discovered that Americans formed voluntary associations to cooperate and get jobs done. "Americans use associations to give fêtes, to found seminaries, to build inns, to raise churches, to distribute books, to send missionaries to the antipodes," he wrote. "In this manner they create hospitals, prisons, schools. Everywhere that, at the head of a new undertaking, you see the government in France or a great lord in England, count on it that you will perceive an association in the United States."[10]

A vast wave of optimism spread through the country, with factories and commerce mushrooming in the North, cotton becoming king in the South, and the frontier always beckoning to the ambitious. Optimism led to the rise of ultranationalism. With each move in the direction of nationalism, politicians discovered their popularity with voters increased. Patriotism had been forged on the frontier, and to be an American was now a mark of pride throughout the land.

★   ★   ★

IN ONLY A FEW years after the War of 1812, the United States solved most of the unsettled problems of its frontiers to the north and south, seized Florida, and established a solid claim to extending the country to the Pacific.

In 1818 Britain accepted the forty-ninth parallel as the American-Canadian frontier to the Rocky Mountains and agreed to leave the Oregon Country in the hands of both countries for ten years, indicating that Britain would be willing to share the country with the United States at some point in the future.

Meanwhile, in March 1818, Andrew Jackson formed a small army that pursued fleeing Indians into Florida and, in the process, seized Pensacola and much of northern Florida. He proposed to James Monroe, who had become president in 1817, that the United States annex the entire province to the United States. Backed by John Quincy Adams, Monroe's secretary of state, Jackson got his way. In November 1818 Monroe issued Spain an ultimatum: either maintain order in Florida or cede it to the United States.

Spain had already decided to make whatever concessions were necessary, for fear of American help to Spain's Latin American colonies, which were fighting for their independence. Spain announced that it would cede Florida if the United States agreed to a satisfactory boundary between the Louisiana Purchase and Mexico. In February 1819, the United States and Spain set the U.S.-Mexico frontier along the Sabine River to the thirty-second parallel (the present boundary between Louisiana and Texas), north to the Red River, along the Red to the 100th meridian, along that meridian to the Arkansas River, along the Arkansas to its source, from its source to the forty-second parallel, which it then followed to the Pacific. By accepting the forty-second parallel as Mexico's northern border, Spain relinquished its claim to the Oregon Country, giving the United States a firm position from which to challenge Britain's attempt to acquire the land.

Although Ferdinand VII of Spain delayed ratification for nearly two years, by 1821 the United States had established a claim that it extended from sea to shining sea. Meanwhile, the frontier had been broken wide open, beckoning to thousands of people to occupy it and make their fortunes.

FOUR

★ ★ ★

LEAVE THIS
CONTINENT TO US

I n the years after the War of 1812, the United States made two right
decisions that profoundly advanced the power and integrity of the
nation. One was to concentrate American energy and attention on
conquering the temperate regions of North America, a choice that virtually guaranteed the nation's rise to greatness. The other decision was
to bar incursions anywhere in the Western Hemisphere by Old World
powers, a resolution that prevented any challenge to us in this hemisphere.

From this second decision stems both the Monroe Doctrine and the
neutrality policy that largely guided the United States until 1917, when
we entered World War I. The idea of both was not new, but the acceptance of them as national policy dates from this era. While the people
turned most of their attention to a rapidly growing economy and to expanding the nation across the continent, the country's leaders focused
on the continued threat of the imperial powers.

John Quincy Adams, secretary of state, shared a deep-seated belief
with most Americans that the New World should insulate itself from
the quarrels, interferences, and colonizing ambitions of the Old. He
told the British minister to Washington in 1821, "Keep what is yours,
but leave the rest of this continent to us." Two years earlier he had

remarked in a cabinet meeting that "it is a physical, moral, and political absurdity" that European colonies "should exist permanently contiguous to a great, powerful, and rapidly growing nation."

Two separate but related dangers emerged at this time. The first was Russia's effort to colonize the north Pacific coast. If successful, this would invite other powers to carve out colonies in America. The second was a threat that the major powers of Europe might intervene to restore to Spain its rebellious colonies in Latin America.

The United States had ignored a trading post the Russians built in 1812 only a few miles north of San Francisco Bay. But it was deeply disturbed by a Russian imperial *ukase,* or decree, of 1821 that extended exclusive claims down the coast to the fifty-first parallel and forbade all non-Russian ships within a hundred miles of the coast. In July 1823 Adams sent a message to Russia and Britain "that the American continents are no longer subjects for *any* new European colonial establishments." The warning was aimed less at Russia than Britain, whose territorial expansion Adams feared most. The next year Russia backed off its claims and agreed not to set up any establishment south of 54 degrees, 40 minutes north latitude.

A greater danger emerged from the policy of the Quadruple Alliance to put down all liberal elements in Europe. The alliance was originally made up of the victors over Napoleon—Britain, Austria, Russia, and Prussia—but Britain opted out quickly because Prince Klemens von Metternich, the reactionary Austrian prime minister and leading figure in the alliance, was determined to destroy democracy wherever he found it. France, under the restored Bourbon monarchy, had demonstrated its extreme conservatism by 1818 and took Britain's place.

Metternich got the alliance to agree that the great powers might suppress revolution in any European state. In 1821 Austria, at the behest of the alliance, smashed liberal outbursts in the Italian kingdoms of Piedmont and Naples, and the next year France, also backed by the alliance, did the same in Spain, where a revolt demanded return of the liberal constitution that Ferdinand VII had abrogated. Ferdinand urged the alliance to help him recover his colonies in Latin America, which, except for Cuba and Puerto Rico, had declared independence. This possibility alarmed Britain, which had taken over most of the trade of the former Spanish colonies and didn't want to lose it. Britain also feared that Ferdinand, out of gratitude, would give some of his colonies to France, thus allowing France to revive its empire in the New World. In that event, all the rivalries and disputes that consumed Europe would be transferred to America, and the United States would inevitably be drawn into the whirlpool of European diplomacy and war. President Monroe was well aware of these dangers and had urged Ferdinand without success to recognize the independence of the Spanish American republics.

George Canning, the British foreign minister, approached Richard Rush, the U.S. minister, and suggested that their governments send a joint statement opposing any attempt by the Quadruple Alliance to restore the American colonies to Spain. When Rush wrote back for instructions, President Monroe asked the opinion of ex-presidents Thomas Jefferson and James Madison. Both were enthusiastic. Jefferson responded that the nation's "first and fundamental maxim should be never to entangle ourselves in the broils of Europe," while our second maxim should be never to allow Europe to meddle in American affairs. Jefferson saw Canning's proposal as a chance to draw Britain "into the scale of free government, and emancipate a continent at one stroke." Jefferson concluded, "With her on our side we need not fear the whole world." Madison wanted to go further. He proposed that the United States condemn French intervention in Spain and also support the Greeks, who were then fighting for independence from Turkey.

John Adams vehemently opposed the joint statement, however. The United States, he asserted, should not "come in as a cockboat in wake of the British man-of-war."

Monroe took Adams's advice. He rejected a joint statement with Canning, knowing that Britain would do as much to prevent European intervention in Spanish America without an alliance with the United States as with it. He decided to announce the U.S. position to the world in a message to Congress. He also omitted any reference to Europe, accepting the argument of Adams and Jefferson that the declaration should make an earnest remonstrance against meddling of European powers in Latin America, but "disclaim all interference on our part in Europe."

Monroe presented his message—which became known as the Monroe Doctrine—to Congress on December 2, 1823. "The American continents," Monroe wrote, "by the free and independent condition which they have assumed and maintain, are henceforth not to be considered as subjects for future colonization by any European powers." Furthermore, "we should consider any attempt on [the part of the Quadruple Alliance] to extend their system to any portion of this hemisphere as dangerous to our peace and safety."

Such a statement by a country of 9 million people appeared presumptuous to the four great powers of continental Europe, not to speak of being galling to Britain. But Monroe and his cabinet knew precisely what they were doing. The powers of Europe could do nothing without mounting a seaborne invasion, and the Royal Navy could sink every ship and transport they sent into the Atlantic. Britain made it plain to the Quadruple Alliance that this was precisely what would happen if they tried it. So the Monroe Doctrine rested on the power of the Royal Navy. And it was *going* to rest on this power until such time as the United States decided to build a world-class navy. In the meantime Britain did the job for us.

Monroe's pronouncement aroused some enthusiasm in Latin America, but the new republics soon discovered that the United States was not prepared to back up its words. With the Royal Navy guarding our Atlantic flank, we did not need such capabilities ourselves, however. Such was the wisdom of the Monroe Doctrine, which remained the bedrock policy of the United States. No other nation was going to dominate the Western Hemisphere.

There's an astonishing parallel between this era in American history and the cold war after World War II. The protection that Britain performed for the United States during its period of weakness was reciprocated a century and a quarter later when the United States did exactly the same thing for the free world. For most of the nineteenth century the Royal Navy kept aggressors away from American shores.

From 1945 until the Soviet Union collapsed in 1991, the United States performed the identical service throughout the world—keeping Soviet totalitarianism away from equally weak democracies in Europe and other continents.

British foreign minister Canning was annoyed by Monroe's message, which gave Britain no credit, seized the protector's role for America, and summarily denied Britain's preeminence in American affairs. Canning later claimed he was the author of the Monroe Doctrine. "I called the New World into existence to redress the balance of the Old," he said, a claim that was true in an indirect way, since the Royal Navy made the Monroe Doctrine valid. But the United States never acknowledged the fact, and few people at the time appreciated what Britain was doing. America at least repaid its debt to Britain in the last half of the twentieth century.

FIVE

★ ★ ★

MANIFEST DESTINY

In the thirty-three years after the War of 1812, Americans got it right in a series of decisions that have influenced the course of American history to the present day. These correct choices gave us a coastline along the Pacific from San Diego to Puget Sound, acquired a region one and a third times the size of the Louisiana Purchase, eliminated Britain as a contender in North America, pushed Mexico out of the path of westward expansion, rejected an effort by a greedy minority to create an empire of subject peoples, like the British Empire, and raised to a national axiom the dream that had inspired Americans from the first—to have a *single* nation, a *single* people, and a unified democratic society.

During this same period Americans established a tradition of army and navy strength, imagination, and leadership that commenced the march of the United States to world military supremacy. The standards and maxims that produced the invincible American army, navy, and air force of the twenty-first century had their origin in the brilliant campaigns of the Mexican War (1846–48).

The conflicts with Britain and Mexico rested on a clear decision leaders made very early in our history to possess the entire West. Secretary of State John Quincy Adams told a cabinet meeting in 1819 that the United States inevitably must absorb all of North America. This, he said, "is as much a law of nature as that the Mississippi should flow to the sea." Britain and Mexico resisted his sweeping aspiration toward the north and the south, but a resolve hardened to accept *no* restraints on expansion due west.

That the United States possessed the *right* to push Britain and Mexico aside no one has ever seriously claimed. That it was the *right* thing to do for the future success and destiny of this nation, however, only the most pacific and docile of persons would dispute. During this period Americans showed the world our willingness to go the extreme test to gain what we had decided we must have. The campaigns were not conducted with the cynical "might-makes-right" arrogance of the Prussian "Iron Chancellor," Otto von Bismarck, who welded divided Germany into one nation by force and threat. Rather, they were an expression of the American people's deeply held belief that the United States was destined to become a nation of continental size and that those states in the way had to yield.

Alexis de Tocqueville figured this out when he came to the United States in 1831. In *Democracy in America* he declared, "There is at least one event that is certain. At the period that we can call imminent, the Anglo-Americans will alone cover the whole immense space included between the polar ice and the tropics; they will spread from the shores of the Atlantic Ocean to the shores of the South Sea."

Tocqueville saw clearly the fate in store for Mexico: "Beyond the frontiers of the Union toward Mexico extend vast provinces that still lack inhabitants. The men of the United States will penetrate into these solitudes even before those who have the right to occupy them. They will appropriate the soil, they will establish a society on it, and when the legitimate proprietor finally presents himself, he will find the desert fertilized and foreigners sitting tranquilly on his inheritance."[1]

Although the idea was quite old, the actual term "manifest destiny" was not coined until 1845. Writing about the planned American annexation of Oregon, the editor of the *New York Morning Sun*, John L. O'Sullivan, asserted on December 27, 1845, that the "true title" to the region was found in "the right of our manifest destiny to overspread and to possess the whole of the continent which Providence has given us for the development of the great experiment of liberty and federated self-government entrusted to us. The God of nature and of nations has marked it for our own."

The final winning of the West consisted of three separate but related campaigns—occupation of the Oregon Country, annexation of Texas, and seizure of California and all the land between it and Texas.

The United States was compelled to fight only one war, against Mexico, to gain these territories, covering 1.2 million square miles, or a region as large as all of Western Europe. But Britain backed down over Oregon only when the United States showed its teeth, and disputes within America were intense, because some wanted no expansion, others wanted no more slave states, and still others were afraid an assertive United States would lose trade with Europe.

The original Oregon Country ran from the forty-second parallel to 54 degrees, 40 minutes north latitude, and from the Pacific to the crest of the Rockies. It was jointly occupied by Britain and the United States. The United States had always been willing to split the country at the forty-ninth parallel, the same line agreed on in 1818 as the U.S.-Canadian frontier from the Lake of the Woods to the Rockies. But Britain refused both in 1818 and in 1827. Agitation increased for the United States to acquire Oregon—by force, if necessary—as more and more Americans made their way west. Beginning in the 1830s American missionaries made the difficult journey along the Oregon Trail, which commenced at Independence, Missouri, led to the bend of the Platte River, through South Pass in the Rockies, to the Snake River, then by a cutoff to the Columbia River. Word of excellent land spread back to the east, and after 1841 hundreds of emigrants gathered each spring at Independence to make the long trek by covered wagon into the new frontier.

For all the interest in the Oregon Country, California clearly was the real prize on the Pacific coast. Passage to Oregon was hard and the region would be slow to develop, but California was more accessible, had one of the world's best harbors at San Francisco, would open the door to the Far East, and was potentially even richer than Oregon.

In 1841 Commodore Thomas ap Catesby Jones, chief of the American squadron in the Pacific, received orders to seize Monterey in the event of war with Mexico. Hearing rumors that a British fleet also had designs on California and convincing himself that the United States was already at war, Jones seized Monterey in October 1842 and ran up the American flag. When he learned that fear of a British invasion was groundless and the United States was not at war, Jones apologized and withdrew. But his action revealed all too plainly the ultimate goal of his government.

The United States collided first with Mexico over Texas, however. Americans began to settle in Texas in 1821. By 1835 about 30,000 Americans were in the region, the great majority southerners, some of whom possessed slaves. The U.S. government tried to get Mexico to sell Texas but saw its feelers rebuffed. Alarmed that the United States might simply occupy the country, the Mexican government commenced ineffectual measures to reduce the American presence, first checking immigration, then prohibiting slavery. The measures were not enforced, but they incensed the settlers, who demanded in 1833 that Texas be made a separate Mexican state to stop the harassment. At this time General Antonio Lopez de Santa Anna came to power, converted the states to mere departments, and made the governors his tools. Texans now took up arms, planning at first simply to recover their old rights. But on March 2, 1836, they declared independence after agents of the U.S. government advised them that only thus could they secure American sympathy.

Santa Anna advanced across Texas with an army of 6,000. At San Antonio he killed every man in the garrison of the Alamo. At Goliad in the south he executed 350 prisoners in cold blood. The entire immigrant population of Texas fled eastward. The main Texan army under Sam Houston met Santa Anna on the San Jacinto River at the northwest corner of Galveston Bay. In the late afternoon of April 21, 1836, Houston formed a line under the cover of trees, and his men rushed upon the Mexicans, shouting "Remember the Alamo" and "Remember Goliad." They caught the Mexicans wholly by surprise, killed, wounded, or captured almost the whole force, and found Santa Anna the next day cowering in high grass. The rank and file were prepared to execute him for the massacre at Goliad, but Houston and other leaders saved his life and later allowed him to return to Mexico by way of the United States. Although Santa Anna agreed to order the Mexican army to withdraw from Texas and to get the Mexican Congress to grant independence, he reneged the moment he was free. But in fact the Mexican army withdrew beyond the Rio Grande, and Texas achieved de facto independence.

Independence was seen everywhere as merely a prelude to annexation by the United States, and in September 1836 the voters of Texas approved a petition almost unanimously. But a number of people in the North opposed taking in another slave state, and the matter was postponed for nine years. During that time Britain tried to form a close relationship with Texas as a market for British goods and as a source of cotton for British mills, which revived efforts to overcome opposition to annexation. In April 1844 President John Tyler proposed taking in Texas, but the treaty was rejected by the Senate, in part because of the slavery issue and in part because Mexico had made clear that annexation would be grounds for war.

Henry Clay, the prospective Whig candidate, and Martin Van Buren, the prospective Democratic candidate, tried to head off making Texas a campaign issue in the presidential election of 1844. Both wrote statements opposing annexation without Mexican consent. But the two men sadly misunderstood the mood of the American people. The Whig convention nominated Clay, but made no mention of Texas. The Democrats passed over Van Buren in favor of James K. Polk of Tennessee, who was wholly in favor of annexation. Moreover, since Britain was refusing to settle the Oregon question, the Democrats astutely combined Oregon and Texas, maintaining that "our title to the whole of the territory of Oregon is clear and unquestionable" and urging the United States to take both Oregon and Texas. Oregon appealed to voters in the Northwest; bringing in free as well as slave territory spared Democrats from the charge of sectionalism; and the idea of forestalling Britain from acquiring Texas as a near colony appealed to almost everyone. Unmentioned, but by no means overlooked, was the possibility of securing New Mexico and California as well.

Polk won a narrow but complete victory. He had a clear mandate in favor of expansion. Just before he left office, on March 1, 1845, President Tyler signed a resolution he had gotten through a now-willing Congress offering Texas statehood.

In June 1845, as soon as he received assurance that Texas would accept, the new president, Polk, ordered General Zachary Taylor to move U.S. troops into Texas to protect it against any Mexican challenge. But Polk had no intention of stopping with Texas. He was prepared from the outset for an aggressive war, to seize all Mexican territory between Texas and the Pacific. He hoped he might simply buy the region from Mexico, however, and sent John Slidell of Louisiana to Mexico City to make an offer. But no one in the capital dared to receive Slidell, and he returned to the United States in March 1846.

Polk had already decided armed conflict was inevitable, now that the United States had annexed Texas. In January 1846 he ordered General Taylor, who had stopped at the Nueces River, to proceed to the Rio Grande, and prepared to ask Congress to declare war. Polk's move asserted Texas's claim that it extended to the Rio Grande, not the Nueces, as the Mexicans insisted. Before the message was sent, news arrived of fighting between Taylor and Mexicans along the Rio Grande. Polk rewrote the message so as to put the blame on the Mexicans, and on May 11, 1846, Congress voted for war.

Meantime, Polk also solved the vexing problem of Oregon. When he became president, he hopefully renewed the offer to Britain to settle the frontier on the forty-ninth parallel. But London rejected the settlement again. It's difficult to understand what the British expected to gain. They wanted to bluff the United States into staying off the Pacific coast, of course. Yet with thousands of Americans already in Oregon and more arriving every year, while only a few fur traders were coming in from Canada, it would not be long before the American presence would be overwhelming. One is forced to conclude that Oregon was another example of British incomprehension of the force of the westward migration, and, more, of their lack of appreciation of the value of land in North America. The emigrants suffered under no such misapprehensions. They knew they could prosper by exploiting the good soil and adequate rainfall in the region west of the Cascades.

Polk was a pugnacious man. When Britain rejected his offer, he asked Congress for permission to tell London that the joint occupation of Oregon would end after a year, and also to set up U.S. military posts throughout the Oregon Country and extend U.S. laws there. The move was designed as a clear challenge to the British, but Congress, more timid than Polk, authorized him only to notify London that the joint occupation would end. Britain nevertheless took alarm, and—perhaps because the United States at the moment was showing extreme aggressiveness against Mexico—decided to accept the forty-ninth parallel as the border, asking only for the whole of Vancouver Island, which the U.S. government accepted. On June 15, 1846, the two countries reached an agreement, and the United States officially extended to the Pacific from the forty-second to the forty-ninth parallel.

★   ★   ★

THE MEXICAN WAR of 1846–48 was proof of a decisive transformation in American military thinking after the War of 1812. The changes turned the United States into a major military power and set in motion the excellent leadership and raw force that have characterized American wars ever since.

The War of 1812 revealed what discerning military thinkers had known from the beginning of warfare: that soldiers everywhere are about the same in terms of courage and resolve, and that the decisive difference between armies is found in their leadership, and especially in their *tradition* of leadership. It is leaders who teach soldiers discipline, skills, and confidence in battle, and leaders who inspire troops to valor. The War of 1812 presented outstanding examples of both atrocious and superb leadership. The politically appointed and generally unskilled officers of the state militias were almost uniformly incompetent and incapable of leading men into battle. But Andrew Jackson at New Orleans and Winfield Scott and Jacob Brown at Niagara had taken the same human raw material—untrained young American men—and transformed them into effective, victorious soldiers.

American political chiefs recognized that Jackson, Scott, and Brown were natural leaders, and were grateful that they had emerged during the war. But a nation cannot depend on the fortuitous appearance of skilled military leaders after war has already started. From the very end of the war, the U.S. government commenced a program to rectify this glaring flaw in the American political system.

They found the vehicle in the United States Military Academy, which had been established in 1802 at West Point, New York, but which had played an insignificant role to date. Under President James Madison, the Military Academy was reorganized and given additional support, and in 1817 received an inspired leader, Colonel Sylvanus Thayer, who, by the end of his tenure in 1833, had built a school that was producing an entirely *new* kind of military leader—an officer drawn from the entire American democracy, educated at public expense, and taught all the professional skills available to soldiers of that day. In other words, Thayer created a *democratic* officers corps composed of citizens who reflected all the concepts of freedom, independence, and equality that suffused the American population.

By comparison, the military schools of Europe were restricted largely to the aristocracy or the extremely well off, and their guiding ethos was not democracy but upholding the social and economic privileges of the upper classes. Both produced qualified officers, but West Point educated officers attuned to the citizen-soldier, and these temporary warriors were the people who were going to make up the armies of the United States. America, for the foreseeable future, was *not* going to be a land of a huge professional standing army, and American officers were *not* going to constitute a separate, aloof social class, like the aristocratic *Junkers* who dominated the Prussian army, or the less professional but still detached gentry who held most of the places in the British army.

In the years leading up to the Mexican War, West Point produced a line of outstanding graduates who were to gain fame in the years ahead— Robert E. Lee, Thomas J. (Stonewall) Jackson, Ulysses S. Grant, William Tecumseh Sherman, and others. During these years they and their less famous fellow alumni built a solid tradition of competence, skill, and leadership, but most of all they established a military structure that could adjust to and exploit the vibrant, fluid, dynamic American society around them.

The concept of the citizen-soldier that they were establishing as the American standard expanded beyond West Point and, in the years just prior to the Mexican War, led to three more institutions modeled on West Point that were going to reinforce and deepen the American system in the years ahead: two state academies—Virginia Military Institute, founded in 1839, and The Citadel in South Carolina, founded in 1842—and a second national school, the United States Naval Academy, founded in 1845 at Annapolis, Maryland. In the Mexican War, these institutions played no part, but later they formed with West Point the central basis and ideal around which the American military tradition consolidated. As the nation grew, their concept of citizenship *and* military service was expanded to the Reserve Officers Training Corps (ROTC), which became the means by which the United States produced military subalterns in the nation's civilian colleges and universities.

★   ★   ★

THE MEXICAN WAR was marked by spectacular campaigns over vast distances, and by audacious and usually successful attacks, often with forces decidedly inferior to the enemy's. In this conflict America did not possess overwhelming power anywhere. But the revolution in leadership that had been going on for thirty years brought about operations that were generally inspired and that foreshadowed the boldness and educated risk-taking that were going to characterize the U.S. military from that point onward.

"Old Rough and Ready" Taylor, although he emerged as the most popular American commander, was the least qualified. After collisions around Camp Texas (Brownsville) and Matamoros, Mexico, Taylor advanced south to Monterrey, despite disease among poorly conditioned recruits, difficulties in getting supplies, and some Mexican resistance. After hard fighting on September 21–23, 1846, his army captured Monterrey, but Taylor permitted enemy troops to evacuate, not surrender, and agreed to an eight-week armistice. These decisions caused Polk to lose all confidence in Taylor, and he disallowed the armistice. Taylor thereupon advanced south to Saltillo. Polk wanted him to drive from there straight to Mexico City, but three hundred miles of desert intervened, and Taylor refused the idea as impracticable.

Meanwhile, Santa Anna led an army three times the size of Taylor's toward Saltillo, losing one-fifth of his men along the same three hundred miles of desert. At Buena Vista, a few miles south of Saltillo, the Americans repulsed Santa Anna on February 22–23, 1847. But the victory was almost entirely due to the valor and the high morale of the Americans, for Taylor allowed himself to be surprised and his conduct of the battle was quite defective.

While this inconclusive campaign was going on, Brigadier General Stephen W. Kearny marched overland from Fort Leavenworth, Kansas, to Santa Fe, New Mexico, with 1,700 men and seized the town on August 18, 1846. His orders were to push on and conquer California. But Kearny received a message that California had been pacified by army captain John C. Frémont and navy commodore Robert F. Stockton, who were on the scene when the war started. Accordingly he took only 120 dragoons with him as he marched by way of the Gila River toward Los Angeles. It turned out that Mexican resistance had not ended in southern California, and it took two fierce engagements, at San Gabriel and the Mesa, on January 8–9, 1847, before Kearny ended resistance and occupied Los Angeles.

Kearny's campaign was one of the most astonishing in history. He marched more than 2,000 miles over desert territory never previously traversed by an organized military force and won decisive battles at the end.

His feat was duplicated by Colonel Alexander W. Doniphan, who took 850 Missouri mounted riflemen from Santa Fe all the way to Chihuahua, scattered a superior Mexican force at the Sacramento River, then marched to Saltillo to join Taylor on May 21, 1847.

But the most spectacular campaign in the war was the march of Winfield Scott with an army much smaller than the enemy's. In March 1847 the small but bold U.S. Navy carried out an extraordinary amphibious landing near Veracruz on the Gulf of Mexico. From there Scott crossed the Sierra Madre and seized Mexico City, winning every engagement and forcing the Mexicans to give up the war. Scott's campaign ranks in nerve and temerity with Alexander the Great's conquering of the Persian Empire in 334–331 B.C. After capturing Veracruz, Scott handed Santa Anna a disastrous defeat at Cerro Gordo in the mountains near Jalapa, rested for several months at Puebla until reinforcements could arrive, then drove on to the central valley of Mexico, where Santa Anna at last challenged him. But the Mexican general was no match for Scott, who defeated him in a series of victories, at Contreras, Churubusco, Molino del Rey, and Chapultepec. In the last stage of the campaign, Scott had fewer than one-third the number of troops arrayed against him, yet was never even checked, much less defeated.

Before Americans occupied Mexico City on September 12, 1847, an American diplomat, Nicholas P. Trist, had been trying to negotiate peace with Mexico. His sole accomplishment was to give Santa Anna $10,000 as the price he demanded for cooperation. Santa Anna then refused to cooperate. Polk was so incensed that he deprived Trist of all authority and ordered him home. Exasperated at Mexico's refusal to accept terms, Polk and his cabinet talked of taking more territory from the enemy than at first was contemplated.

While Polk tried to deal with Mexico, a new movement arose to annex the entire country. This was a wholly different concept from any American aspiration in the past. It would mean creating a colony with a subordinate population, no different from the way Britain ruled over the millions it held in subjection in India. Hitherto, the people living in lands the United States acquired—the French in Louisiana and the Spaniards in Louisiana and Florida—were accepted as full and equal American citizens. Now a sinister drive to create an American empire surfaced.

James Buchanan, secretary of state, and Robert J. Walker, secretary of the treasury, were leaders in this imperial movement, known as the "Continental Democrats." They tried to get Polk to claim the whole country in a message to Congress. Polk refused to say any more than that Americans should "take the measure of our indemnity into our own hands," but that was ambivalent enough. Although some critics thought this was an underhanded way for southerners to gain new slave territory, it was quickly apparent that the climate of Mexico was unsuitable to support the plantation system, and that slavery would never exist there.

Actually the "all-Mexico" movement was neither pro-slavery nor anti-slavery—it was almost wholly imperial. The most vocal support came from New York and in the western states from Ohio to Texas. A party magazine, the *Democratic Review* of October 1847, stated, "Until every acre of the North American continent is occupied by citizens of the United States, the foundations of the future empire will not have been laid." Similar ideas were spread by the *New York Herald* and *Sun*. These American imperialists invented the identical excuses that the British conjured up wherever they found a people they wanted to subjugate. The "all-Mexico" adherents cited the supposed "incapacity for self-government of the Indian race." Since Indians formed a large part of the Mexican population, the people were ipso facto incapable of ruling themselves. The *New York Evening Post* editorialized, "The aborigines of this country [the United States] have not attempted and cannot attempt to exist *independently* alongside of us. The Mexicans are *aboriginal Indians*, and they must share the destiny of their race."

Nicholas Trist knew something of the "all-Mexico" movement and suspected that Polk was in sympathy. To him, the choice lay between making peace at once with moderates who were in temporary charge in Mexico and conducting a protracted military occupation, including guerrilla warfare, which would possibly end in annexation of the whole country. Trist, along with John C. Calhoun of South Carolina and many others, believed that this would be a calamity—turning the nation away from its ideals and transforming it into an imperial tyrant.

In an unprecedented act of insubordination, Trist decided to stay on in Mexico and negotiate a peace. On February 2, 1848, in Guadalupe Hidalgo, a suburb of Mexico City, he signed a treaty in which Mexico acceded to America's minimum territorial demands—all of the region from the Rio Grande westward to the Pacific, including the whole of California.

Back in Washington, Polk had not aligned himself with the "all-Mexico" faction, but he was getting increasingly exasperated. Then quite unexpectedly a messenger arrived bearing the peace treaty. Polk was indignant at Trist, but the diplomat had delivered what the United States had originally set as its conditions. If Polk rejected the treaty, he would be fiercely criticized—for the drumbeat to annex all of Mexico was countered by a growing realization that the nation was in peril of heading down the wrong road.

Polk now made the right choice. Whatever his private feelings, he turned the nation away from empire and inequality. He sent the treaty to the Senate. There, after a bizarre battle between a minority faction that wanted *less* Mexican land and the "Continental Democrats," who wanted *more,* the Senate approved the treaty by a vote of 38–14 on March 10, 1848. The Mexican Congress accepted minor changes the Senate had made, and on June 30, 1848, the last American soldiers embarked from Veracruz.[2]

Five years later, the United States secured even more land from Mexico with the Gadsden Purchase, the region south of the Gila River in what are now Arizona and New Mexico. President Franklin Pierce authorized the $10 million purchase to acquire a suitable route for a railroad to the Pacific coast, but the transaction was even more significant in that it completed the boundaries of the original forty-eight states. It had been a mere seventy-five years since the United States had declared independence, and the nation had fulfilled its "manifest destiny" to possess the whole of the West from the Appalachians to the Pacific Ocean.

★ ★ ★

SIX

OUT OF THE DARKNESS

In just a few generations, the United States had made a remarkable journey from small colonial outpost to powerful nation that spanned an entire continent. Americans had boldly challenged the traditional powers of Europe to stay out of their affairs—indeed, to stay out of their *hemisphere*. But only a few years after the United States achieved its "manifest destiny" of occupying the land from Atlantic to Pacific, it nearly fell apart. This would be the darkest period in American history.

The calamity of the Civil War occurred because of intransigence on both sides. Simply put, Americans forgot our genius for compromise. Republicans, guided by Abraham Lincoln, elected president in 1860, took an adamant stand to stop the advance of slavery in the territories, arousing deep suspicions among slave owners that they were bent on eradicating slavery altogether. The Southern aristocracy, meanwhile, refused to face up to the fact that the nation could no longer tolerate the iniquity of human bondage and could not endure half slave and half free. Instead, they dug in their heels and tried to protect their selfish economic interests.

No national leader proposed the only equitable solution—for the U.S. government to buy the slaves and set them free. Yet Senator

Henry Clay of Kentucky proposed just this solution for the District of Columbia in 1850. Lincoln himself proposed it for the four slave states that remained in the Union in 1862, but by then North and South were already at war. The conflict, in money alone, cost at least twice what it would have taken to purchase all the slaves and give every freed family forty acres and a mule.[1] Far worse, the war cost 600,000 lives, one person in sixty in the entire population, and left wounds and animosities that endured for a hundred years.

There was time for compromise even after South Carolina seceded on December 20, 1860, followed by six other Deep South states. The urgent need at that point was not for an immediate solution but for dialogue. The longer the parties talked, the more the sensible voices would be heard rather than the firebrands (both North and South).

At the end of 1860, Senator John J. Crittenden of Kentucky produced a compromise that would allow everyone to save face. Crittenden's committee of thirteen senators, representing all sides, agreed to prohibit slavery all across the United States north of 36 degrees 30 minutes north latitude—the old line of the Missouri Compromise of 1820—and protect it south of that line. It was a sop that would have appeased the Deep South and ended the crisis. The only territory that actually could have theoretically become slave was New Mexico, but every informed person knew the dry climate there was unsuitable for plantation agriculture. Thereafter cooler heads could have come to a rational agreement, perhaps setting a future date when slaves would be free, perhaps reaching a purchase agreement after all. In short, such a compromise would not simply have delayed an inevitable clash, it would have allowed both sides to come together to achieve a solution. But the compromise did not happen because Abraham Lincoln refused to accept any extension of slavery, although he admitted he didn't "care much about New Mexico."[2] With no support from the incoming president, Congress allowed the plan to die.

Crittenden then urged that the compromise be submitted to the people for approval or rejection at the polls. Faced with the alternative of compromise or secession, most Americans North and South probably would have voted for Crittenden's solution. There was no machin-

ery to conduct such a referendum, but this could have easily been rectified if Lincoln had endorsed it and pulled the leaders of the Republican Party behind it. But this Lincoln would not do.

Instead, Lincoln made the worst of all decisions. In his inaugural address on March 4, 1861, he flung down the gauntlet to the seven seceded states: either come back into the Union or fight to stay out.[3] He
then precipitated war by ordering a relief expedition to Fort Sumter, a
federal facility in the harbor of Charleston, South Carolina. This was
an unnecessary provocation, designed to inflame demagogues North
and South. When Confederate forces fired on Fort Sumter on April 12,
1861, Lincoln called out 75,000 militia in all the states to suppress the
"rebellion." Having thus been directed by Lincoln to take part in an
invasion, four of the slave states that had held loyally to the Union—
Virginia, North Carolina, Tennessee, and Arkansas—chose to join the
Confederacy. This was a grave strategic blunder on Lincoln's part. Four
border states added to the Deep South meant that victory would be
much more difficult. Moreover, Virginia and North Carolina were by
far the most powerful southern states, and their adhesion to the Confederacy guaranteed a long and costly war.

Although the central issue going into the crisis was slavery, the four
upper South states seceded because they refused to invade the Deep
South. Destroying the homes and property of fellow Americans was
more than the people of these states could bear. It was *this* issue, not slavery, that caused the war to last for four years and caused southerners to
resist so bitterly. It did not have to be. The longer talks went on, the more
isolated the seven Deep South states would have become and the more
their people would have insisted on finding a way back into the Union.

★   ★   ★

THE TERRIBLE CIVIL WAR that followed at last delivered the
slaves their freedom. But nearly everything else about the war was
tragic: it left pain, suffering, and destitution in the South, and it required a century of conflict and denial before the nation at last brought
African Americans fully under the equal protection of the law with the
civil rights acts of 1964 and 1965.[4]

In one strange and unforeseen aspect, however, the Civil War produced a profound benefit for the United States. The war solidified and
strengthened the superb professional standards and traditions of the
army that had been established in the Mexican War and transformed
the United States into a formidable military power long before the nations of Europe recognized it and long before Americans were aware of
what they had done.

For four years, two of the greatest armies in the history of the world
fought each other to utter exhaustion and deadlock. There had never
been anything like the collisions between the Union Army of the Potomac and the Confederate Army of Northern Virginia before, and
there has never been anything like them since. In most wars, one army
somehow defeats the other and the political leaders come to a resolution and make peace. This did not happen in the fantastic campaigns
that spread over Virginia, Maryland, and Pennsylvania from 1861 to
1865. Time after time the Army of Northern Virginia defeated the
Army of the Potomac. But after every defeat, the Union army picked
itself up, licked its wounds, and went back into the fight.

Faced with Confederate leaders who outwitted and outmaneuvered
the Union commanders at every turn, the Federal army shifted to massive power and sheer numbers to overwhelm the South. With three
times the population and eleven times the industry of the South, the
North was able to bring immense force to bear on the battlefield.[5]

Unable to match this insurmountable weight of arms, the Confederacy turned to audacity and inventive leadership to win its battles.

Thus the two cardinal elements that would make up American military supremacy in the years ahead—overwhelming power and dazzling leadership—came together in the battle between the Army of the
Potomac and the Army of Northern Virginia. What is more, each side
perfected and refined its particular advantage, and each carried the implementation of its principle to the extreme limits.

The North, for example, produced far more rifled cannons than the
South, and in battle after battle—especially in what the southerners
called "artillery hell" at Antietam on September 17, 1862—it used its
huge superiority to slow Rebel movements or shatter defenses. Yet it

was the Confederacy, particularly under its gifted artillery leader Porter Alexander, that created the most effective and flexible artillery organization—the so-called corps artillery that permitted all the guns of a corps to be concentrated quickly on a particular target. This system became the standard in the U.S. Army for the next century and was adopted immediately after the war by Prussia, Austria, France, and Britain.[6]

Robert E. Lee, the commander of the Army of Northern Virginia from June 1, 1862, to war's end, was far bolder than most men. Joseph Christmas Ives, who had served on Lee's staff, described him thus: "If there is one man in either army, Federal or Confederate, who is head and shoulders far above every other one in audacity that man is General Lee. Lee is audacity personified. His name is audacity."

Lee sought from first to last to fight an offensive war—that is, a war of battles and marches against the armies of the North. This offensive war ultimately failed, but it provided the nation and the U.S. Army an ideal of boldness and daring that influenced every war and every campaign thereafter. Not by greater power but by aggressive action and by movements forcefully and confidently carried out, Lee defeated or neutralized superior Union forces time after time. Only after slow, costly attrition was the North able to hobble Lee. By 1865, the Army of Northern Virginia had become only a shadow, and at Appomattox it not so much surrendered as vanished into legend. The Civil War is nearly unique in military history in that a single man, Lee, by his audacity, was able to stymie over a period of years the greatest efforts of an extremely powerful state, the Union.

The South possessed, in Stonewall Jackson, an authentic military genius, and his ideas and actions raised inventiveness, daring, boldness, and execution to levels never before seen in this country and matched only by the greatest captains of world history, such as Alexander the Great and Napoleon. Where Lee established standards of action, swift movements, and sudden attacks that became axioms of how commanders could use imagination, not power, to succeed, Jackson produced campaigns so stunning and so cerebral that they established hitherto unimaginable concepts of what could be achieved by brainpower in war.

Early in the conflict Jackson wanted to sweep around Washington, D.C., and sever the rail lines connecting the capital with the North. Such a move, especially after the Confederate victory at First Manassas in July 1861, would have taken few troops, would have eliminated the food supply of the capital, and would have forced the Lincoln administration to abandon the city. A fugitive president who had lost his capital would have left the North with shrunken faith in the war and probably would have brought peace. But the Confederate president, Jefferson Davis, refused to go ahead with the plan because he was convinced the North would tire of the war and grant the South its independence. Thus the campaign was never undertaken.

In the Shenandoah Valley campaign in the spring of 1862, Jackson maneuvered a tiny army, but he nevertheless convinced Lincoln that his men threatened Washington. As a result, Lincoln called off the planned drive of a 40,000-man corps under Irwin McDowell from Fredericksburg to the Confederate capital of Richmond; Jackson thereby prevented a Union triumph that would have ended the war within days.

In the summer and fall of 1862, Jackson tried to induce Lee to place the Confederate army athwart the Union line of supply and retreat to force the Federals to attack. Since the Minié ball rifle, new to warfare, had a range four times the old smoothbore musket of the Mexican War, Jackson was certain that any Union attack against an emplaced and waiting Rebel army would fail, with tremendous casualties. The Confederates could then sweep around the flank of the demoralized Union army and either cut it off and force its surrender or compel it to flee in disorder. Lee refused to undertake this maneuver three times and once—at Second Manassas, in August 1862—waited too long to carry it out. Only at Chancellorsville, in May 1863, did Lee at last employ Jackson's strategy. Though Jackson achieved a brilliant victory there, his plan to destroy the entire Union army was foiled because he suffered a mortal wound in the battle.

The astonishing fact is that Union general William Tecumseh Sherman won the Civil War by following in Georgia exactly the model that Stonewall Jackson had built in Virginia. In his 1864 march through the mountains from Tennessee to Atlanta, Sherman refused to challenge Joseph E. Johnston's Confederate army and instead simply swung around it, threatening its retreat and forcing Johnston to withdraw all the way to Atlanta. Jefferson Davis replaced Johnston with John Bell Hood, who foolishly shattered his army in precisely the kind of frontal attacks that Jackson had tried to avoid with Rebel forces and had tried to induce with Union forces. Now with no effective army to block him, Sherman marched almost unmolested to Savannah, splitting the Confederacy in two and ending any hope of victory.

The strategic lessons of the Civil War were little heeded in Europe and were slow to be appreciated in the United States in the welcome peace that came in 1865. But in 1898 a British army colonel, G. F. R. Henderson, published a two-volume work, *Stonewall Jackson and the American Civil War,* that laid out Jackson's unique contributions. The book commenced a process that incorporated into American doctrine not only the ideal of great leadership exemplified by Robert E. Lee but also the brilliance and innovation demonstrated by Stonewall Jackson and William T. Sherman.

Therefore, when the United States came into the twentieth century, its army possessed a solid tradition of leadership and massive force. As the world was going to find out, it was a devastating combination.[7]

★   ★   ★

ALTHOUGH THE SOUTH was destitute at the end of the war, the nation as a whole had advanced immensely. The war had even forced the South to build numerous factories—cotton mills, boot and shoe factories, munitions plants, and many others—since the Union blockade prevented southerners from relying on imports. Upon these foundations rested the vast industrialization of the "New South" after the war. The textile industry largely migrated from New England to the Piedmont uplands of North and South Carolina. Furniture-making and the new cigarette industry concentrated in North Carolina and Virginia. A large iron and steel center grew up around Birmingham, Alabama. In the North the industrial advance was much greater. With so many men in the army, manufacturers had to make use of new labor-saving machines to increase output, and this pattern accelerated after the war.

The railroads, which had grown to 35,000 miles of track in 1865, at last welded the entire nation together in 1869, when the first transcontinental line was completed at Promontory Point, near Ogden, Utah. Other cross-country lines followed, and the United States was transformed by rails in the space of a few years into by far the largest common market in the world.

The railroads revolutionized American industry, because a factory anywhere could get its products to customers wherever located. Business on a local scale gave way to business on a national scale. Gigantic corporations tended to drive smaller operators out of existence. They were protected from most foreign competition by a high tariff that Northern business interests had been able to establish after Southern delegations withdrew from Congress in the Civil War. In time, the government took action to restrain the monopolies that industrialists and railroad owners had built, but throughout the last years of the nineteenth century and the first years of the twentieth, the American economy experienced stupendous growth.[8]

The numbers are astounding. In 1860 the United States possessed 7.2 percent of the world's manufacturing output; at the time Britain led the world with almost 20 percent. By 1900 America's share had tripled to 23.6 percent. And by 1913, just prior to World War I, the United States produced nearly one-third of the entire world's manufacturing output, while Britain's portion had fallen to 13.6 percent. In the years between the end of the Civil War and the Spanish-American War of 1898, American wheat production increased two and a half times, corn more than twice, miles of railroad track over five and a half times, coal production eight times, and steel from fewer than 20,000 tons to nearly 9 million tons. By 1890 American invested capital per person was three times that of Britain. American corporations like International Harvester, Singer, Du Pont, Bell, Colt, and Standard Oil were equal to any in the world, sometimes better. As the economist Paul Kennedy points out, when Andrew Carnegie sold out his factories in 1901 to J. P. Morgan's colossal United States Steel Corporation, Carnegie alone was producing more steel than the whole of England. It was therefore not surprising that the national income of the United States in 1914 was more than three times that of Britain or Germany and six times that of France. The American population of 98 million was more than twice that of Britain or France, half again as large as Germany's.[9]

★   ★   ★

AT THE TURN of the twentieth century the United States entered into a vast new world. It had become the preeminent economic power on earth and was separating itself further from the rest of the world every year. Americans didn't know it yet but we had all the elements that would make us the paramount military power on earth. But the United States had so far played only a minor role in world affairs. This was about to change.

On July 12, 1893, a young professor from the University of Wisconsin, Frederick Jackson Turner, read a paper before the American Historical Association in Chicago. This event was one of the most telling moments in American history. It caused Americans to wake up to the fact that we and our forebears had actually accomplished the immense and splendid task that the explorers had dimly foreseen centuries before when they looked out from the Appalachians and beheld another new world stretching westward far beyond their imagination.

The Census of 1890 announced that the frontier had ceased to be. This brief notation marked the closing of a great historic movement. "Up to our own day," Turner said, "American history has been in a large degree the history of the colonization of the Great West. The existence of an area of free land, its continuous recession, and the advance of American settlement westward, explain American development."[10]

In by far the biggest task we had ever set for ourselves, we had built the greatest nation in a century and a quarter of existence, and we had become a people steeped in individualism, self-reliance, and self-confidence. So America had got it right. But the frontier was gone. What now?

SEVEN

★ ★ ★

IMPERIAL INTERLUDE

In the last decade of the nineteenth century, leaders in the United States were astounded by the revelation of an American naval officer, Alfred Thayer Mahan. His book, *The Influence of Sea Power upon History*, published in 1890, proved that a superior fleet can sweep all lesser navies from the seas. Mahan showed that this was how the Royal Navy had dominated the oceans for two and a half centuries and why Britain had been able to accumulate the largest empire in history. Mahan concluded that without sea power no nation could attain a position of first importance. He was anxious to see his own country profit by the British example.

Only four years after the book came out, Japan graphically demonstrated Mahan's principles when its twenty-three fast, modern warships sank four of the Chinese fleet's eleven slower, older ships in the Yellow Sea and drove the remainder into a harbor, where they didn't dare come out again. The results of this one short battle were monumental—Japan gained dominance of Korea, a tributary Chinese kingdom that it absorbed in 1910; annexed the Chinese island province of Taiwan; and received the Liaodong Peninsula at the tip of Manchuria (northeastern China). Possession of Liaodong with its deepwater ports of Lüshun and Lüda (Dalian) gave Japan dominance of Manchuria. What's more, since Lüshun was only three hundred miles from the Chinese capital of Beijing, it would provide a perfect base for future Japanese aggressions against China.

Russia had been coveting the same port, however, and it got the help of France and Germany to force Japan to relinquish Lüshun. Russia then took over the peninsula, renamed Lüshun "Port Arthur," and built a large naval base there. Japan was livid, and plotted revenge.

Until the 1890s Americans had largely been able to ignore the worldwide implications of sea power. We had never built a world-class navy, protected as we were by the Royal Navy while we were conquering the continent. But now the frontier was gone, the continent had been tamed, and Mahan's lessons, combined with disturbing events like Japan's aggressions, revealed a much more sinister world. In Europe, a powerful, recently united, and dangerous Germany was threatening to challenge Britain's world trade and build an empire of its own. In the Far East, not only was Japan emerging as another threat, but also the European powers were circling like buzzards around the decaying Chinese empire, hoping to pick off parcels of it and end America's Open Door policy of guaranteeing free trade to all in China.

Although the Royal Navy still guarded the Atlantic approaches to the United States, a new feeling of unease spread among American leaders. What if the British got bogged down in a war with Germany? Or what if we got into a real confrontation with them about China? Who would protect the Western Hemisphere then? And what about the Pacific? Mahan had prophesied that this ocean would be the theater of a gigantic struggle between the Western and Oriental civilizations and that the United States would be in the front position to meet this challenge. All at once the world did not seem as safe as it had been.

An influential group of "navalists" emerged. They focused on the need to protect the United States *beyond* its shores. This group, led by Mahan and his principal disciple, Theodore Roosevelt, held, first, that the American navy must be modernized and vastly enlarged. Second, a ship canal had to be built between the Atlantic and the Pacific in Central America so American warships could move quickly from one coast to the other as the need arose. Third, the Caribbean approaches to a canal and the oceanic approaches to the West Coast had to be protected by naval bases — Hawaii in the Pacific and any of several islands in the West Indies, especially Spain's last two possessions there, Cuba and Puerto Rico. Fourth, a string of naval coaling and repair stations should be occupied, particularly in the Pacific. Without them, Mahan wrote, U.S. warships would "be like land birds, unable to fly far from their own shores."

The first direct response to Mahan's treatise came in the administration of Republican President Benjamin Harrison, 1889–93. His secretary of the navy, Benjamin F. Tracy, proposed an up-to-date fighting fleet of twenty battleships—twelve in the Atlantic, eight in the Pacific, all equal to the best in the world in armor, guns, and speed. Congress actually authorized, and shipyards speedily built, four of these battleships: *Indiana, Massachusetts, Oregon,* and *Iowa.*

At the same time another movement commenced in the United States, led by individuals who believed that Charles Darwin's theories on evolution could be applied to society.[1] Where Darwin argued that higher life forms evolved through natural selection and spoke of the "survival of the fittest" and the "struggle for existence," Social Darwinists believed that a similar struggle existed among the races and nations. In their view, Anglo-Saxons represented the Darwinian "fittest," and they—that is, the British and the Americans—had some divine right to rule the world. These notions, of course, were perversions of the American dream of equality, democracy, and freedom, and the antithesis of everything the nation had strived for from its birth and had etched on its character in the Civil War. Nevertheless, Social Darwinists used them to justify a ruthless international competition in the name of "progress" and to create an "American empire" in the same fashion as the British had done. Historian John Fiske, for example, announced that the "English race" was destined to dominate with its language, politics, and blood all regions of the earth not already the seats of old civilizations. And Josiah Strong, a Protestant clergyman, proclaimed that the Anglo-Saxon was "divinely commissioned to be his brother's keeper" and that "this race of unequaled energy will spread itself over the earth."

★   ★   ★

WHILE SOME HAD been vocally advocating a strong U.S. presence on the world stage, it would be a civil war in Cuba that thrust the

United States into imperialism. In 1895 Cuban insurgents rebelled against the Spanish colonial government, destroying cane fields, sugar mills, and other property in the hope of rendering the island worthless to Spain. In February 1896 a new Spanish captain-general, Valeriano Weyler, ordered the entire population of large districts in central and western Cuba into concentration camps surrounded by trenches, barbed wire, and blockhouses. There he provided neither adequate food nor sanitation. Cubans who disobeyed the "reconcentration" were shot on sight. Famine and disease spread in the camps. By spring 1898 200,000 *reconcentrados* had died out of total population of only 1.6 million.

The plight of the Cuban people aroused tremendous sentiment in the United States. The public got vivid, often exaggerated accounts through the "yellow press" led by William Randolph Hearst's *New York Journal* and Joseph Pulitzer's *New York World*. Reporters played up Spanish atrocities but ignored insurgent crimes. It was easy to see that the newspapers were pushing an expansionist agenda, although most papers disclaimed selfish designs on Cuba. To artist Frederic Remington in Havana, Hearst reportedly wired: "You furnish the pictures, and I'll furnish the war." A rising demand came from Americans to intervene, but they wanted no U.S. colony, only a free Cuba.

Any chance for compromise was ruined by the explosion of the U.S. battleship *Maine* in Havana harbor on February 15, 1898, in which 260 American seamen lost their lives. The ship was in Cuban waters on a "courtesy call"—really a not-so-subtle device to intimidate the Spanish authorities. Divers who examined the wreckage concluded that the bottom plates had been blown inward and upward, indicating that the cause was a submarine mine. By that time, American newspapers had already adjudged Spain as guilty. Later investigations would question whether a mine really had caused the explosion, but that didn't matter; "Remember the *Maine!*" had become a popular cry long before.

On March 28, 1898, President William McKinley demanded independence for Cuba. The Spanish government desperately sought allies in Europe. But Britain refused, and all the other capitals said they'd act only if *someone else* took the lead. Spain tried to compromise but rejected

Cuban freedom. When the U.S. Congress passed a resolution recognizing the independence of the island, Spain declared war.

The conflict was pathetically one-sided. The Spanish navy had nothing to match the four new U.S. battleships that had been authorized under President Harrison, and Spanish crews were wretchedly inefficient. Theodore Roosevelt, the assistant secretary of the navy, had already targeted the Spanish-owned Philippine Islands for occupation and had alerted Commodore George Dewey, chief of the Asiatic squadron, to move immediately after war was declared. Dewey sank or burned the entire Spanish flotilla at Manila, and at the end of July, 11,000 American troops entered Manila against only token resistance. On the way, Americans occupied Guam in the Marianas, another Spanish colony.[2]

Meanwhile the main Spanish fleet slipped into Santiago harbor on the south coast of Cuba but was promptly blockaded by the U.S. Atlantic fleet. Spain's main strength, four old wooden-decked armored cruisers, altogether could not fire as many shells as a single American battleship. An American army landed a few miles east of the city, and on July 1, 1898, in a hard-fought engagement at El Caney and San Juan Hill, it reached the high ground above Santiago. Two days later the Spanish squadron made a dash for a safer haven farther west, but in a running fight U.S. ships sank all the Spanish vessels or ran them ashore as burning hulks. On July 16 Santiago surrendered. While all this was going on, another American expeditionary force landed on Puerto Rico and took possession against minuscule resistance.

The Spanish asked for peace.

Roosevelt, who had resigned his post as assistant navy secretary to go to Cuba as a lieutenant colonel in the "Rough Riders" regiment, urged leaders in Washington to keep the Philippines, Puerto Rico, and Guam. President McKinley, Senator Henry Cabot Lodge, and Admiral Mahan, among other leaders, were of the same opinion. There was no dispute about acquiring Guam and little about annexing Puerto Rico, a relatively small island inhabited mainly by people of European culture, though they spoke an alien tongue. Puerto Rico's strategic location at the outer edge of the Caribbean could shield any ship canal in Central America, and this reason alone was sufficient to ensure its annexation.

Nor did the U.S. government waste much time discussing annexation of another group of islands, Hawaii. Dewey's victory at Manila had turned American eyes on the Pacific, and it would be essential to keep a naval base at Hawaii. With little argument a joint resolution passed both houses of Congress, and on August 12, 1898, Hawaii passed formally under the flag of the United States.

But the Philippines were another matter. The archipelago was 6,000 miles from San Francisco, and its 7 million people were Malays, with a vastly different culture. Many of the people were pagans and Muslims. Moreover, the Filipinos had also been trying to win independence from Spain and didn't want to become subjects of the United States. Here was a dangerous venture into imperialism, a violation of time-honored American principles. While the Social Darwinists endorsed annexing the islands, opponents formed an Anti-Imperialist League, and in the Senate many Democrats and a few Republicans made clear that they would vote against annexation.

Then a couple of disturbing events took place. Japan proposed that it join with the United States and a third power to administer the Philippines. In light of Japan's recent aggressions against China, no one in the U.S. government wanted Japan to have any hand in the islands, for its intentions were obviously to gain a permanent position there. Then Germany sent a naval squadron to Manila. It became abundantly clear that if the United States abandoned the islands, Germany would take over. Indeed, Germany exacted from Spain a secret promise not to cede its Caroline and Marshall Islands or any of the other Mariana Islands except Guam to the United States; it later bought the islands.[3]

A major power play was developing in the Far East. Britain much preferred the United States to either Japan or Germany in so strategic a place as the Philippines. There a hostile power could threaten China and all of Southeast Asia. Accordingly, Britain advised Washington to keep the archipelago. Of course, London's advice carried very much a tone of irony. The United States had been berating Britain for a century and a quarter for its sinful colonialism, and here it was about to join the imperial club.

Only a few months later, Rudyard Kipling, Britain's greatest poet of empire, wrote a poem that spelled out what the United States was getting into:

Take up the white man's burden—
Send forth the best ye breed—
Go bind your sons in exile
To serve your captives' need;

To wait in heavy harness
On fluttered folk and wild—
Your new-caught, sullen peoples,
Half devil and half child.

Take up the white man's burden
And reap his old reward:
The blame of those ye better
The hate of those ye guard. . . .

The debate in the Senate was long and hard. But on February 6, 1899, the Senate voted 57–27 to acquire the Philippines, just one vote above the two-thirds necessary for approval. Two days before, the Filipinos had opened hostilities in Manila against the Americans. It was not until July 1902 that resistance finally subsided.

The Philippine insurrection soured most Americans on the idea of empire. The Social Darwinists' dream of joining with Britain and establishing "Anglo-Saxon" domination of the world evaporated in the reality of a nasty guerrilla war in a faraway tropical archipelago. The insurrection took 4,200 American lives, and 2,800 more were wounded; in contrast, the Spanish-American War itself had claimed just 379 American lives. Americans also killed 16,000 Filipinos in battle, and as many as 200,000 civilians died, victims of disease, famine, and cruelties on both sides. Possessing the islands became an embarrassment to the United States. We toyed with plans to free the Filipinos on several occasions, and in 1934 Congress finally passed a bill that promised independence. On July 4, 1946, less than a year after the end of World War II, the United States actually granted it.

The decision to free the Philippines was right, but the decision in 1899 to annex the islands was also right. It kept imperial competition in the Far East from getting any worse than it already was. Japan had embarked on a drive to acquire a great empire and to oust the Western powers from the Far East.[4] That Japan was intent on aggression was proved in the Russo-Japanese War of 1904–05, when it defeated Russia, primarily because its superior fleet sank almost the entire Russian fleet in the Strait of Tsushima in 1905, thereby proving Mahan's thesis once again. Japan finally took the Liaodong Peninsula back from the Russians, and then planned a murderous program aimed at absorbing China.

Theodore Roosevelt, who by this point had entered the White House, after the September 1901 assassination of President William McKinley, decided to give Japan what it wanted most of all—control of Korea—in exchange for a Japanese promise to back off from the Philippines. This was an immoral act. It delivered an innocent people into the grasping hands of an avaricious empire. Roosevelt knew, however, that Japan could be thwarted only by force, and neither he nor any European power were willing to apply this force. He decided to make the best of a bad situation and signed the agreement in July 1905, with the United States accepting Japanese "suzerainty" in Korea and Japan disavowing any interest in the Philippines.

Roosevelt then offered to broker a peace between Russia and Japan, setting up a conference in Portsmouth, New Hampshire, in August–September 1905. Largely because of Roosevelt's pressure, Japan gave up its demand for the whole island of Sakhalin, accepting the southern half, and it also gave up its demand for a huge indemnity. Even so, Japan took over Port Arthur and the South Manchuria Railroad (Harbin to Port Arthur, or Lüshun) from Russia and got a firmer hold on south Manchuria. Despite this, the Japanese people held the United States directly responsible for their failure to gain better terms, and from this moment they focused on the United States as their principal enemy.

Japanese anger intensified when the San Francisco school board, fearful of the "Yellow Peril," ruled in October 1906 that the children of Japanese residents could not attend white schools and must go to the school reserved for Chinese and Korean children. This decision brought vociferous protests from Tokyo and threats of war in the Japanese press. President Roosevelt talked the school board into withdrawing the decision in exchange for a "gentlemen's agreement"—Japan would refuse passports to laborers coming to the mainland United States, while the United States would bar Japanese from coming in from Hawaii, Canada, or Mexico.

Roosevelt now committed another immoral act. He tacitly accepted Japan's supremacy in south Manchuria in 1907, despite the fact that Manchuria belonged to China and the United States had previously supported Chinese territorial integrity. President Roosevelt had decided to appease Japan in the hopes of creating a balance of power in East Asia to counter the European empires. But he had discovered that he could not contain Japan without concessions.

And even these concessions to Japan's greed did him no good. The next year the Japanese became incensed when the California legislature nearly passed a bill prohibiting Japanese from owning land in the state. Though Roosevelt managed to derail the bill's passage, California passed the same anti-Japanese measure a few years later, as did several other western states.

From 1905 on, the United States confronted an intractable foe and ambitious competitor on the western edge of the Pacific Ocean.

★   ★   ★

IN THE 1890S the nation had achieved some of Admiral Mahan's goals. First, of course, it had started to build a modern navy. It had also gained a series of bases and coaling stations in the Pacific, along with two bases to protect any canal dug in Central America—Puerto Rico and Guantánamo Bay, on the southeastern corner of Cuba, which was acquired after the United States gave the island its independence.

Still, much remained to be done. When Mahan's apostle Roosevelt became president, he set about to achieve all of the admiral's objectives. After inheriting a navy with seventeen battleships already built or being built, he accelerated the growth of the U.S. fleet. By 1904 the United States was the fifth-largest naval power on earth, by 1914 the third-largest (behind Britain and Germany).

Roosevelt focused even more attention on Mahan's final objective: to build a canal across Central America. Although Americans had recognized the growing strategic importance of the Pacific, the U.S. Navy remained a one-ocean fleet. And with Japan threatening from one ocean and Germany threatening from the other, the navy had to have a canal to get to whichever coast was most in danger.

The German threat had become clear when U.S. officials caught the German kaiser, Wilhelm II, making two different incursions into Latin America. In 1902 Kaiser Wilhelm sent German warships to survey Margarita, an island just off Venezuela's coast, with the idea of buying it and establishing a naval base there. U.S. secretary of state John Hay delivered a démarche to Berlin, and the German vessels withdrew. The next year, however, Wilhelm tried to set up another naval base by buying all the land around the Bay of Magdalena in the southern reaches of Mexico's Baja California peninsula. When word of his efforts got out, Wilhelm backed off. But it was obvious that Germany, given the chance, would expand into Latin America and defy the Monroe Doctrine.

With Germany aggressively moving toward America, the need for a canal became acute. The question remained, however: where to build it? A French company had started trying to dig a canal in 1881 through the isthmus of Panama, a province of Colombia, but the rainforest created such difficult construction conditions that the company was bankrupt by the early 1890s. Only a small part of the work had been completed. Meanwhile, the United States had toyed with building a competing canal through Nicaragua, but nothing had come of it. By the time Roosevelt became president, many in the United States refocused on Panama, since a canal there would be much shorter than one in Nicaragua. But several senators still pushed hard for the Nicaraguan route. In June 1902, champions of a Panama canal placed on the desk of every senator a Nicaraguan postage stamp featuring a smoking volcano in the middle of Lake Nicaragua, through which the canal was to run. Volcanoes had become a terrifying danger, because, only the month before, Mount Pelée on Martinique had erupted, destroying the town of St. Pierre and killing thousands of people. With that fearful image before it, Congress voted to build a canal through Panama.

At this moment the national interests of the United States collided with the special interests of Colombian politicians. Colombia was in the midst of a civil war. Its president, José Manuel Marroquín, an aging intellectual, was thrown on the horns of a dilemma. If he made the necessary concessions to the United States, he would risk impairing his nation's sovereignty and be accused of buckling under to "Yankee imperialism." If he did not take advantage of the bonanza being offered, he would be charged with economic idiocy.

Marroquín vacillated, but at last he told Dr. Tomás Herrán, his minister in Washington, to get the best deal possible. Herrán and John Hay signed a treaty that the Senate approved on March 17, 1903. It was heavily weighted in favor of the United States, which was to have exclusive rights to the canal for a full century, renewable at the sole discretion of the United States. Not only that, but the United States was to receive an exclusive zone for five kilometers on either side of the canal. For these privileges, the U.S. government agreed to give Colombia a lump sum of $10 million and $250,000 a year beginning in nine years.

The civil war in Colombia had ended, and Marroquín submitted the treaty to his newly elected Senate. There intense opposition erupted. The money offered was not enough. The perpetually renewable grant of rights and the exclusive zone infringed on Colombian sovereignty. Colombian leaders decided to hold out for a better deal. When this got back to Secretary of State Hay, he warned that any rejection might result in action Colombia would regret. The Colombian Senate, infuriated at Hay's threat, voted down the treaty 24–0.

Here again, President Roosevelt exhibited unworthy motives. From his earliest days as a politician, Roosevelt had disparaged and vilified persons who opposed him, and he thought of himself as invariably right, his opponents as always wrong. There were, besides, elements of jingoism in Roosevelt that caused him to belittle those living in less-advanced countries. Roosevelt was certainly an imperialist, and he possibly had absorbed some of the Social Darwinist ideas about the innate superiority of the "Anglo-Saxon race" and its "divine right" to rule. He was livid at the Colombians, announcing that he was not going to be "held up" by Colombian politicians. He described them as "jack rabbits" and "contemptible little creatures." No, he asserted forcefully, he would not negotiate with them further.

The solution, of course, was to induce the people of Panama to secede and then to sign a quick treaty with them. Roosevelt thought this was a good idea, but "for me to say so publicly would amount to an instigation of a revolt, and therefore I cannot say it."

On September 3, 1903, Dr. Manuel Amador, leader of a group of self-seeking Panamanian conspirators, met in the United States with Philippe Bunau-Varilla, former chief engineer of the French company that had tried to build the canal, who had a material interest in getting the United States to finish the job. Bunau-Varilla promised Amador $100,000 for expenses and secured interviews for himself with President Roosevelt and Secretary Hay. On the strength of these interviews, Bunau-Varilla assured himself that the United States would prevent Colombia from suppressing a Panamanian revolt, although he asked no inconvenient questions and received no incriminating promises. Bunau-Varilla sent Amador back to Panama with assurances that the United States would protect the conspirators if they revolted.

Roosevelt later asserted that no one connected with the U.S. government had any part in the revolution. But as the revolution was brewing, U.S. naval vessels arrived at Colón and Panama, on either side of the isthmus. Once there they got an order to "prevent landing of any armed force, either government or insurgent, at any point within fifty miles of Panama." The skipper of the *Nashville* at Colón did not get the message in time to prevent the landing of four hundred Colombian troops, but officials of the Panama Railroad delayed their transportation to Panama, where, on November 3, 1903, the conspirators declared independence. The four hundred Colombians went back home, and the revolution succeeded without bloodshed.

On November 18, 1903, in a bald-faced power play, Secretary Hay signed with Bunau-Varilla a Panama-U.S. treaty, even more favorable to the United States than the treaty with Colombia had been. It made Panama a protectorate of the United States, and the United States got in perpetuity a sovereign canal zone ten miles wide. The *New York Times* denounced Roosevelt's policy as "the path of scandal, disgrace, and dishonor." There were other critics, but a surprisingly large number of papers supported the president. Roosevelt defended his handling of the case to his dying day, but his bullying of the Colombians was detestable. And it was unnecessary, for he could have continued negotiating with Colombia, offering more money and at least a veneer of residual sovereignty. Roosevelt's mistreatment of the Colombians caused ill feelings that lasted for years.

Nevertheless, the United States had its canal zone. Construction proceeded rapidly, and on August 15, 1914, the canal opened to traffic.

America handled acquisition of the Panama Canal Zone badly, but the decision to build the canal was right, because the United States had an imperative need to gain quick access to both oceans. The advantages afforded by the canal would serve America well in the years ahead, when the mounting threats around the globe would call the United States to assume an active role in world affairs.

★   ★   ★

ALTHOUGH THEODORE ROOSEVELT made certain troubling decisions during his presidency, he also upheld important traditions established by his predecessors and guided the United States on its path toward becoming the world's preeminent military and political power. Building up the navy and beginning the Panama Canal prepared the United States militarily, but he took another important step to protect America's national security. Specifically, he enunciated what became known as the Roosevelt corollary to the Monroe Doctrine.

In 1904, the Dominican Republic was so deeply in debt to Europe that European powers threatened to forcibly intervene. Recognizing that such intervention would flout the Monroe Doctrine, which the Americans had held sacred for some eighty years, Roosevelt declared in December, "Chronic wrongdoing, or an impotence which results in a general loosening of the ties of civilized society, may in America, as elsewhere, ultimately require intervention by some civilized nation, and in the Western Hemisphere the adherence of the United States to the Monroe Doctrine may force the United States, however reluctantly, in flagrant cases of such wrongdoing or impotence to the exercise of an international police power." In short, to prevent European countries from interfering in Latin America, Roosevelt asserted that the United States itself could and would intervene to impose order. At the same time the message served as a warning to Latin American countries to keep the peace and honor international obligations or else run the risk of U.S. occupation.

Where James Monroe had given Europe a simple message—*keep out*—Theodore Roosevelt lent muscle to that declaration.

In the immediate term, the Roosevelt corollary prompted the United States to appoint a customs receiver to deal with the financial crisis in the Dominican Republic. Soon, however, it would be used to justify even more "preventive interventions." Before World War I began, the United States would take action in Cuba, Haiti, and Nicaragua, among other places.

In time, too, the "international police power" that Theodore Roosevelt first suggested in 1904 would become an important part of America's reasoning for venturing into the world as a decisive leader after Europe descended into war in 1914.

EIGHT

★ ★ ★

WAR AND ISOLATION

The United States moved reluctantly into the role of world power in 1917. When it did so, it acted decisively, and it has never abandoned its leadership role since, despite an atavistic effort after the disillusionment of World War I to withdraw behind its oceans.

During a crucial five-year period, from 1917 to 1922, the United States made three profoundly right decisions that saved the world from autocracy and oppression. It entered World War I and stopped the aggression of Germany. It rejected membership in the League of Nations and preserved American sovereignty. And it took on the burden of building the world's greatest military power to foil future attempts by aggressive nations to enslave other peoples.

When World War I started in 1914, we saw it as another terrible outgrowth of the entangling alliances that the Founding Fathers had warned against. We wanted to stay out of the maelstrom. Woodrow Wilson, who became president in March 1913, lectured the Europeans like the schoolteacher he was on why they should make peace without either side gaining victory. This angered both the Allies and the Central Powers. Each wanted to devastate the other side. But it suited the Americans. In early 1917 three-quarters of the population still regarded the war in Europe with indifference or aversion. Only a tiny fraction wanted to get into it. (Hence the popularity of Wilson's reelection campaign slogan in 1916, "He kept us out of war.")

Our misgivings were a product of a deep lack of appreciation as to how important and powerful the nation had become. The world now could not do *without* the United States. To our surprise, we had become the indispensable nation. We were by far the largest economy in the world, by far the richest nation. What we did affected decisively the fates of all other countries. The forces of history were driving the United States into taking a crucial role in world affairs. We at last recognized our responsibility and began acting as the preeminent power on earth. It was a hard decision to give up the security and isolation that we had enjoyed since our founding. But it was the correct decision, and Americans by an overwhelming majority made it definitely and with little backward glance.

★   ★   ★

WORLD WAR I was a pivotal turning point in Western civilization. By entering into the conflict, European nations—out of selfishness and obduracy—inflicted a crippling blow on their own wealth and power. No European nation thenceforth ever possessed more than a third of the economic capacity of the United States. Twenty years after the war, the United States, with much of its industry idle because of the Great Depression, still commanded almost as much war potential as all five of the European great powers put together.

Until the war occurred, the imperial powers of Europe—notably Britain, France, and Russia—controlled much of the world's underdeveloped territory and most of the world's seaborne trade. Britain was incomparably the leader. It had outperformed all other countries industrially until the last few years of the nineteenth century. Moreover, by means of the Royal Navy, it had seized a quarter of the earth's surface, which made Britain the paramount force in world commerce, commanding trade with the new dominions of Canada, Australia, New Zealand, and South Africa, with its crown jewel, India, and with most of Latin America.

Since its unification in 1871, however, Germany had become a major contender, seeking a large colonial empire of its own and expanding its trade, especially at the expense of Britain. Right-wing political leaders began to claim for Germany status as a world power—*Weltmacht*. Around the turn of the century Germany passed Britain in industrial development and overall economic power. At the same time it began a fatal program of building a modern fleet to challenge the Royal Navy, which set in motion a fierce naval arms race. By 1909 Britain had won the contest. Its navy was double the size of Germany's, and the disparity was growing, not shrinking. Nevertheless, the damage had been done. Fearful of Germany's economic growth, Britain signed a series of agreements with France in 1904 that grew into a secret military alliance, and it signed a similar agreement with Russia in 1907. Meanwhile Germany had allied itself with Austria-Hungary. Thus two powerful coalitions arose in Europe, each ready to challenge the other.

In 1907 Arthur Balfour, British prime minister from 1902 to 1905, told an American diplomat, "We are probably fools not to find a reason for declaring war on Germany before she builds too many ships and takes away our trade."

This trade rivalry was the reason for World War I. As President Wilson put it in 1919, "This war was a commercial and industrial war. It was not a political war." About the same time, the English economist John Maynard Keynes wrote that, in the war, Britain had destroyed a trade rival. The automaker Henry Ford understood as well. "Do you want to know the cause of the war?" he asked. "It is capitalism, greed, the dirty hunger for dollars."

All that was needed to set off conflict was a spark. It came when a cell of Serbian terrorists bent on creating a "greater Serbia"—the same purpose that would lead to "ethnic cleansing" murders of non-Serbs in Yugoslavia eight decades later—shot down the Austrian archduke Franz Ferdinand and his wife on a street in Sarajevo, Bosnia, on June 28, 1914. Austria blamed Serbia, but Serbia refused to back down because it was supported by Russia, which wanted to expand its influence into the Balkans. Austria wanted precisely the same thing, however, and exploited the assassinations in a secret plan to destroy Serbia. Germany covertly assured Austria of its support.[1] After a month of intense negotiations, Austria-Hungary declared war on Serbia, Russia mobilized, and Germany, after the Russians refused to restrict their troops to the

Austro-Hungarian frontier, declared war on Russia on August 1. Within a few days Britain, France, and Russia were at war with Germany and Austria-Hungary. Italy soon joined the Allies, hoping to get land from Austria, while Turkey and Bulgaria, also hoping for spoils of war, sided with Germany and Austria-Hungary.

Thereafter erupted a series of bloody battles that settled nothing and led to stalemate amid the trenches, barbed wire, and fortifications that faced each other along the western front from the Belgian coast to the Swiss frontier. The war was characterized by hopeless frontal assaults into impregnable defenses. In the opening stages, the French, adhering to their misguided concept of *offensive à outrance,* or all-out attack, shattered nineteen divisions in direct assaults against machine guns and rapid-firing cannons. But the worst and most flagrant case of official blindness occurred on the Somme River. There the British lost 60,000 men, 19,000 of them dead, in a single day of frontal assaults on July 1, 1916.

The Germans did better in the east, driving the Russians back into their country and defeating Romania in 1916. But by 1917 both sides were paralyzed. Although the Allied armies could not break through in the east or the west, the British navy's blockade was slowly starving the German people. By 1916 all foods except turnips were scarce in Germany, milk was available only by prescription to persons over six years old, and eggs were doled out at one per person every two weeks.[2] On the other hand, the Russian armies were tottering from atrocious leadership, insufficient supplies, and German military pressure. The nation would soon burst into revolution and drop out of the war. Britain and France likewise were almost at the end of their endurance.

British leaders knew that Europe could be saved only if the United States joined the Allies. But President Wilson was unshakable in his neutrality and in his efforts to mediate peace. Wilson had declared American neutrality when the war started, although sentiment was overwhelmingly with Britain and France, and huge purchases by the Allies gave the United States instant prosperity.

Relations with Germany deteriorated swiftly after a German U-boat, or submarine, sank the British passenger liner *Lusitania* without warning off the coast of Ireland on May 7, 1915, costing 1,200 lives, 128 of them American. Sinking on sight defied established international rules, which required the attacking warship to provide for the safety of noncombatant passengers and crew. This, of course, a submarine could not do. If it surfaced, it became a sitting duck to attack, and a U-boat had space for no more than a few extra people. Because of this, Wilson held that the submarine was an illegal weapon and told the German government that a repetition would be regarded as a "deliberately un-friendly" act. This was a threat of war, but Germany repeated the of-fense on August 19, 1915, when a submarine sank the *Arabic,* claiming two American lives.

At this point the German ambassador, Count Johann-Heinrich von Bernstorff, promised the State Department that ocean liners would not be sunk "without warning and without safety to the lives of non-combatants." Then, either by accident or intent, a few more attacks oc-curred, notably on the English Channel steamer *Sussex* on March 24, 1916. Wilson renewed his threat and Germany reiterated its promise. This time Germany kept it.

From May 31 to June 1, 1916, the German High Seas Fleet chal-lenged Britain's Grand Fleet in the North Sea in the Battle of Jutland, inflicting serious losses on the British (three battle cruisers, three cruisers, eight destroyers). This was a harsh wake-up call for the Amer-icans. Although the German navy slipped back to safety in its harbors, the battle showed that British command of the seas might be threat-ened. Congress quickly passed the National Defense Act, increasing the standing army to 175,000 men and the National Guard to 450,000 men. More important, the Naval Appropriation Act provided for the immediate construction of four battleships and four battle cruisers to add to three capital ships, *Nevada, Oklahoma,* and *Pennsylvania,* that had just been completed. America's leaders were heeding Alfred Thayer Mahan's lessons.

Nevertheless, Wilson—who successfully campaigned on the slogan "He kept us out of war" in the 1916 election—would not abandon America's neutrality. On December 18, 1916, he took on the mantle of peacemaker, calling on the Allies and the Central Powers to state their war aims so differences might be bridged and peace achieved.

Germany had already announced on December 12 that it was willing to take part in a peace conference. But the dominant authoritarian coalition in Germany—the kaiser's court, the landowning Junkers, the industrialists, and the military—demanded total conquest, simply because having to pay the exorbitant costs of the war would bankrupt Germany. In short, someone else would have to pay for the war. Germany's war aims were so outrageous that its leaders refused to list them. They wanted to keep all the territory Germany had overrun— Poland, part of Russia, Romania, Belgium, and northern France—*and* annex a part of France the Germans had not occupied, the French coast opposite the English Channel.

The Allies were indignant at Wilson's inquiry. They realized the American president didn't understand that Germany could not afford to make peace unless the Allies paid for it; in addition they thought he was presumptuous interfering in their affairs without offering anything but advice. Nonetheless, they replied to Wilson. Peace, they said, must carry restitution of all conquered territories, full reparations for damages done, and guarantees that German aggression would not happen again. These were the only conditions the Allies would accept, and a peace on such terms would end the German Hohenzollern dynasty and the governing class.

With neither side offering the slightest opening for negotiation, Wilson, in an address on January 22, 1917, turned to the idea of a "peace without victory." This implied a simple cease-fire and some kind of equitable settlement. Yet the Allies ignored the proposal, realizing that any peace leaving the autocrats in control in Germany would never last. As the historian Barbara Tuchman writes, "The facts would have forced themselves on anyone but Wilson, but the armor of fixed purpose he wore was impenetrable. He chose two main principles— neutrality for America and negotiated peace for Europe—as the fixed points of his policy and would allow no realities to interfere with them."[3]

The military leaders of Germany had already resolved to seek a decisive victory over the Allies. Their weapon was the U-boat. In August 1916 Paul von Hindenburg and Erich Ludendorff had been elevated to command of the General Staff, becoming in effect dictators of Germany. While the generals were focused on fighting through to victory, the civilians in the government were convinced that victory would be impossible to achieve and that Germany had to make peace soon even to achieve the status quo ante. But the civil government, in the face of an adamant military, fell into line; soon it contrived its own plan to prevent American participation in the war.

Though Germany had stopped U-boat attacks because of Wilson's protests, its navy had been industriously building new submarines. By the fall of 1916, the submarines were ready and the military was contemplating unleashing them to sink every ship approaching the British Isles and thereby starving Britain into surrender in a matter of weeks. To do so, however, would abandon any chance for peace and risk U.S. entry into the war. Germany's military leaders assumed the risk, believing that the United States was not a military power worth reckoning with. Army leaders argued that America could neither train nor transport enough troops in time to affect the outcome of the war. The chief of the German navy asserted that no American would set foot on the continent of Europe before the U-boats had beaten Britain into surrender. Nevertheless, the decision was, as a German statesman put it, Germany's last card. "And if it is not trumps, we are lost for centuries."[4]

On January 31, 1917, Ambassador Bernstorff announced to Robert Lansing, the U.S. secretary of state, that Germany was beginning indiscriminate submarine warfare. The challenge was flung in America's face. For three days the world waited while Wilson wrestled with himself. On February 3 he decided: diplomatic relations with Germany were broken off. But Wilson made this move without malice. The same day, he announced to Congress: "I refuse to believe that it is the intention of the German authorities to do in fact what they have warned us they will feel at liberty to do. Only actual overt acts on their part can make me believe it even now."

But Germany had already initiated an underhanded act of treachery, and this was to change everything. The previous month, a telegram from German foreign minister Alfred Zimmermann had come into a secluded British naval counterintelligence office in London. One of countless messages intercepted and read by the crack team of British decoders in Room 40, the Zimmermann telegram was a top-secret letter to the president of Mexico, inviting Mexico to join Germany and Japan in an invasion of the United States. Mexico's reward would be recovery of the territories it lost in the Mexican War. Japan would presumably gain territory on the West Coast. Germany's goal was to keep America fully occupied on its side of the Atlantic while unlimited German submarine warfare crushed the Allies.

On February 23, 1917, after carefully concealing the fact that Britain had broken the German diplomatic code, Foreign Secretary Arthur Balfour presented the telegram to the American ambassador in London.

President Wilson's eyes were at last opened to Germany's perfidy, and he released the telegram to the public. On March 1, 1917, the news burst across the newspapers of America. The *New York Times* headline, running all the way across the top of the page, read: "GERMANY SEEKS ALLIANCE AGAINST U.S., ASKS JAPAN AND MEXICO TO JOIN HER."

The Zimmermann telegram led most advocates of war to demand immediate hostilities. But the vein of neutrality ran so deep in America that many did not accept that the letter was authentic. Then, unbelievably, Zimmermann admitted at a press conference on March 3, 1917, that he had indeed written the letter, that he had—while still at peace with the United States—tried to forge an alliance with Mexico and pull Japan on the side of the Central Powers against the United States. The admission was a blunder of colossal proportions, because it settled the matter in American minds. No one knows why Zimmermann did not keep his mouth shut. Probably he had decided that the Americans had acquired documentary proof of his actions and that denial would make him look foolish. This was logical, but incorrect. The British had not revealed to Washington the full truth about how they had acquired the telegram.

The "Prussian Invasion Plot," as the newspapers named it, conveyed as nothing else Germany's deliberately hostile intent. Here was a country, while still ostensibly friendly, proposing an attack on the United States, conspiring with a neighbor to snatch American territory and plotting with Japan to stick a dagger in America's back. There could no longer be a question of neutrality. This became even more clear on March 18, when German U-boats sank three American ships without warning.

Then, on March 19, came the preliminary revolution in Russia that overthrew the czar and established a parliamentary government under Alexander Kerensky. With the disappearance of the czar, the only autocratic member of the Allies had vanished; the war, it could now be said, was about saving democracy.

President Wilson called a special session of Congress for April 2, 1917. Before Congress, Wilson announced that neutrality was no longer possible. Germany, he said, was a "natural foe of liberty." He declared that "the world must be made safe for democracy," that "the right is more precious than peace," and that America must fight "for the principles that gave her birth." A roar like a storm greeted the president's address. By a huge majority Congress voted for war.

In the frenzied days between the revelation of the Zimmermann telegram and the president's speech before Congress, it became clear that the fate of the world now rested on the United States. The United States—for that matter, the world—could not tolerate a German victory. Every astute leader recognized this.

President Wilson certainly recognized it, albeit belatedly. The night before his address to Congress, talking in the White House with Frank Cobb, liberal editor of the New York World, the president had said that he feared Germany would be beaten so badly that there would be a dictated peace. No longer was he talking about "peace without victory." His statement to Cobb implied a peace of retribution, a peace so heavily weighted in the Allies' favor that Germany would be shattered.

Indeed, Germany would have to be shattered, for if the Allies lost, Germany would assume the status of dominant world power. An old military axiom now applied: A nation with a great navy but a weak army can strike far but not hard. A nation with a great army but a weak navy can strike hard but not far. But a nation with a great navy and a great army can strike both hard and far. The Allies needed to prevent Germany from becoming the last type of nation.

Elihu Root, who had been Theodore Roosevelt's secretary of state, saw plainly what was at stake for the United States. If Germany won, he said, not only would it destroy the balance of power in Europe, but perhaps more important, there would no longer be a British fleet to support the Monroe Doctrine and protect America.

The protection of the Royal Navy would, indeed, be one of the casualties of World War I. America would be compelled thenceforth to protect itself and its hemisphere.

★   ★   ★

THE DOUBLE-BARRELED American method of waging war refined in the Civil War combined overwhelming power with imaginative, inspired leadership. In World War I the United States exhibited its immense power element in full. Brilliant leadership was less apparent, since the United States joined an old coalition whose leaders already *thought* they knew everything there was to know about waging war and were not much interested in listening to the upstart Americans. Still, American military leaders made some remarkable decisions that demonstrated they were true recipients of the brilliant heritage of the Civil War.

A notable example was the American admiral who played a major role in solving the problem of unrestricted U-boat attacks, the single greatest danger facing the Allies. In April 1917 submarines sank 875,000 tons of British shipping, driving Britain almost to the brink at the very outset of the campaign. British and neutral sailors refused to sail. Admiral Sir John R. Jellicoe, the First Sea Lord, calculated that at this rate of loss, Britain would run out of food and other needed materials by July. Nevertheless, the British Admiralty rejected proposals to place merchant ships in convoys closely protected by warships, calling convoys an unsound waste of cruisers and destroyers. Only after Prime Minister David Lloyd George and his strongest ally, American admiral William S. Sims, insisted on creating convoys did the Admiralty back down.

The results were spectacular. British escort vessels, joined by American destroyers in May 1917, provided good protection, since multiple U-boats had to concentrate their attacks to target convoys and thus could be located and destroyed more easily. American naval officers also laid minefields across the Strait of Dover and across the opening of the North Sea. Cruising destroyers hunted down U-boats and sank them with depth charges. All these measures crippled submarine activity. By the end of the war, about half the German U-boat flotilla had been destroyed.

In ground operations in France, General John J. Pershing insisted that the American Expeditionary Force operate under a wholly separate American command—*not,* as the Allies wanted, by brigading them with existing French and British divisions. Pershing was convinced that three years of defensive fighting had weakened the Allies for effective offensive tactics. He forced the Allies to give in. The United States transported 2 million soldiers to France. It placed forty-two divisions into combat. In June 1918 American troops helped stop the German offensive at Château-Thierry. Half a million Americans reduced the Saint-Mihiel salient southeast of Verdun. Americans advanced down the Meuse River through the Argonne Forest toward Sedan as part of a larger campaign across the front to smash the German Hindenburg Line. German resistance collapsed, and Germany sued for an armistice on November 11, 1918. By the end of the war, the Americans held one-fourth of the entire battle line, more than the British. Total American deaths were 125,000, fewer than half in battle. By comparison, Russia lost 1.7 million men dead, Germany 1.6 million, France 1.4 million, Britain 900,000, and Austria 800,000.

Americans made immense material contributions to winning the war. Indeed, American supplies of all kinds made Allied victory certain. Even before the first American soldiers arrived in France in June 1917, ships had delivered 10,000 tons of wheat to France. In advance of the flood of troops, U.S. workers dredged French harbors, built docks, created debarkation depots, repaired railroads and freight yards, laid telegraph and telephone lines, and erected hospitals, barracks, and warehouses.

Back in the States, the material contributions were far greater. Much of the $9.4 billion the United States lent to the Allies paid for arms, food, and supplies produced in America. The U.S. government virtually took over the economy, launching programs that increased production immensely in all fields. The number of acres in agricultural production increased by 10 percent, production of mines by 30 percent, total manufactures by 35 percent. Much of the gain went abroad to feed Allied soldiers and civilians and supply Allied armies. But the resulting increase in basic productive facilities pointed to a much higher standard of living in the United States in postwar years. By 1920 U.S. manufacturing production stood at 122 percent of its level in 1913, whereas Europe's manufacturing production by 1920 was only 77 percent of its level in 1913. By 1928 the United States produced more than 39 percent of the whole world's manufactures, while Britain produced less than 10 percent, Germany less than 12 percent, and France just 6 percent.[5] In other words, World War I dramatically increased America's economic dominance of the world.

★   ★   ★

THE PARIS PEACE CONFERENCE began in January 1919. President Wilson himself went to Paris, hoping he could provide the basis for the peace treaty with his idealistic "Fourteen Points."[6] Wilson was a utopian. He wanted a world federation, a parliament of man, a global organization to abolish war. His fourteenth point called for "a general association of nations for mutual guarantees of political independence and territorial integrity." His instrument for this was to be a League of Nations. The two most powerful Republicans, Senator Henry Cabot Lodge of Massachusetts and Theodore Roosevelt, believed in traditional balance-of-power politics and sneered at Wilson's idealism.

The aims of the European leaders, David Lloyd George of Britain, Georges Clemenceau of France, and Vittorio Orlando of Italy, were closer to Senator Lodge's and Roosevelt's than to Wilson's. They represented constituents who had suffered greatly at the hands of the Germans and Austrians and who were burning for revenge. They also were bound by secret treaties negotiated early in the war. France had long sought to reclaim Alsace-Lorraine (which Germany had taken after the Franco-Prussian War in 1870–71), and it also wanted the coalfields of the Saar basin and Syria and Lebanon. Britain wanted most of the German colonies and a free hand in Egypt, Iran, and Iraq. Italy wanted the southern Tyrol of Austria and control of the Adriatic Sea.

Utopian Wilson was unequal to the cynical Allied leaders. Wilson was expert in dealing with the written word. As Frederick Lewis Allen, the great historian of this era, writes, "In the oral give and take about a small conference table he was at a disadvantage. When Clemenceau and Lloyd George and Orlando got him into the Council of Four behind closed doors, where they could play the game of treaty-making like a four-handed card game, they had already half-defeated him."[7]

The result, the Treaty of Versailles, reflected little of the idealism of the Fourteen Points. On June 28, 1919, Germany was forced to accept the loss of its colonies, Alsace-Lorraine, the Saar for fifteen years, a corridor to the sea for Poland, and border areas to Belgium and Denmark. It had to agree to a demilitarized Rhineland and to provide reparations set in 1921 at $33 billion, well beyond its ability to pay. These reparations included the full cost of pensions for Allied soldiers. The German army was limited to 100,000 men, and the navy reduced to insignificance.[8] The Paris conference produced precisely the dictated peace that Wilson had feared—begetting an angry Germany thirsting for retribution. Niccolò Machiavelli, the sixteenth-century Italian political theorist, prescribed two ways to deal with an enemy: destroy him altogether, or treat him so generously that he will become your friend. A middle course is dangerous. Wilson and the Allies chose a middle course—and begat a whirlwind.[9]

Wilson and other Americans were repelled by the avarice and venality of European leaders. Italy walked out of the conference briefly because Wilson would not grant it the city of Fiume on the Adriatic. It later seized the city by a coup. Large minorities of different nationalities were taken against their will into various states—Germans into Italy, Romania, and Czechoslovakia; Hungarians into Romania and Czechoslovakia; Russians and Ukrainians into Poland, Romania, and Czechoslovakia; and whole congeries of Slavs and Albanians of different religions and cultures into the new Yugoslavia. All of these minority populations would cause trouble in the years ahead.

Instead of settling conflicts in Europe, the Paris conference created new divisions and animosities. Clemenceau talked Wilson and Lloyd George into an alliance to protect France against any future attack from Germany. This was a radical departure from the American tradition of nonintervention into European affairs and would have allowed a dispute in Europe to decide whether America went to war. The U.S. Senate quite properly rejected the idea.

Wilson had pinned his hope on a League of Nations to adjust differences among nations and preserve world peace. He insisted on including the League in the Treaty of Versailles. The League was to have an assembly of member nations, a council of five great powers plus four others chosen by the assembly, and a permanent secretariat. The heart of the League was Article 10 of its covenant. It committed member nations, in case of aggression, to impose sanctions or go to war to force a decision of the league.[10]

This provision aroused intense opposition from a group of mostly Republican senators led by Lodge. They insisted on amendments that reserved to the U.S. Congress—not the League—the right to decide whether the United States would carry out any military or economic actions under Article 10. They were entirely correct. If the United States had accepted Article 10, the League would have had the power to decide American policy and even how American military forces would be used. President Wilson, in his desire to preserve peace, was proposing to sign away American sovereignty. Under the U.S. Constitution, treaties are expressly declared "the supreme law of the land." Only under very narrow circumstances can the Supreme Court alter a properly ratified treaty.[11]

There was no guarantee that the interests of the League of Nations would be those of the United States. Opponents saw the League as a "superstate" that would destroy American independence, subject the American people to international control, and drag the United States into quarrels with which it had little concern. For example, Article 10 would nullify the Monroe Doctrine. Under it, the United States could not resolve a problem in the Western Hemisphere on its own but instead must refer it to the League of Nations.[12]

Senator Lodge held views little different from those of most Americans today. "He believed that the essence of American foreign policy should be to keep the country clear of foreign entanglements unless our honor was involved," Frederick Lewis Allen writes, "to be ready to fight and fight hard the moment it became involved, and, when the fight was over, to disentangle ourselves once more, stand aloof, and mind our own business."[13] Lodge treated honor and prerogatives as one and the same. If any other country assaulted our prerogatives—that is, the rights, privileges, and options we had gained—it assaulted our honor.

Senator Lodge and other opponents were willing to accept the Treaty of Versailles *provided* that the League of Nations was stripped of the supranational authority that Wilson wanted. If this had happened, the League would have been about as powerful as the United Nations today.

But Wilson refused to make any amendments that would protect American sovereignty. Having failed to embody in the treaty the ideals that he had preached, he glossed over its failure to follow the Fourteen Points and argued that the United States should fully accept the League of Nations. As Allen writes, "He pictured the world, to himself and to others, not as it was, but as he wished it to be."[14] Wilson took his case to the people in the summer of 1919. In a railroad tour through the Midwest and the Far West, he made thirty-six formal addresses and numerous "whistle-stop" back-platform speeches. Wilson won enthusiastic responses from the audiences but swayed no votes in the Senate. The grueling travel in intense heat (there was no air-conditioning) wore on the president; in Pueblo, Colorado, on September 29, his health gave way. He was rushed back to Washington, where he suffered a paralytic stroke that made him an invalid for months and from which he never fully recovered.

On March 19, 1920, the Senate rejected the treaty by a vote of 49–35.

Wilson was an impractical idealist, unable to balance protection of

American independence with his sincere desire to prevent new aggressions in Europe. He was trying, in effect, to create a world state, and he could not see that in such a state—in which the United States would be only one of many voices—the greed and self-interest he had experienced in the Paris Peace Conference would prevail. This was shown clearly in his agreeing along with Britain to an alliance to protect France from future attacks. In other words, he was willing to draw the United States into precisely the sort of armed league that had brought on World War I in the first place. The Senate recognized Wilson's blindness, rejected the alliance and also the League of Nations, and made the right decision for America.

In the presidential election of 1920, the American people cast a solid majority vote in favor of disentanglement from Europe and in support of the Senate's rejection of the League of Nations. The Republicans declared that their party stood "for agreement among the nations to preserve the peace of the world without the compromise of national independence." The Democrats called for immediate ratification of the Versailles Treaty and the League. Although there were other issues in the campaign, the vote against the League was unequivocal. The Republican candidate, Warren G. Harding, gained 16 million votes, while the Democratic candidate, James M. Cox, received only 9 million.

The United States, therefore, renewed its historic insistence on being master of its own destiny. It sent only "unofficial observers" to League of Nations commissions and conferences. Furthermore, it refused to join the Permanent Court of International Justice, or World Court, in The Hague, because of its power to give advisory opinions on the legality of actions not yet taken and without the affected nation's consent. This would have constituted a clear curb on American sovereignty.

In World War I and its aftermath, America struck down Germany's attempt to dominate the planet and refused to give up its independence to the universal state that President Wilson wanted to create. The American people got it absolutely right with these deliberate and

profoundly important choices. And we would also get it right with a
third decision that quickly followed—taking on the responsibility of
creating sufficient military power to protect ourselves and other lands
from future aggressors. Because of these three decisions, we set up the
conditions that allowed us to save the world from totalitarianism in the
troubled and tumultuous decades that lay ahead.

NINE

★ ★ ★

A WORLD NAVY

When World War I ended, the Royal Navy stood to become by far the dominant naval power on earth. This was because it expected to add to its numbers the warships of the German navy, second-largest in the world, which surrendered to the British at the Firth of Forth in Scotland.[1]

The prospect alarmed the United States, because, since 1902, Britain had been allied with Japan, which now moved up to the third-largest navy. Britain was a friend, yes, but with a fleet (counting the German ships) three times the size of the U.S. Navy, the United States was in an extremely vulnerable position. Every informed person knew Japan was spoiling for a fight because of American opposition to Japan's aggressions in the Far East. If friction between the United States and Japan should lead to war, Britain might be obliged by treaty to side with Japan.

This was totally unacceptable. When the German navy surrendered, the U.S. Navy Department proposed a building program to give the United States a fleet equal to the existing strength of all other navies on earth combined.

British prime minister David Lloyd George recognized that the proposal would force Britain into an arms race with the United States—a race the British could not win. In return for some concessions to President Wilson on the League of Nations, he got assurances that Wilson would not pursue the navy's expansion plan.[2] The urgency of the building program subsided when the German crews conveniently scuttled their ships on June 21, 1919, two days before Germany accepted the terms of the Versailles Treaty. This abruptly reduced the potential size of the Royal Navy.

Even without all-out American naval expansion, Britain faced an impossible challenge to maintain the traditional "two-power standard" of the Royal Navy—that is, a navy bigger than the next two largest fleets combined. The war had cost the British Empire one and a half times more than it had cost the United States, and Britain's economy was only a third the size of America's. Britain was close to bankruptcy.

In the spring of 1921 Britain faced up to its reduced status in the world. The Admiralty announced that it would accept parity with the U.S. Navy. For the first time Britannia was willing to share the waves with another power. But American naval experts knew Britain's concession was far greater than that. Britain was declining rapidly relative to the United States. Accepting a U.S. fleet the size of its own was merely clutching at straws as British naval supremacy went down. Britain could not possibly *maintain* parity with the United States. Britain was inevitably going to step into the second rank of naval powers.

Britain gave up what it had struggled to maintain for two and a half centuries—command of the seas. The British had fought World War I to prevent the Germans from sharing the oceans with them, but they gave up their preeminent position to the United States without a fight. Perhaps they were reassured by the community of values they shared with Americans. But they did so *only* because they had no choice. What Adam Smith had predicted in 1776 had come to pass: Britain had become merely an appendage to the greater whole. The center of the English-speaking world had moved to America, and America had outstripped not only the Mother Country but every other country on earth.

Although a potential naval competition with Britain had been avoided, the danger of Japan still remained. The empire was industriously building its fleet in an attempt to match the power of the U.S. Navy. It was in no one's interest for this to continue. American leaders hoped to deflect Japan away from conquest and a challenge to the

United States. A conference on armaments offered a way. After taking office, President Harding invited Japan, Britain, France, and Italy to an assembly in Washington on limitation of armaments, beginning November 11, 1921. Other countries also came: China, Portugal, Holland, and Belgium.

The conference also reflected a renewed American desire to end imperialism in the Far East. Empires were perpetuating selfish policies and power rivalries, especially at the expense of China and the newly established and still-weak Soviet Union. The United States wanted to annul all deals among the powers and establish new principles to govern their conduct in China, and to thwart an attempt by Japan to annex eastern Siberia. The aim was not to help Soviet Russia, which had become a pariah state because of its aspirations to foment a world Communist revolution, but to keep Japan from seizing territory, resources, and power. America wished to stay out of the affairs of Europe, but we had not abandoned our anxiety to settle matters in the Far East.

★   ★   ★

SECRETARY OF STATE Charles Evans Hughes produced a series of diplomatic triumphs at the Washington Naval Conference that were awesome and unparalleled. He stopped the naval race, cooled the war fever gripping the United States and Japan, caused Japan to back off in its attempt to gain hegemony in East Asia, forced it to withdraw from Siberia, and returned to China not only some of its territory but also much of its dignity. Hughes was a consummate politician, an excellent diplomat, and a shrewd negotiator. When Japan tried to employ its usual obstreperous methods to continue its selfish policies, Hughes repeatedly isolated the island empire in world opinion and forced Japan, much against its will, to back down. Republican Hughes had almost beaten Woodrow Wilson in the presidential election of 1916 after he resigned as a Supreme Court justice to run. Judged by how he handled the Washington Naval Conference, he would have been a superb American president.

Hughes made a number of crucial preliminary decisions. He decided the conference would focus on naval limitation, the issue of most concern to war-weary people around the world. And he decided to concentrate on ratios of capital ships (battleships, battle cruisers) between the United States, Britain, and Japan based upon the existing sizes of their navies. Hughes seized on capital ships because all the navies of the world believed these ships with the heaviest guns and the longest range were the decisive weapons in naval warfare.[3]

Hughes proposed from the outset a 5:5:3 ratio of capital ships for Britain, America, and Japan. It was a preemptive strike and, moreover, was eminently fair. Britain and the United States had to defend more than one ocean apiece, whereas Japan had to defend just one. The Japanese had no grounds for argument. Japan was able only to extract promises from the United States and Britain not to fortify their bases in the western Pacific.

Part of the reason for Hughes's success was that the American cryptographer Herbert Yardley, located in the ultrasecret "Black Chamber" at 22 East Thirty-sixth Street, New York City, had broken the Japanese diplomatic codes. On November 28, 1921, Yardley's group intercepted a radio signal from Tokyo to its negotiators to avoid any clash with Britain and especially the United States over arms limitation. Hughes, holding this trump card, stared down the Japanese delegates and insisted on the 5:5:3 ratio.

Credit also must be given to Japanese foreign minister Kijuro Shidehara, chief delegate to the conference. Although he drew much hostility from ultranationalists at home, Shidehara believed that Japan's interests lay in markets, not in conquests and colonies. He supported conciliation toward both China and the Soviet Union. He expressed this attitude in Washington, and with Hughes pressuring Japan, he was able to force the hard-liners in Tokyo to back down. (Ultimately, in 1927, the militarists would oust Shidehara, but throughout the early and mid-1920s he helped keep Japan's foreign relations rather tranquil.)

The treaty also limited the numbers of aircraft carriers, a new type of ship that would become *the* definitive weapon in the next war. Admirals didn't realize this at the time, but aircraft launched from a carrier could give the carrier even longer range than the largest gun on a battleship, and bombs dropped by carrier aircraft could deliver heavier blows than the biggest shell. The carrier was destined to be far more powerful than the battleship, because it was going to have the longest reach, and *reach* is the decisive factor in naval warfare. The treaty authorized 135,000 tons each of carriers for the United States and Britain, 81,000 tons for Japan. The United States turned two battle cruisers under construction into the aircraft carriers *Lexington* and *Saratoga,* which would gain renown in coming years.

The broader implication of the conference was that the United States took over responsibility from Britain for governing the world's oceans. This was never spelled out, but every naval expert on earth knew it. Only five years after we stepped fully on the world's stage in World War I, we decided as a matter of policy that *wherever* an enemy might appear, we would project superior naval power against him — to prevent this enemy from ever reaching our own hemisphere.

The decision to deploy the greatest navy occurred at the precise moment the United States was withdrawing from close relations with Europe. This step back into isolationism resulted from our dismaying experience with avaricious, grasping Allies after the war and with the efforts of President Wilson to draw us into a world government with these same avaricious, grasping countries. A liberal myth developed in later years. It held that the reason we decided to go out into the world to fight major wars *must have been* to remake the world in our image.[4] Yet in truth we never had any goal to Americanize, let alone liberalize, the world by military action. Our goal was merely to *stop* unacceptable, disruptive actions by aggressors so that the United States could exist in peace.

The retreat behind our oceans expressed our atavistic longing for a return to simpler times, although in truth they were lost forever. Yet this withdrawal did *not* deter us from making the decision to destroy any potential enemy anywhere who might try to strike the United States. This was proved by our resolve to build the world's greatest navy. It went little noticed at the time, but in fact we had transformed our nation's fundamental strategy. Our oceans had ceased to be the shield they had been since our nation's founding. They had now become avenues over which we would project our power. We didn't address the matter at the time, but the decision meant that we also had to create an army and an air force that could *win* on whatever islands or continents our fleets reached and where an enemy challenged us. Thus a world navy implied a world army and a world air force as well. In the relative peace that descended after the Washington Naval Conference, we put the ramifications of our decision out of our minds. But we remembered them with a start when bullies began to walk over weak peoples in the following decade.

★   ★   ★

A GREAT VICTORY at the Washington Naval Conference came when Charles Evan Hughes finessed Japan out of its alliance with Britain. Hughes substituted a mere consultative pact with three powers—Britain, the United States, and France. The four powers agreed to confer in a joint conference if a controversy arose between any two of them. It *sounded* good, but Senator Henry Cabot Lodge got it through the Senate by pointing out the promise to consult meant that and nothing more. Japan had exchanged a dangerous weapon it could use against the United States for a meaningless scrap of paper.

With both the Chinese and Japanese delegations in Washington, Hughes saw an opportunity to force Japan to discuss with China the issue of Shandong Province, which Japan had occupied during the war. President Wilson had done a great wrong to China at the Paris Peace Conference when he accepted Japan's control of the province. Hughes got the support of the British chief delegate, Arthur Balfour, and they offered their good offices to bring Japan and China together. The Japanese could scarcely refuse to talk, but they argued from December 1 to December 20, 1921. They finally capitulated after seeing that their position had been hopelessly eroded because Hughes had maneuvered them into the talks and because Baron Shidehara felt Japan should have no designs on Chinese territory. On February 4, 1922, China and Japan signed a treaty abrogating Japan's rights in Shandong.

Hughes also pushed through a treaty that embodied for the first time all the major policies the United States had advocated in China since the Open Door policy took form around the turn of the century.

The treaty condemned spheres of influence and called on the signatories to respect the sovereignty and territorial integrity of China, maintain "the principle of equal opportunity for the commerce and industry of all nations" in China, and "refrain from taking advantage of conditions in China in order to seek special rights or privileges." Japan, to avoid being an outcast, signed. This was the Nine-Power Treaty, solemnized February 6, 1922. Despite its seeming strength, it remained, as historian A. Whitney Griswold described it, "a self-denying ordinance rather than a collective-security pact. The only sanction behind it was the good faith of its signatories."[5] Although it locked Japan publicly into support for a free China, it did not change the Japanese militarists' drive to dominate the country.

In addition, Hughes used the Washington Naval Conference to force Japan to make a public statement denying that it had any ambitions for the parts of eastern Siberia it had occupied after the Russian Revolution. Hughes didn't want the Japanese to use the new Soviet Union's present weakness to carve out an empire in Siberia from which it would be difficult to extract them without a dangerous war. Japan did not fix a date for withdrawal from the Siberian maritime province (around Vladivostok) and from northern Sakhalin, but it renounced all claims to territorial aggrandizement. Japan had no option but to withdraw. It took its troops out of eastern Siberia in October 1922 but kept them in northern Sakhalin until 1925.

The agreements Secretary of State Hughes and his colleagues worked out at the Washington Naval Conference marked the most gains the United States had ever achieved in East Asia. Part of the reason was that the world was tired of war and people everywhere, including segments inside Japan, sought ways of resolving conflicts and living in peace. Even so, much of the credit must go to Hughes. He saw the opportunities and he seized them.

Liberal opinion in Japan supported the results in Washington, and some agreed with Baron Shidehara in wanting to substitute a program of economic expansion in place of the drive for a bigger empire. But newspaper accounts assailed a "hateful and haughty America" for forcing upon Japan "a peace without liberty, a slavish peace." As the

Japanese scholar Hugh Borton writes, Japan was in the throes of "an unquenchable aggressive nationalism which was to sweep everything before it."[6]

The Washington Naval Conference kept Japan from overt aggression for the rest of the 1920s, but the Japanese threat would not go away, of course. Nor would other threats to America and to international security. For a time after the Washington Naval Conference, however, the United States would for the most part turn a blind eye to these threats.

TEN

★ ★ ★

THE LOCUST YEARS

Winston Churchill called the 1930s "the locust years," an apt and eloquent phrase. He was referring to the terrible losses, mistakes, and failures that devoured all hope of peace during that tragic decade. The words came from the Old Testament book of Joel, which described a period of calamity in ancient Israel as "the years that the locust hath eaten."[1] When today we look back on those sad times leading up to World War II, we are dismayed at the inability of well-intentioned people to see what should have been plainly evident—that Germany, Italy, and Japan were bent on aggression of the most ferocious and destructive kind, and that they had to be stopped.

Whole libraries have been written trying to explain why the leaders of the Western democracies appeased the dictators and allowed the crimes to happen—fear of another bloodletting like the first world war; belief in the peaceful intentions of Adolf Hitler, Benito Mussolini, and the Japanese militarists; paralysis caused by the Great Depression that began in 1929; the wish that a pact "outlawing war" would actually be obeyed; and, among Americans especially, the hope that the murders would occur in places far away, and that we could remain safe and unaffected behind our oceans.

The decade of the 1930s stands out as the longest and most sustained period of willful blindness in American history. During those years our leaders refused to accept either reality or the duty that bound them to protect their nation and their civilization. During the entire reach from the Japanese occupation of Manchuria in 1931 to the German defeat of France in the spring of 1940, America did *not* get it right, and we and the world suffered immeasurable harm because of it. It is no consolation that the other democracies did no better than we did, for if America had stood up resolutely, the weaker and more timid democracies would have been emboldened, and the world could have avoided the most terrible war in its history. The 1930s should serve as a cautionary tale to guide our future conduct—if we allow *some* aggression to get by, it almost certainly will grow into *more* aggression.

Today we tend to look back on the sellout of Czechoslovakia to Nazi Germany in 1938 as the worst and most disgraceful failure of the decade. But in fact this appeasement of Hitler was by no means the most horrible of the atrocities we allowed to happen. We let Japan take over Manchuria and north China and murder hundreds of thousands of innocent Chinese civilians in Shanghai, Nanjing, and other cities. We did nothing when Mussolini's Italy bombed villages in harmless Ethiopia in 1935–36. We took no action when Hitler rearmed Germany in 1934–35 and remilitarized the Rhineland in 1936, both in defiance of the Versailles Treaty, and we stood idly by when he annexed Austria in 1938.

★   ★   ★

IN THE PEACE that descended on the world after the Washington Naval Conference of 1921–22, we Americans turned our attention inward on our own booming, contradictory, and rapidly changing nation.

Much of that rapid change resulted from two constitutional amendments ratified in quick succession: in 1919 the states approved an amendment prohibiting alcoholic beverages, and the very next year approved another amendment giving women the vote. Both derived from perhaps noble intentions—we were taking a firm moral stand for equality and also for sobriety—but they produced startlingly different results.

Although both political parties opposed women's suffrage in 1914, attitudes changed during the war. Many women went to work in factories and on the farms and volunteered as nurses and in other ways to support the war effort. In September 1918 President Woodrow Wilson urged Congress to approve the women's vote, saying the measure was "vital to winning the war." This broke the back of the opposition. Congress and then the states approved the amendment in time for the presidential election of 1920.

Though men at last accepted women as qualified to vote, a deep vein of puritanism still ran through the population. *Baltimore Sun* columnist H. L. Mencken defined this austerity as "the haunting fear that some-one, somewhere, may be happy." To protect the morals of young sol-diers, during the war the U.S. government closed down (temporarily) every red-light district in the country, including fabled Storyville in New Orleans. But continence could not be so well enforced in France. Soon everyone was singing, "How you gonna keep 'em down on the farm, after they've seen Paree?" French premier Georges Clemenceau volunteered to share his nation's prostitutes with the Americans. When social worker Raymond Fosdick informed Secretary of War Newton D. Baker that willing mademoiselles had been proffered not only from Armentières but from all over France, Baker cried, "For God's sake, Raymond, don't show this to the President or he'll stop the war."[2]

It was the war that got the prohibition amendment into the Consti-tution. The drys argued that alcohol dimmed the wits of doughboys and war workers, and that outlawing beer saved barley.

But we soon realized things were not so clear-cut. Whereas giving women the vote changed the nation vastly for the better, outlawing al-coholic beverages changed the nation vastly for the worse. Prohibition, which brought us mobsters and speakeasies and bathtub gin, eroded what most Americans saw as solid verities of the nation's life, like re-spect for the law and respect for the individual. Puritanism thus led not to morality but to immorality. We learned our lesson, however. In 1933 we stripped prohibition from the Constitution.

Women's suffrage and prohibition were not the only profound changes during the 1920s. Early in that decade the novelist F. Scott Fitzgerald wrote that "an infinite and unbridgeable gap" divided his gen-eration from the generations that had gone before.[3] Cheap automobiles, much-improved highways, the movies, tabloid newspapers, confession magazines, radio, jazz, liberated women—all this and more transformed society. "Flappers" bobbed their hair, discarded the corset, danced the Charleston, drank bootleg liquor, smoked cigarettes, and discussed sex in public. Skirts went up, and morals went down.

The poets Ezra Pound and T. S. Eliot looked at the terrible losses of the war and felt a deep depression and sense of man's wickedness. Most Americans had precisely the opposite reaction. We were sick and tired of the whole European mess and wanted to be done with it.[4] Americans were confident and had high hopes for the future. This optimism produced an explosion of creativity. Eugene O'Neill brought revolutionary improvement to the theater. More talent appeared on Broadway than in any previous era—Maxwell Anderson, Elmer Rice, and others. A whole pantheon of writers and poets emerged—Ernest Hemingway, William Faulkner, Sherwood Anderson, F. Scott Fitzgerald, Willa Cather, Ellen Glasgow, Sinclair Lewis, Thomas Wolfe, Langston Hughes, Ring Lardner, Dorothy Parker, Robert Frost, E. E. Cummings, Carl Sandburg, and others. As historian William E. Leuchtenburg remarks, "The 1920s produced a literature that no era since has been able to match." Talents burst forth in other fields as well. Georgia O'Keeffe created brilliant paintings in New Mexico, Edward Hopper equally brilliant paintings in the city, and George Gershwin incorporated jazz rhythms into symphonies.[5]

Also fueling change was the staggering economic growth. Industrial production almost doubled during the 1920s. The number of telephones rose from 1.3 million in 1900 to 20 million in 1930. By 1929 the United States was generating more electric power and also paying out more for education than the rest of the world combined. Vast numbers of new products appeared—cigarette lighters, oil furnaces, antifreeze, Pyrex glass, rayon, cellophane, Bakelite, lacquer for car paint, the artificial silk celanese, and much more. In 1916 the federal government offered to match state highway funds, turning road-building into the largest employer in the country, and Americans into a nation of nomads. By 1928 a tourist could drive from New York to St. Mary's, Kansas, on paved roads. In the United States there was one car for every 5 people, in Britain one car for every 43 people, in Italy one for every 325.[6]

By the end of the decade, the United States had a larger economic output than all the other six great powers combined. The value of manufactures per head was twice that of Britain or Germany, eleven times that of the Soviet Union or Italy. In 1929 America produced 4.5 million motor vehicles, compared to 211,000 in France, 182,000 in Britain, and 117,000 in Germany. The United States constituted by far the greatest common market on earth. Americans consumed 92 percent of all goods manufactured in the country, a mark of how little trade with the rest of the world mattered economically.

In the nineteenth century, the United States had paid for much of its industrial growth by borrowing capital from abroad. Now, no longer needing foreign money, we became the leading creditor nation. To function as a creditor nation, the United States had to import more than it exported. The country moved in the opposite direction, however, raising tariffs in 1922 higher than prewar levels, making it difficult for Europe to sell its products in the United States. The only way the Allies could repay their debts to America was by getting reparations from Germany.

Those reparations were exacting a heavy cost on Germany. In 1923 Germany defaulted on its payments, crippled by reparations and by the excessive national debt Imperial Germany had incurred during the war. Runaway inflation ensued, impoverishing working-class and middle-class Germans. The resulting disillusionment helped bring on Adolf Hitler a decade later. The situation was alleviated only when the United States lent money to Germany, which subsequently paid the Allies . . . who then paid the United States! As Leuchtenburg writes, "It would have made equal sense for the United States to have taken the money out of one drawer in the Treasury and put it into another."[7]

Since the United States was unwilling to allow in substantial imports, it kept up world trade by private investment abroad. The center of world finance moved to New York. American corporations began investing and building plants in Europe, South America, Asia, and the

Middle East. Many Europeans put their funds into American securities, where they got high speculative profits.

As dollars flowed to Europe to pay for development, European nations had to turn to the United States for still more borrowing, since they couldn't repay the debts through exports. In 1928 the American domestic boom sharply curtailed this outflow of capital. On September 19, 1929, prices on the New York Stock Exchange achieved record highs. But then they began to slip. Speculators who had bought stocks on margin were forced to sell to cover their losses. This brought down prices further and produced a chain reaction of ever more selling and ever-lower prices. To bring home needed funds, England raised the interest rate to 6.5 percent. Many European holdings were thus thrown onto the U.S. market, reducing prices even more. The American banking system lacked a "lender of last resort" to stabilize such temporary disjunctions in international accounts. The Bank of England had done this job prior to the war. As frightened speculators frantically unloaded, panic set in. During October 1929 the value of stocks on the New York Exchange fell from $87 billion to $55 billion. By March 1933 the value was down to $19 billion.[8]

The stock market crash set off the most devastating economic depression in modern times. Contributing greatly to the disaster was the Smoot-Hawley Tariff of 1930, which placed prohibitively high duties on imports. This made it even more difficult for other countries to earn dollars and led to reprisals that ruined American exports. "Hard times" blighted the entire decade of the 1930s. Indeed, only the start of heavy military spending with the onset of World War II finally brought the Depression to an end.[9]

★   ★   ★

THE SLIDE INTO the locust years was preceded by an astonishingly naive international treaty that "outlawed war." This was the Kellogg-Briand Pact of 1928, signed by most nations, which renounced war "as an instrument of national policy."[10] It sounded good, but was meaningless. As Senator Carter Glass of Virginia commented, "I am not willing that anybody in Virginia shall think that I am simple enough to suppose that it is worth a postage stamp in accomplishing permanent international peace."[11] Senator Glass was correct, of course. But it is a measure of the hopefulness of the era that millions of people throughout the world put their faith in the treaty.

Perhaps the most telling testimony to the times was the decision by Henry L. Stimson, secretary of state in Herbert Hoover's administration, to dismantle the State Department office that broke the codes of foreign radio transmissions on the ground that "gentlemen do not read each other's mail."

The first great travesty took place in Manchuria in September 1931. The Japanese army cooked up an incident to take over this huge northeastern region of China. A bomb exploded on a railway track north of Mukden. The damage was minimal, but a Japanese patrol claimed that Chinese soldiers opened fire from nearby fields and the patrol had to fight back. It was a well-planned conspiracy, because more than 10,000 Japanese troops swung into action almost simultaneously, and by late November 1931 they had occupied all of Manchuria.

The world's response was astonishing. It took until December for the League of Nations to appoint a commission to investigate, and until January 7, 1932, for Secretary Stimson to declare that the United States would not recognize Japan's occupation of the region.

The Hoover administration's failure to respond to Japan's aggression in 1931 is the single greatest cause for the disasters that came in the years ahead. The Japanese move directly challenged China and foreshadowed further aggression. If the United States had resolved on firm action, the other democracies would have fallen into line, and all the aggressions that plagued the world could have been prevented. Instead, American inaction led the Japanese to believe they could bully China without international repercussions — and signaled to Hitler and Mussolini that America was a paper tiger.

Another outrage came quickly. The Chinese, incensed at the occupation of Manchuria, launched a boycott of Japanese goods, which cut exports by 95 percent to central and south China and 72 percent through Hong Kong. Seeking an excuse to intervene, the Japanese army secretly sent one of its officers to incite Chinese workers to beat up five Japanese in the International Settlement in Shanghai on January 18, 1932. One of the Japanese died. Demanding retribution, the Japanese moved a flotilla, including an aircraft carrier, to Shanghai and sent 2,000 marines into the Chinese suburb of Zhabei, just north of the settlement. Chinese Nationalist leader Chiang Kai-shek, more concerned with the threat of the Chinese Communist Party than the danger from Japan, had decided not to fight. But a military force of a regional warlord, the 19th Route Army, did not consider itself bound by Chiang's orders, and its machine guns opened fire on the Japanese. Unable to dislodge the Chinese, the Japanese launched carrier planes in methodical bombing runs over Zhabei.

This brought something new—and ghastly—to the world: heavy bombing attacks directly on unarmed civilians in tightly packed residential areas. The Japanese then moved up artillery and tanks and turned Zhabei into a flaming no-man's-land. Thousands of civilians died. Even this overwhelming response was not enough. An additional 50,000 Japanese troops were needed to force the Chinese soldiers to withdraw on March 2–3.

Despite this unequivocal example of Japan's aggression, no other nations protested. In October 1932, more than a year after Japan's invasion of Manchuria, the Lytton Commission, the League of Nations inquiry group, finally presented its report.[12] The commission recommended not that Manchuria be returned forthwith to China, but that it be governed by an autonomous regime with foreign advisers and that "a substantial proportion should be Japanese." It was disgraceful, the merest slap on the wrist for Japan. When the League of Nations brought the Lytton report to a vote in February 1933, only Japan opposed. The Japanese delegation left the hall, and a month later Japan withdrew from the League.

In 1935, when the Washington Naval Treaty of 1922 was coming up for renewal, Japan would accept nothing less than parity with Britain and the United States, and finally it renounced the treaty as of the end of 1936. Japan, it was clear, was bent on dominating the Pacific Ocean, and possibly challenging the democracies directly.

The Japanese then made a critical miscalculation that would cost them in the future. They concentrated on creating the world's best battleship fleet, for Japanese admirals, like their counterparts in the American and British navies, believed the battleship and its big guns were the keys to naval power. As time was to show, however, battleships could not compete with aircraft carriers in their reach. Hence, Japan built a navy that was largely obsolete by the time the war started.

U.S. leaders were anxious about the impending Japanese naval buildup but were mollified by one glaring weakness in Japan's strategic position: the nearest source of abundant oil was the Netherlands East Indies, nearly 3,000 miles from Tokyo. American naval experts figured, if worse came to worst, the United States could always close off the Indies, blockade Japan's home islands, and starve Japan into submission. This dangerously facile argument led American leaders to underestimate the Japanese threat.

Japan went on to attack China directly in 1937, occupying all of north China and all the Chinese seaports. Japanese soldiers massacred several hundred thousand Chinese civilians in cold blood in Nanjing and committed terrible atrocities in other cities. Chiang Kai-shek at last began to resist, and he withdrew deep into the interior, setting up his capital at Chongqing in Sichuan Province. By 1937, Japan's intention to dominate East Asia had become crystal clear.

★   ★   ★

WHILE MILITARISTS WERE LAUNCHING Japan on a career of violent aggression, similar developments were taking place in Europe. Benito Mussolini founded the antidemocratic, totalitarian Fascist Party in Italy and took over the country in 1922, but he seemed to be no threat beyond Italy's borders until the mid-1930s, when he conquered Ethiopia, then occupied Albania in 1939. Italy was weak militarily, however, and Americans soon sized up Mussolini as mostly bluster and little substance. And so he was.

Adolf Hitler was another matter entirely. Winston Churchill describes how Hitler, a corporal in the German army, lay temporarily blinded by chlorine gas in a military hospital just as Germany was in the process of surrendering in 1918. The son of an obscure Austrian customs official, Hitler had failed as an artist in prewar Vienna. He joined a Bavarian regiment at the outbreak of war and served for four years on the western front.

"As he lay sightless and helpless in hospital during the winter of 1918," Churchill writes, "his own personal failure seemed merged in the disaster of the whole German people. The shock of defeat, the collapse of law and order, the triumph of the French, caused this convalescent regimental orderly an agony which consumed his being."[13]

Hitler became obsessed with the idea of reviving and extending German strength. His first bid to overthrow the government, the Munich beer hall putsch of 1923, failed completely. Nevertheless, to a large degree because Germany was hard hit by depression and unemployment, he and the National Socialist (Nazi) Party that he led came to power on January 30, 1933—five weeks before Franklin D. Roosevelt became president of the United States. In March 1933 the Reichstag (parliament) gave Hitler dictatorial powers, and when President Paul von Hindenburg died in 1934, Hitler united the powers of president and chancellor in himself.

In his book *Mein Kampf,* Hitler outlined his aims—totalitarianism, turning the German people into a nation of warriors, transforming them into a "master race," eliminating democracy, suppressing the Jews, and vastly expanding Germany at the expense of its neighbors, especially in Poland and Russia to the east. It was a recipe for world conquest, and an essential part of Hitler's plan was mass murder of Jews and all the other people he hated. In the butchery that followed in the years ahead, Hitler and his willing German executioners killed 6 million Jews, 1 million Poles and Gypsies, thousands of persons who had mental or physical disabilities or who objected in any way to his ideas, 7.7 million Soviet civilians, and 5 million Soviet soldiers whom Hitler starved or murdered in prisoner-of-war camps.

But in the early stages of his dictatorship, Hitler veiled his malignant thoughts. Though he promptly deprived German Jews of their citizenship, his initial moves in the international arena were circumspect, and democratic leaders at first failed to see that he was dead serious and a grave menace to the world.

By 1935 Hitler's intentions were becoming evident. Still, Britain and France were unwilling to challenge him alone, and they refused to join with the Soviet Union, although the Soviet dictator Joseph Stalin, aware of Hitler's animosity, was hunting for allies. President Roosevelt was on the side of the European democracies, as well as China, but he was wary of saying so against the overwhelming isolationist sentiment in Congress. The United States rejected collective security and chose instead to insulate itself from war by passing a series of neutrality acts. They were hopeless gestures, like trying to stop the tide by ordering it to go back. But for the whole of the 1930s neutrality was the policy of the United States.

Americans came to this viewpoint because of a distorted and incomplete appraisal of the nation's involvement in World War I. As the outstanding political scientist Julius Pratt writes, most Americans felt that their "former associates had used the war and the peace settlement for their own selfish advantage, had repudiated the ideals for which America had fought, and had shown neither gratitude for American aid nor a disposition to pay their just debts."[14] Lost in this argument was the fact that the victory over Germany had saved America quite as much as it saved any European state. The United States should have written off all the wartime debts of its allies and forced these same allies to release Germany from its intolerable burden of reparations.[15]

Primarily because no power stood up to oppose him, Hitler rang up a string of victories unprecedented in world history. He achieved most of them by his remarkable political skills, and without the use of force. Over the course of seven years, Hitler withdrew Germany from the League of Nations in October 1933; commenced massive secret rebuilding of German military power in 1934; introduced conscription in violation of the Versailles Treaty in 1935; reoccupied the Rhineland, a German border region demilitarized under terms of the Versailles Treaty, in 1936; seized the sovereign state of Austria and joined it to Germany on March 10, 1938; bullied the leaders of Britain and France into dismembering Czechoslovakia at the Munich conference, September 29–30, 1938; occupied the Czech portions of Bohemia and Moravia on March 15, 1939; and shattered Poland in a lightning campaign beginning on September 1, 1939. The attack on Poland finally drove Britain and France to go to war against him, but Hitler also struck a deal with the Soviet Union to divide Poland between them. Stalin signed a nonaggression pact on August 23, 1939, out of desperation, hoping that by appeasing Hitler, he could stave off or prevent an attack on his own country.

★   ★   ★

THE WORLD TURNED upside down in May 1940, when the Germans launched an offensive against France and Britain. In April of that year, German forces had occupied Denmark and seized Norway, thereby protecting that flank against British naval action, as well as securing deliveries of Swedish iron ore, vital to Germany's war effort, by way of the Norwegian port of Narvik.

The German offensive in the west bewildered the Allies. Instead of launching it where they expected it to come—with a frontal attack in northern Belgium—Heinz Guderian led the main German panzer, or armored, assault through the lightly guarded Ardennes Mountains of eastern Belgium and Luxembourg, and appeared only days later at Sedan, France, *behind* the Allied army, which meanwhile had rushed pell-mell into Belgium. Now striking due west to the English Channel, the panzers sealed off the Allied formations and forced them to surrender or to evacuate, without their weapons, from Dunkirk. Within six weeks France had capitulated, and the British were thrown back on their islands with virtually no land weapons and only the twenty-one miles of the Channel to prevent them from being conquered as well.

A few weeks later Hitler launched his Luftwaffe, or air force, against Britain in the first great aerial battle in history. British radar, a secret weapon that tracked incoming German aircraft, and the Spitfire and Hurricane fighters of the Royal Air Force saved Britain from defeat, but the damage to London and other cities was enormous, and for months the issue lay in doubt.

The effect on the United States was instantaneous and profound. All at once the danger from Nazi Germany became clear and present, and the fear that Britain would lose the war made the Atlantic seem less a zone of safety than a potential avenue of attack. Three immediate responses came from the government and the people: a visceral urge to withdraw into a "Fortress America," the realization that the United States had to rearm and do it fast, and the need to help Britain by all measures "short of war."

President Roosevelt, speaking at the University of Virginia on June 10, 1940, the same day Italy declared war against France and Britain, reflected the mood of the country precisely. "The hand that held the dagger," he said, "has struck it into the back of its neighbor." He announced that the United States would extend aid to "opponents of force" and would speed up rearmament to defend America.

Before that awful summer was out, Roosevelt had signed a law to create by far the greatest navy on earth (doubling the fleet), begun building an air force of 7,800 combat aircraft, called the National Guard into federal service, begun increasing the regular army from 280,000 to 1.2 million men, and passed the first peacetime draft in American history. It was a belated awakening, but an awakening all the same. From this point onward, the United States, while still hoping for peace, girded itself for war.

That same summer, Roosevelt offered fifty overage American destroyers to the British to help them hunt U-boats and convoy merchant ships. But he coupled this aid to Britain with a move to protect the Western Hemisphere—in return, he secured permission to occupy eight bases on British possessions from Newfoundland to British Guiana.[16] In other words, FDR helped Britain to shield itself from the storm of attack from Germany. But in case Britain lost, the United States would have a powerful defensive barrier in front of the American coastline.

American resolve was strengthened when Germany, Italy, and Japan signed the Tripartite Pact on September 27, 1940. With this, the three powers aimed to keep the United States on the sidelines by raising the prospect of a two-front war—against Germany and Italy in Europe and against Japan in the Pacific. But this threat had the opposite effect than intended: it *increased* American leaders' determination to arm the nation. It also encouraged Japan to risk an attack on the United States in the belief that in a two-front conflict Americans would be unable to defeat the Japanese navy. The decision to sign the treaty probably cost Germany and Japan the war. By seeming to offer Japan the opportunity to exclude the United States from the western Pacific, the pact encouraged Japan to plan a campaign to seize the colonies of Britain, France, and the Netherlands in Southeast Asia.

Roosevelt was seeking any way possible to support Britain's war against Hitler. His hand was strengthened greatly on November 5, 1940, when he became the first (and only) American president elected to a third term.

Knowing Britain could not possibly pay for its military needs, and remembering the hostility that World War I loans had engendered among lenders and borrowers alike, he came up with Lend-Lease. Instead of *selling* goods to allies, the United States would *lend* them. Roosevelt compared the idea to lending a garden hose to a neighbor to put out a fire that might otherwise spread to one's own house. The fact that few if any of the "lent" goods would ever be returned was passed over in silence. Everyone knew it was just a device to give untrammeled aid to "opponents of force." Congress approved the Lend-Lease Act on March 11, 1941.

The act set American factories producing goods at full capacity. American economic power dwarfed that of any other country. In 1938, with the economic depression cutting its potential output in half at least, the United States still produced almost 29 percent of the world's manufactured goods, more than twice what Germany generated, even though German factories were operating at maximum capacity. In 1937 the United States possessed almost 42 percent of the entire world's war-production potential. Germany's share was 14.4 percent, the Soviet Union's 14, Britain's 10, France's 4, Japan's 3.5, and Italy's 2.5.[17]

During the same winter of 1940–41, high British and American military officers met in Washington at secret "ABC-1" talks (short for "America-British conversations") to coordinate efforts in the event the United States was compelled to enter the war. At the conferences the two nations agreed that Germany was the number one enemy, since it was by far the most dangerous. It had to be defeated first, even if Japan entered the war.

As America moved into the fateful year of 1941, it had at last cast off the illusion that it could remain unprepared while war and aggression were consuming Europe and China. The nation's "locust years" were ending. It was arming as fast as its factories could produce weapons and its military could train recruits. The hope that America could remain neutral was fading. As had happened in 1917, Americans realized we once more stood as the greatest bulwark against the totalitarianism and oppression that were flooding the world. Whether we wanted to or not, we were rushing toward a rendezvous with destiny.

★ ★ ★

MILITARY SUPREMACY

By the spring of 1941, President Franklin Roosevelt had abandoned any pretense of neutrality. His political savvy kept him from showing his hand publicly, since isolationism still gripped the Congress. But he ordered the U.S. Navy to patrol the North Atlantic west of Iceland and inform the Royal Navy of any German submarines it discovered. In April he sent American forces to occupy Greenland. That summer he also occupied Iceland and began escorting British convoys to the island from Canada.

But new dangers arose when, on June 22, Hitler invaded the Soviet Union. Panzers led a frontal assault all along the frontier from the Baltic to the Black seas. The German military reputation was so awesome that many observers believed the Soviets would collapse in a few weeks. Indeed, the German panzers advanced so far and so fast that the doomsayers' predictions seemed about to come true. But the Russians resisted bitterly and, though losing literally millions of soldiers, withdrew deep into the interior and continued to fight.

Faced with this new challenge, Roosevelt sent his closest confidant, Harry Hopkins, to Moscow to see if the Russians were about to surrender. Hopkins found the Soviet dictator, Joseph Stalin, with high morale and an unbounded determination to win. This positive report convinced Roosevelt to supply Russia whatever goods it needed through Lend-Lease.

Meantime, Hitler was pressing the Japanese to honor their alliance with Germany and attack the Soviet Union in Siberia. Yosuke Matsuoka, the Japanese foreign minister, strongly urged his government to do so. The Soviet Union probably would not survive sustained offensives on two fronts. If the Axis powers conquered the Soviet Union, they would control the Eurasian heartland, make most of Africa untenable for Britain, cripple the British Empire, and force the United States to use its strength to defend the Western Hemisphere.

It was a recipe for victory, but only if the United States continued to allow oil and other raw materials to be shipped to Japan. Because of Japan's continued aggression in China, however, the United States had been on the verge of ending all trade with Japan for a year. If Japan attacked the Soviet Union, the Americans would close off trade at once and induce Britain and the Dutch East Indies (now Indonesia) to follow. Without imports, an offensive into Siberia would run out of oil and raw materials within months. Therefore, the United States in effect prevented the Japanese from attacking the Soviet Union. Realizing this belatedly, Japan's leaders decided to use force to seize the oil and other materials they needed from Southeast Asia.

The Japanese hoped the United States would not oppose this move with anything more than words. But if it did, Japan resolved to go to war. It was a bizarre intellectual progression. Japan refused to back down on its primary goal, to conquer China. To get the oil and materials it needed, Japan was prepared to challenge the United States, the most powerful nation on earth. This was madness. Worse, the Japanese resolved to go to war even if Roosevelt merely cut off trade.

Failure was virtually assured, but not once did Japan's leaders stop and consider what they were getting into. A Japanese army study in April 1941 concluded that Japan did not have the means to carry on a sustained war, "but we will manage by one means or another." Shortly afterward, Japanese officials were incensed rather than sobered by a message from Winston Churchill pointing out that the United States in 1941 would produce 75 million tons of steel and Britain 12.5 million tons. Churchill asked, "Would not the 7 million tons of steel production of Japan be inadequate for a single-handed war?"

Roosevelt and other American leaders hoped the Japanese would give up their attempt to conquer China and rely like normal nations on trade to secure the materials they needed for their industry. But whatever Japan elected to do, the United States made the right decisions—refusing to sanction Japanese aggression against China (although the League of Nations had accepted it) and standing solidly against Japanese expansion into Southeast Asia. These two positions brought war to the United States, but in the end they also brought the destruction of Japanese and German tyranny.

In July, American cryptanalysts, using the decoding program "Magic," intercepted and deciphered Japanese cables revealing that France had capitulated to Japan's demand to occupy eight air bases in southern French Indochina and to use France's naval base at Cam Ranh Bay. The intelligence intercepts convinced Roosevelt, on July 25, to freeze all Japanese assets and instantly end all trade with Japan. Britain, the dominions, and the Dutch East Indies quickly followed suit.

Early in August, Roosevelt met with Winston Churchill in Placentia Bay, Newfoundland, the first meeting between the two leaders. There they affirmed an informal British-American alliance. FDR, despite opposition from America First isolationists, had aligned the nation solidly on the side of democracy and freedom. At the conference Roosevelt and Churchill concluded that Japan would await the outcome of the battles for Russia and Britain before attacking Southeast Asia. But they were wrong. The embargoes actually made the Japanese more determined to go to war.

As the Japanese attempted to get the United States to lift the trade restrictions, the Americans learned that Tokyo had secretly set a firm deadline for the negotiations. On November 5, Magic picked up a flash from Tokyo to Japan's U.S. ambassador, Kichisaburo Nomura, reporting that Japan needed an agreement with the United States by November 25. From this cable, Secretary of State Cordell Hull concluded that the Japanese had decided on war if the United States did not meet their demands by that date.

Nomura gave Hull the first set of those demands—Plan A—on November 10. In the proposal, Japan refused to withdraw from China or give up its alliance with Germany, and it demanded to keep troops in French Indochina. The United States rejected the entire plan. On November 20, Nomura and another Japanese envoy sent over to handle these last-minute negotiations, Saburo Kurusu, presented Plan B. It would require the Dutch East Indies to provide raw materials to Japan and the United States to supply Japan necessary oil and give Japan a free hand in China. This proposal, too, was completely unacceptable to the United States, which wanted the Japanese to back off of first Indochina and then China. A message from Tokyo, intercepted by Magic, warned that the new deadline, November 29, was absolute. "After that things are automatically going to happen."

FDR attempted a last-minute compromise in which Japan would withdraw from southern Indochina while the United States would modify the July freeze order slightly. But Secretary Hull learned that five divisions of Japanese troops had been sighted on transports headed south from Taiwan. With that news Roosevelt decided to "kick the whole thing over" and draw a hard line. The United States now demanded that Japan withdraw all troops from both China and Indochina. It was an open invitation to war.

On November 25, a secretly assembled strike force of the six newest aircraft carriers of the Imperial Navy departed the Kuril Islands, northeast of Hokkaido, headed for the American naval base at Pearl Harbor in Hawaii. In strict radio silence, the force traversed a part of the North Pacific generally avoided by merchant shipping.

Roosevelt told his cabinet on November 28 that negotiations had ended and that hostile Japanese action was possible at any moment. Both the War and Navy Departments in Washington sent out warning messages to stations in the Pacific, but the radio intercepts pointed toward Japanese attacks in Southeast Asia, and no one imagined that a blow would be aimed at Pearl Harbor.

The Japanese did not know it, but the commander of America's Pacific Fleet had sent his three aircraft carriers away from Pearl Harbor— *Enterprise* to deliver fighter planes to Wake Island, *Lexington* to take scout bombers to Midway Island, and *Saratoga* back to the West Coast for repairs. The United States had nine battleships in the Pacific, eight of them lined up on "battleship row" at Pearl Harbor.

At 6 A.M. on December 7, with the Japanese armada having arrived within 275 miles of Pearl Harbor, the commander, Admiral Chuichi Nagumo, launched 183 aircraft toward the Hawaiian base to the south. They arrived over Oahu at 7:55 A.M. and commenced their attack. Nomura and Kurusu didn't deliver their message declaring war to Hull until fifty-five minutes after the attack started. By then Hull knew it was under way.

The assault, which ultimately employed 360 aircraft, shattered the American fleet. The Japanese sank four of the battleships and severely damaged the other four. They destroyed 188 American aircraft, most of them on the ground, and killed 2,327 American servicemen and wounded 1,143. Japan, meanwhile, lost only 29 aircraft and not many more men. The fleet turned back toward Japan.

Though the Japanese did indeed destroy much of the American fleet, the attack proved to be an enormous blunder. December 7 became for the American people "a date which will live in infamy," as Roosevelt told Congress. Pearl Harbor unified the American people in an instant, ended isolationism, and created an unquenchable resolve to destroy Japan. Most Americans fervently agreed with Roosevelt when he said, "No matter how long it may take us to overcome this premeditated invasion, the American people in their righteous might will win through to absolute victory."

The attack had a psychological effect on Americans exactly opposite to what the Japanese had expected. Japanese triumphs dismayed but never defeated the American people. The evidence of wanton Japanese brutality against American and other prisoners, combined with the anger inspired by the Pearl Harbor sneak attack, created a hatred that led to the internment of thousands of innocent Japanese Americans and, beyond that, something very like a racial war against the Japanese people.

Beyond strengthening American resolve, the Pearl Harbor attack also spurred the United States to rebuild its fleet. And the fleet that emerged—based around the aircraft carrier—would be far more advanced than what the United States had possessed previously. Pearl Harbor, and the subsequent attacks that sank the British battleship *Prince of Wales* and battle cruiser *Repulse* off Malaya, demonstrated that battleships were mortally vulnerable to aerial bombs and torpedoes. This at once made the aircraft carrier the capital ship and nullified the Japanese dominance in battleships. As the United States adjusted its priorities, the tremendous American manufacturing capacity permitted a massive construction program focused on large, fast fleet carriers and smaller escort carriers. Japan had nothing like U.S. capacity to build new carriers, so it had to depend on its existing fleet, a fleet heavily weighted with largely unusable battleships. Thus the silhouette of Japan's defeat appeared quite soon as a result of its own victories in the first four days of the war.

In the years after December 7, conspiracy theorists invented all sorts of scenarios trying to show that Roosevelt had known the attack on Pearl Harbor was coming and allowed it to happen in order to pull the United States into war. There is no evidence whatsoever of this. Pearl Harbor was not on alert, it is true, but that failure reflected inefficiency by the commanders there and the widely held conviction that an attack, when it came, would occur in Southeast Asia.

★ ★ ★

HITLER GRATUITOUSLY DECLARED war on the United States on December 11, 1941, dragging Mussolini along with him. It was a foolish decision by the German leader. With American attention and anger focused on the Japanese, Roosevelt would have had difficulty getting Congress to declare war on Germany.

Churchill exclaimed joyfully, "Hitler's fate was sealed. Mussolini's fate was sealed. As for the Japanese, they would be ground to powder. All the rest was merely the proper application of overwhelming force."

The United States began at once to create this overwhelming force. It started building the carriers to take the war directly to Japan, as well as other weapons to defeat Germany. The formidable combination of American military strength that had emerged in the Civil War—

immense material power and brilliant leadership—now came into play.
The nation went on a war footing overnight. Production of every sort
of weapon and ammunition received top priority. Detroit stopped
building automobiles and started building trucks and tanks.

Well before Pearl Harbor, President Roosevelt made a decision that
was one of the greatest examples in America's history of getting it right,
because it preserved democracy and freedom on the planet. The judgment also showed how Americans can combine great leadership and
great material resources. FDR's decision was to embark on a vast secret
undertaking to develop the atomic bomb. On October 11, 1939, Roosevelt received a letter from Albert Einstein, a German-born Jew now
living in the United States, a refugee from Nazi oppression. Einstein,
who had conceived the theory of relativity, informed Roosevelt that
theoretical physicists, including the Italian Nobel laureate Enrico Fermi,
had discovered that an atom bombarded with neutrons could release
great amounts of energy and that a chain reaction of this process could
create a bomb of unimaginable power. Einstein and other physicists
feared that German scientists might develop this bomb and destroy
any possibility of defeating Hitler.

Roosevelt at once saw the peril facing the free world and set in motion a vast program called the Manhattan Project to develop the atomic
bomb before the Germans. Although FDR allowed Britain to share in
the program, the overwhelming bulk of the work was done in the
United States.

Fermi produced the first self-sustaining nuclear chain reaction at
the University of Chicago on December 2, 1942. Over the next three
years the United States assembled an immense number of scientists
and workers and built huge facilities—at Oak Ridge, Tennessee; Han-
ford, Washington; and Los Alamos, New Mexico—to work out the
theory of the atomic bomb and to produce it.

Despite the fears that Germany would get the bomb first, Hitler
failed to appreciate the possibilities of atomic power and did not push
through a program in Germany. Joseph Stalin was not so mindless,
however. He exploited Soviet spies—Klaus Fuchs and Julius and Ethel
Rosenberg—in or around the Manhattan Project.[1] They ultimately

transmitted its secrets to the Soviet Union. If Roosevelt had *not* instituted the atomic-bomb project, Stalin most certainly would have done so, with disastrous consequences for humankind.

While the Manhattan Project was going forward in supersecrecy, more conventional weapons programs burgeoned. In 1942 U.S. shipyards delivered six fleet carriers and fifteen escort carriers. In 1943 they built eleven fleet carriers and twenty-five escort carriers. In 1944 they produced nine fleet carriers and thirty-five escort carriers. Japanese shipyards came nowhere close to matching these figures. For example, between 1941 and 1943 the United States built 331 destroyer escorts, which were designed to locate and eliminate submarines; Japan built none during that time. The Japanese, consequently, did not protect their vital lines of supply from the East Indies to Japan. American submarines by 1944 had virtually severed this connection, and by sinking food ships, they were threatening to starve the Japanese people by 1945. The Japanese seldom used their own submarines, armed with accurate and lethal torpedoes, to hunt down U.S. warships and convoys. Instead they wasted them as scouts for battle groups and to run supplies to garrisons on isolated islands.

The United States also produced the new weapons needed to win a modern war. From 1942 through 1944 the United States built 230,000 aircraft, many of them heavy four-engine bombers like the B-17, B-24, and B-29. During the same years Germany and Japan together built only half as many aircraft. Between 1941 and 1943, U.S. arms output increased eightfold. By 1943 Allied arms production was three times that of Germany and Japan, and the disparity became greater as the war went on. American gross national product (GNP) doubled between 1939 and 1945, and the physical plant in the United States increased by 50 percent. America was the only country that actually became richer because of the war. By war's end more than half the world's manufacturing production took place within the United States, and a third of the world's goods came from there.

Although Germany carried out successful campaigns over great distances and its leadership was in general excellent, it was ultimately overwhelmed by the sheer mass of Allied firepower. Japan was even more overmatched, particularly because its conquests from Burma to the Solomon Islands in the South Pacific had vastly overextended Japanese strength.

Overwhelming military force was one anchor of American power. Superb leadership was another. This element was less apparent in the war against Germany and Italy than against Japan. Against Germany and Italy the United States formed a coalition with the British. Although Dwight D. Eisenhower, an American, became supreme commander, Americans were hobbled by the British, whose principal leaders were extremely timid. For example, the senior British field commander, Bernard Montgomery, insisted on assembling overwhelming material forces before he would launch an attack; even when the enemy was reeling he would advance only at a snail's pace.

Nevertheless, in the key decisions leading to Germany's defeat, Americans overcame British leaders' often overly cautious approach, which emphasized saving British lives. In the principal dispute, the British wanted to attack Germany through the Mediterranean, which Churchill called the "soft underbelly" of the Axis powers, whereas the Americans, led by George C. Marshall, army chief of staff and Roosevelt's primary military adviser, wanted to put nearly all Allied power into an invasion across the English Channel. Once landed, the Allied forces would advance through France and the Low Countries into the heart of Germany.

The "soft underbelly" concept would not have led to a quick victory over the Nazis. An invasion by way of either the Adriatic Sea or the Aegean Sea would have encountered large mountain barriers and profoundly inadequate railroad and highway networks. These obstacles would have made it extremely difficult to advance into Germany at any speed and without enormous casualties.

Later, enthusiasts for the Mediterranean strategy overlooked these military difficulties and insisted that such an approach would have prevented the Soviets' postwar domination of Eastern Europe. These advocates contended that the political goal of occupying Eastern Europe had been uppermost in Churchill's mind, but there is little evidence Churchill was looking so far ahead. Until quite late, he believed in the goodwill and honesty of Joseph Stalin. In the last months of the war, with the support of FDR, he agreed to give the Soviet Union primary influence over Bulgaria and Romania, in exchange for primary British influence in Greece. That arrangement not only guaranteed Communist governments in these two Balkan countries but also made it easier for Russia to place Communist regimes in Yugoslavia and Hungary, and to dominate Czechoslovakia.[2]

Americans were finally able to concentrate most Allied power on a cross-channel invasion, but Churchill and his generals weakened the effort by getting the Allies to invade Italy in 1943. This invasion led to a terrible step-by-step advance through the Italian mountains that consumed huge amounts of Allied manpower and material but achieved little. Worse, Field Marshal Sir Alan Brooke, chief of the British Imperial Staff, told General Eisenhower just prior to the invasion of Italy that he wanted to avoid any wider land front than the Allies could sustain in Italy. Instead of invading France, Brooke said, the Allies should apply air and naval power to blockade Germany and destroy its industry.

As a result of British hesitation, the Anglo-Americans generally assembled massive force and then attacked the enemy headlong, using little finesse or imagination. That is why U.S. commanders in this theater did not have much opportunity to showcase the brilliant leadership that had characterized American warfare since the Civil War.

One notable exception was U.S. 3rd Army commander George S. Patton Jr., who led the spectacular breakout from the Normandy beachhead in August 1944. Patton was a commander in the tradition of Stonewall Jackson and William Tecumseh Sherman. His fast offensive through France rolled back the German armies in chaos all the way to the German frontier by September 1944. When the Germans launched their last desperate offensive into the Ardennes in December 1944, Patton's forces came up so fast from the south that the offensive collapsed within days. That defeat sped Germany's collapse.

The army air force also demonstrated inspired leadership in overcoming Germany's highly effective aerial defenses. Early in the war, American doctrine held that the long-range, four-engine B-17 bomber, heavily armed with machine guns, could deliver precision strikes on selected targets while flying in close formations, or "combat boxes." American leaders believed that German fighters could not penetrate these boxes. They were wrong. On August 17, 1943, German fighters shot down 36 of 183 B-17s on a raid against ball-bearing factories at Schweinfurt, and 24 of 146 bombers attacking the Messerschmitt fighter works at Regensburg, both far beyond the range of escorting P-47 fighter planes. On the return flights, German fighters shot down 60 bombers, 17 crashed into the sea or in England, and 36 were damaged beyond repair—a single-day loss of 38 percent. The devastation spurred doubts about whether daytime bombing could be continued.

But U.S. commanders recognized the value of the North American P-51 Mustang fighter. Until then the P-51 had played only a minor role in the war, but it had acquired a new engine that increased performance dramatically. Its top speed of 440 miles an hour was comparable to the best German fighter, the Focke-Wulf 190. With extra fuel tanks on the wings that could be dropped off in flight, the Mustang could reach a range of 2,200 miles. American airmen turned at once to the P-51. Soon they were launching daily B-17 raids, pounding German industry deep into the interior.

The Germans used up nearly all of their fighter reserves, as well as their pool of trained fighter pilots, in their vain attempts to challenge the Mustang. By the spring of 1944 the German fighter force had been virtually eliminated. When the invasion of Normandy came on June 6, 1944, the Germans had practically no aircraft to send against the invasion beaches. The Allies now possessed air supremacy over western Europe. This supremacy contributed greatly to Allied victory in Europe.

The primary reason for the success of the air campaign was American leadership. Airmen spotted the problem, searched for and found a solution, and then applied it. In the manner of the great leaders of the Civil War, commanders ignored established doctrine, conventional wisdom, and—in the case of the Mustang—pessimists who insisted that no fighter aircraft could possibly accompany long-range bombers all the way to their targets and all the way back.

★   ★   ★

IT WAS IN the Pacific that the true dimensions of American military leadership became most apparent. With most American resources being diverted to defeat Nazi Germany, only a portion could be concentrated against Japan. After Pearl Harbor, Japanese forces occupied all of Southeast Asia—Burma, Thailand, French Indochina, Malaya, and the Philippines—and spread over the South Pacific from the Dutch East Indies and northern New Guinea to the Solomons, some 500 miles farther to the east. To overcome these challenges, American commanders wisely chose to bypass huge Japanese garrisons on islands in the South Pacific and seize islands closer to Japan.

Ignoring Japanese garrisons on hundreds of islands, and then gaining new bases on islands beyond, permitted the Americans to drive deep into the enemy rear and to position ships and aircraft *between* the Japanese-occupied islands and Japan. This cut off the garrisons from succor except by occasional submarines. More important strategically, the garrisons were unable to do anything militarily because they could not get off the islands. In other words, the Americans imprisoned the Japanese on the islands and turned them, in effect, into Allied prisoner-of-war camps in which the inmates were obliged to support themselves.

The authors of this brilliant strategy were Chester W. Nimitz, Pacific Fleet commander, and other officers around him, especially Admiral William Halsey, who commanded naval forces in the southwest Pacific. General Douglas MacArthur, senior army commander, also adopted the island-hopping concept by jumping from one position on the northern coast of New Guinea to the next, often hundreds of miles to the west.

Their decision came in response to Japanese soldiers' unwillingness to surrender even when their situation was hopeless. This insistence on fighting to the death portended enormous and probably prohibitive Allied casualties if every Japanese-held island had to be conquered. Indeed, that was the Japanese strategy—to ensure so many American losses that the United States would agree to less than unconditional surrender.

The Japanese first made their intentions clear on Guadalcanal, in the southern Solomons, in August 1942. After losing four fleet carriers, two battleships, many smaller craft, and hundreds of aircraft in the battles of the Coral Sea (May 7–8) and Midway (June 4–6), 1942, Japan was forced to go on the defensive, hoping to retain the lands it had occupied and keep the Allies from breaking through the barrier it had erected around the Solomons and across the central Pacific west of Hawaii. On Guadalcanal, then, the Japanese engaged U.S. Marines in gruesome fighting under terrible jungle conditions; the Americans finally secured the island and its airfield in February 1943.

That type of brutal warfare complicated the U.S. strategy for defeating Japan, which was to strike directly at the cities and industries of the home islands of Japan with overwhelming force. The vehicle for these strikes would be the B-29, an extremely long-range aircraft that Admiral Nimitz and the outstanding group of leaders he had assembled decided to base in the Mariana Islands. But getting across the central Pacific to the Marianas—which were well over 2,000 miles from the Solomon Islands but only 1,400 miles from Japan—represented an enormous problem. There were no land bases on which to build invasion forces, and the individual islands along the way bristled with thousands of Japanese troops.

At first the idea was to attack each island individually. But when U.S. forces invaded the island of New Georgia on July 3, 1943, they encountered resistance just as stiff as they had met a year earlier on the island immediately to the south, Guadalcanal. Just as had happened on Guadalcanal, the 9,000 Japanese troops who garrisoned New Georgia refused to surrender, and virtually all had to be killed.

The next island to the north, Kolombangara, was even more heavily garrisoned than New Georgia. Admiral Halsey boldly decided to bypass it. Instead, on August 15, 1943, he landed on the next island beyond, Vella Lavella, where his forces met almost no opposition. The 10,000-man Japanese garrison on Kolombangara was left to sit out the war. This set the strategy for the rest of the war.

Indeed, after taking the coral atolls of Tarawa and Makin in the Gilbert Islands, 2,200 miles southwest of Honolulu, Nimitz targeted the Marshall Islands just to the north, but he insisted on skipping a direct attack on the nearest, most easterly of the Marshalls. Instead he pinpointed as his target Kwajalein Atoll, 400 miles farther on. The Japanese played into the Americans' hands by sending what reinforcements they could to the easterly Marshalls, assuming they would be the next hit.

By now American naval power was greatly superior to Japan's. The U.S. invasion fleet included, in addition to transports for two divisions, twelve fast fleet carriers and eight battleships (which had taken on a new role of bombarding enemy-held islands). Besides, Nimitz could assemble American ships where needed, whereas the Japanese, not knowing where the next attack would come, had to keep their naval power far to the rear, mainly at the huge naval base at Truk in the Carolines, 1,100 miles west of Kwajalein.

The main attack against Kwajalein came on February 1, 1944. The Japanese garrison of 8,000 men assisted in their own destruction by launching numerous suicidal "banzai" charges straight into American guns. As a result, only 370 Americans were killed.

With that battle proceeding better than expected, on February 17 the expedition commander, Admiral Raymond A. Spruance, sent the reserve force of 10,000 men to seize Eniwetok Atoll at the far northern end of the Marshalls. The Japanese garrison held out only briefly against the Americans. The same day, Spruance launched a strike by nine fast carriers against Truk, 700 miles southwest of Eniwetok. Though Japan had already moved most of its warships 1,200 miles westward to the Palau Islands, American air strikes sank two cruisers, four destroyers, and twenty-six tankers at Truk. Japan also lost 250 aircraft, whereas the Americans lost only 25, thanks primarily to our pilots' superior training.

The blows revealed that American carrier forces could cripple a major enemy base without occupying it. The United States had forced the Japanese fleet back another 1,200 miles to the west, and now all of the garrisons in the Carolines could be bypassed. The building of new airfields in the Marshalls now proceeded apace.

The Marianas, a thousand miles ahead, became the next target.

Although the Japanese fleet tried to contest the American invasion of the Marianas, it lost 218 aircraft in the Great Marianas Turkey Shoot of June 19, 1944, while the Americans saw only 29 of our planes destroyed. Seizing the islands of Saipan, Tinian, and Guam in the Marianas proved costly (3,500 dead and 13,000 wounded on Saipan alone), but those victories sealed Japan's fate.

Construction crews quickly built or repaired airfields on the Marianas, and B-29s commenced raids on Japan. The bombers began routinely destroying huge sections of Japanese cities. Just one night's attack, the Tokyo fire raid of March 9, 1945, killed 90,000 Japanese civilians and destroyed 267,000 buildings.

Finally, by June 1945 the Americans had liberated the Philippines and seized the island of Okinawa. These were the final stepping-stones to invasion of Japan.

★   ★   ★

WITH THE DEFEAT of Germany assured, Roosevelt, Churchill, and Stalin met at Yalta in the Russian Crimea on February 4–11, 1945. Roosevelt had been elected to a historic fourth term as president in November, but his health had plainly deteriorated badly. Whether his poor health affected his decision making is not clear, but FDR accepted a number of propositions that had tragic consequences for the world. He agreed to divide Germany into four zones of occupation— British, French, American, and Soviet—a decision that ultimately led to a democratic West Germany and a Communist East Germany. He agreed to assign eastern Poland to the Soviet Union and for Poland to compensate by annexing eastern Germany, with the implication that all the Germans inhabiting these regions would be evicted. He accepted Stalin's demand to use Germans for slave labor in the Soviet Union. And he abandoned the entire premise of America's policy in the Far East by allowing Russia, as payment for Soviet entry into the war against Japan, to take over Japan's exclusive and dominant role in Manchuria, including the railroads and possession of the ice-free ports of Lüshun (Port Arthur) and Lüda (Dalian) at the southern tip of

Manchuria. He also agreed to take southern Sakhalin Island and the Kuril Islands from Japan and give them to Russia.

By the time of Yalta, Soviet forces had overrun Poland, Romania, Bulgaria, Hungary, and Yugoslavia—and were soon to sweep into Czechoslovakia. FDR and Churchill, accordingly, had little bargaining power in eastern Europe. Both still relied on the goodwill of Stalin, and both still believed his assurances that he would allow democratic governments in the region. This despite the fact that Stalin had already made fairly evident his intention of setting up a Communist government in Poland.

Giving Russia all the privileges in Manchuria that Japan had enjoyed—and that the United States had condemned—was morally reprehensible. At the time, however, American military leaders still believed they needed Soviet assistance to eliminate Japanese resistance in Manchuria and China. Accordingly, they were willing to grant Stalin concessions to enter the war in the Pacific. Roosevelt also wanted to make sure that Stalin recognized Chiang Kai-shek's Nationalist government in China, not the insurgent Communist movement in north China under Mao Zedong. Stalin did not, in fact, recognize Mao's regime. When peace came, therefore, the Chinese Reds—seeing that Stalin was no friend of theirs—moved into Manchuria, seized weapons from the surrendering Japanese, launched a civil war against Chiang Kai-shek that gained all mainland China by October 1949, and ultimately pressed the Soviet Union to give up all its privileges in Manchuria. So because of the actions of the Communist regime in China, the rights FDR had granted to Stalin in Manchuria amounted to nothing.

★   ★   ★

AFTER GERMANY SURRENDERED in May 1945, the Allied leaders assembled for a conference at Potsdam, a suburb of Berlin. There, on July 16, a stunning alert came to Harry Truman, who had become president a few months earlier when Roosevelt died of a massive cerebral hemorrhage on April 12. The message stated that the world's first atomic explosion ("Trinity") had occurred at 5:30 A.M. that day at

Alamogordo, New Mexico. The blast was equal to 20,000 tons of TNT, four times greater than the most optimistic estimates, and was clearly visible to witnesses 180 miles away. General Leslie R. Groves, chief of the Manhattan Project, told Truman that scientists were certain the bomb would work in combat. A specially trained B-29 group was preparing to leave for Tinian in the Marianas.

Truman decided to use the bomb after Japan refused to surrender. Churchill supported him, and wrote later: "The historic fact remains, and must be judged in the aftertime, that the decision whether or not to use the atomic bomb to compel the surrender of Japan was never even an issue. There was unanimous, automatic, unquestioned agreement around our table; nor did I ever hear the slightest suggestion that we should do otherwise."[3]

President Truman was right to use the atomic bomb. Although Japan was hopelessly defeated, its cities being burned to the ground and its population on the verge of starvation, Japanese military rulers were determined to sacrifice millions of their own people in a suicidal fight to the bitter end on the home islands. Such a battle would have cost at least a million American casualties, and Truman was absolutely correct in avoiding these losses for his nation.

The atomic bomb constituted the final disaster for Japan.

Early on the morning of August 6, a single B-29 by the name of *Enola Gay* rose from the tarmac on Tinian. Bearing one of the two atomic bombs the United States possessed at the moment, it set a course for Hiroshima, a city of some half a million residents and refugees near the southwestern tip of Honshu. At 8:15 A.M. the B-29 released the bomb. Shock waves destroyed two-thirds of the city. Only three hulks of concrete buildings remained in all of the central part. Much of the city and many people were vaporized. Nearly everything else was laid flat. Total casualties reached above 300,000. The official postwar figures showed 92,000 dead or missing. But 80,000 soldiers were stationed at Hiroshima. At least half perished and many of the more slightly injured succumbed later to radiation poisoning or radiation-induced diseases.

On August 9, another B-29 dropped a second atomic bomb on the western Kyushu city of Nagasaki, destroying about half of the urban area. The blast killed many thousands of people, but high hills confined the damage to a smaller area than at Hiroshima.

The destruction of Nagasaki at last showed the emperor and senior leaders that Japan, unless it surrendered, could literally be destroyed. Without further delay, the emperor called for peace. The final surrender was signed on the battleship *Missouri* in Tokyo Bay on September 2, 1945.

Even before the bombs dropped, however, the Japanese had been shattered by the island-hopping strategy. The United States had neutralized all the garrisons on the Pacific islands. The advance to the Philippines had closed off any movement or action by Japanese troops in the East Indies, in Southeast Asia, and in southern China. American forces had bypassed nearly 2 million Japanese soldiers, leaving only 1.8 million troops on the home islands to defend against invasion. The island-hopping strategy in the Pacific was one of the most successful and brilliant in world history, and it was entirely the brainchild of American leaders.

★   ★   ★

DURING WORLD WAR II, 405,000 American troops were killed and 572,000 were wounded. These were severe costs, but in fact the United States suffered far less than its enemies did. More than 2.8 million German forces were killed and 7.3 million were wounded, while about 500,000 German civilians died. Some 1.5 million Japanese military personnel were killed and 500,000 were wounded, and at least 300,000 Japanese civilians were killed. Those were staggering losses, but the United States had got it right during the war by standing up to aggression and tyranny.

By war's end America had emerged as the world's supreme military power, which meant that no other nation could embark on a path of destruction without encountering the United States. America's military strength was awesome: at the end of the war it had 12.5 million persons in uniform, 7.5 million of them overseas. With its 1,200 major warships, the U.S. Navy was more powerful than all the other navies of the world combined. The United States had 2,000 heavy bombers, including 1,000 B-29s. It possessed (for the time being) a monopoly on nuclear weapons and, as peace came, was building a large nuclear arsenal.

But America did not lead the world in military might alone. It had also become the preeminent economic power, making half the world's manufactured goods in 1945, and was on the way to expanding its economic power even further in the years ahead. In addition, the United States was the major political power, a role that would become even more important in the postwar world, when it would have to stand up to Soviet efforts to extend the Communist system.

By 1945 the United States had become not only the greatest power on earth, but in fact the indispensable power on earth.

TWELVE

★ ★ ★

COLD HARBOR

Six days after the bombing of Hiroshima, the radio commentator Edward R. Murrow put into words the dread and foreboding that seized people all over the world when they perceived that the atomic bomb could literally wipe out civilization. "Seldom, if ever, has a war ended leaving the victors with such a sense of uncertainty and fear, with such a realization that the future is obscure and that survival is not assured," Murrow said.[1]

We live today in the shadow of the nuclear clouds that rose over Hiroshima and Nagasaki on August 6 and 9, 1945. But we owe to a trail of dedicated and determined leaders the wondrous fact that the tragedies of those terrible two days have never been repeated, and that the world has not been turned into a totalitarian nightmare.

The "uncertainty and fear" that pervaded the United States was vastly intensified when it became clear soon after the war that Joseph Stalin's sole interest in an alliance with the West had been to help him destroy Nazi Germany. That accomplished, Stalin abandoned cooperation and refocused on his goal of extending dictatorial rule throughout the world. No serious observer doubted that the Soviet Union would break the American atomic monopoly. It did so in August 1949, greatly increasing the chance of a nuclear holocaust.

Nevertheless, over a five-year period, 1945 to 1950, the United States not only didn't buckle to Stalin's aggression, but in a series of decisions saved the world from oppression, deterred the Soviets from using the bomb, and set in motion the forces that caused Communism to collapse four decades later. The architect of these decisions was Harry S. Truman, a president whom nearly all his opponents underestimated, but who—in most cases—made the right choices almost automatically. Truman took responsibility for his actions and expected others to take responsibility for theirs. He had a sign on his desk: "The buck stops here." He was honest. "I never give the public hell," he said. "I just tell the truth, and they think it's hell."

Truman's correct decisions included arming long-range B-29 bombers with A-bombs, thus deterring Russia from overt aggression; preventing the Soviet Union from taking part in the occupation of Japan; adopting a containment policy to keep the Soviet Union from expanding; conceiving the Marshall Plan to revive prosperity in Europe; joining the three western zones of Germany to form the democratic state of West Germany; undertaking the Berlin Airlift to prevent Russia from absorbing Berlin and demoralizing the Western world; forming the North Atlantic Treaty Organization (NATO) as a barrier against Soviet aggression; and stopping North Korea's effort to conquer South Korea and thereby start a march of Communist conquest in the world.

Truman made some mistakes as well, but in large measure he compensated for these blunders by the right decisions he made. Truman erred by going along with President Roosevelt's agreement to a four-power occupation of defeated Germany and Austria; misperceiving Communist China as a tool of the Soviet Union, not the independent force it was; agreeing to France's selfish determination to keep Indochina as a colony; trying to conquer North Korea after its attempt to absorb South Korea had failed; and refusing to end the Korean War when he had the chance in 1951.

Truman made none of his decisions in a vacuum. His actions reflected the democratic consensus-making that has marked American political life from the beginning. This process suffered only one almost fatal lapse, the argument over slavery in the nineteenth century. But our very failure then, our choice of war instead of compromise, taught a priceless lesson. Except with the issue of slavery, our guiding axiom has always been to seek and find agreement. It is the fundamental reason why America works, and why America usually gets it right in foreign affairs.

A Massachusetts congressman, Fisher Ames, put his finger on the strength of America in 1795. "A monarchy," he said, "is a merchantman which sails well, but will sometimes strike on a rock, and go to the bottom; a republic is a raft which will never sink, but then your feet are always in the water."[2]

We achieve consensus by thrashing everything out as we slosh along in the raft. Every TV news program, every national newspaper, every radio talk show is an arena where the opinions, charges, complaints, fears, and plans of politicians, special interests, experts, and plain citizens are debated, often with great heat. In the lobbies of Congress and the White House, all these elements—organized into trade associations, voting groups, ethnic and religious blocs, and single-issue advocates— exert pressure to get their particular points of view enacted into law or carried out in national policy. That's how both domestic and foreign issues are resolved in the United States.

The final result more or less reflects the wishes of the society as a whole. "Although social interest groups perceive themselves as engaged in a constant struggle," Walter Russell Mead writes, "the net effect of all those struggles is to keep society constantly seeking the point at which dissatisfaction is minimized."[3]

Tennessee Williams put into words a deeply embedded belief of Americans when he described his play *A Streetcar Named Desire,* which opened on Broadway in December 1947. His explanation crystallizes why we respect the opinions of others, and why we are willing to compromise. "There are no 'good' or 'bad' people," Williams wrote. "Some are a little better or a little worse, but all are activated more by misunderstanding than malice. . . . Nobody sees anybody truly but all through the flaws of their own egos. . . . Vanity, fear, desire, competition—all such distortions within our own egos—condition our vision of those in

relation to us. Add to those distortions in our *own* egos the correspond-
ing distortions in the egos of *others* and you see how cloudy the glass
must become through which we look at each other."[4]

In the years after World War II, Truman absorbed the consensus
that formed in the debates, made it his own, and carried out an agenda
that received the overwhelming support of the American people.

Running as a leitmotif throughout this period was a remarkable process the United States carried out to build a new and better world. The
aim was not merely to counter the aggression of Stalin. A broader purpose was to bring together a commonwealth of independent states,
many of them former colonies of imperial powers, in a vast cooperative
system of free trade under American protection and hegemony. This
system contributed vastly to the great economic renewal in the West
after the war, a renewal that also brought many economic gains in the
emerging countries of the third world.[5]

★   ★   ★

STALIN'S AGGRESSIVE POLICY was foreshadowed by his attitude regarding the United Nations, which the victors set up in the
spring of 1945 at San Francisco. At the Yalta Conference in February
1945, Stalin had agreed to take part in the United Nations, but only if
the Soviet Union had an absolute veto in the action part of the United
Nations, the Security Council, composed of five permanent members
(Russia, the United States, Britain, France, and China) and six (after
1965, ten) temporary members.

The United States also insisted on a veto, but to prevent any U.N.
action that infringed on American sovereignty, not as a means of bullying other lands. At San Francisco, therefore, all five permanent members of the Security Council got the veto. This meant that any
controversy between two or more of the Big Five could paralyze the
United Nations. Thus from the moment of its birth the United Nations was never a vehicle to solve any significant international problem.

Signs of Soviet aggression were already evident at the Potsdam Conference in July 1945. Soviet armies had gained control of eastern Europe. Stalin was pushing Turkey to give him the Dardanelles Strait

between the Black and Aegean seas. Soviet-dominated Poland had occupied Germany east of the Oder and Neisse rivers. Some 9 million Germans had been expelled from this region; another 2.5 million Germans had been ousted from Czechoslovakia; and 500,000 Germans had been evicted from Hungary. These 12 million refugees crowded into the borders of a shrunken Germany.

The Soviets agreed that Germany would be administered as a single economy. But it quickly became apparent that Russia had little interest in cooperating with the three other powers that had occupied Germany—Britain, France, and the United States.

With suspicions about the Soviets growing every day, American leaders were not willing to give the Russians any more advantages in the Far East. But they could not prevent Soviet troops from moving into Manchuria on the heels of the atomic bomb burst on Nagasaki. Nor could they keep the Russians out of Korea, which bordered Manchuria. The United States made the best of a bad situation by arranging for the Russians to take the surrenders of Japanese troops north of the thirty-eighth parallel, while Americans were to take the surrenders south of the line. The Russians had assented to administer Korea as a single economy, but the example of Germany aroused great doubts.

Truman, accordingly, was determined not to allow the Russians to have any role in the occupation of Japan, or to permit a German-style partition of the country. With the U.S. Navy controlling the seas, the Soviets—though they protested mightily—could do nothing about it. Washington set up General Douglas MacArthur as a vice-regent who acted through the emperor and the Japanese government to carry out American demands. That American strategy rehabilitated Japan, ousted the military elements, led to a democratic constitution and a flourishing market economy, and transformed the nation into a firm ally of the United States.

The situation in Korea was just the opposite. The Soviets refused to allow Allies north of the thirty-eighth parallel and blocked an all-Korea administration. This led the United Nations to hold elections in South Korea that set up a government under the reactionary politician Syngman Rhee in 1948. The Soviet Union created a rival Communist state in North Korea under Kim Il Sung. The two Koreas were deadly antagonistic, each threatening to invade the other. Despite this threat, the United States gave no offensive weapons and no effective defensive weapons to the South Korean army that it had created. As it turned out, however, the Soviet Union did not give the North Korean army many offensive weapons either.

During this same period, President Truman made a mistake that had devastating consequences in the decades ahead: he allowed France to recover French Indochina (Vietnam, Laos, and Cambodia). A Communist-influenced leader, Ho Chi Minh, had declared the independence of Vietnam immediately after the Japanese surrender in 1945. Truman, alarmed at Ho's sympathy with Communism and wanting French support in Europe against Russia, permitted the French to return. This led to a merciless civil war. France was supported by a native elite that had gained power and wealth by allying itself with the French. France and the elite were opposed by the vast majority of the Vietnamese people, mostly poor peasants, who were exploited with high rents on farmland, high taxes, and almost no rights.[6]

On the other hand, Truman made the right decision in 1946 when he pressed Britain to allow European Jewish refugees who had survived Nazi death camps to be admitted into Palestine.[7] Britain had taken over Palestine from Turkey after World War I and was trying to limit Jewish immigration because of intense Arab opposition. But the Nazis' murder of 6 million Jews had aroused ardent support for a Jewish state in Palestine. At Truman's instigation, Britain set up an Anglo-American Committee of Inquiry that recommended immediate admission of 100,000 Jews and the establishment of a binational Palestinian state. The British rejected the proposal, found themselves in a war, and turned the matter over to a special U.N. General Assembly committee in 1947. The only solution, the committee found, was partition. Inevitably, this displaced many Palestinian Arabs from homes they had occupied for centuries. Thus, to rectify partially the injustice Adolf Hitler had done to European Jews and to give the Jews a country of their own, the United Nations perpetrated another injustice on the Palestinians.

On May 14, 1948, the state of Israel, consisting of half the territory of Palestine, was proclaimed; the United States and the Soviet Union recognized the new state that same day. Surrounding Arab countries attacked Israel but were thoroughly bested by Jewish troops, who seized additional territory. More than a million Palestinian Arabs fled. If the neighboring Arab states had given these refugees citizenship and material aid, the issue would have left bitter memories, but would have been solved. It didn't really happen, however. Instead, most of the Palestinians were confined to huge refugee camps in Gaza, the West Bank, southern Lebanon, and Syria, where anger germinated into a great and enduring conflict.[8]

★   ★   ★

IN GERMANY AND in Austria, both divided into four occupation zones, deadlock developed quite soon. Although the Soviet Union permitted the Austrians to elect a single government, it continued to occupy the country; in fact, it rejected a peace treaty until May 1955, ten years after the end of the war. In Germany the Russians repudiated the promise at Potsdam to treat the whole country as an economic unit. In 1946 Secretary of State James F. Byrnes tried to get the Soviets to agree to a unified economy by offering a treaty to guarantee German disarmament. But they spurned the proposal. The new secretary of state, George C. Marshall, made another bid for German political and economic unification at a conference of foreign ministers in Moscow in March 1947. Again the Soviets refused.

The Moscow Conference marked the final U.S. effort to cooperate with the Soviet Union. American leaders were convinced at last that Russia was incorrigible. From this point on, they saw the dispute with Communism as a sort of Manichaean contest between the forces of light and the diabolical powers of darkness.

The policy adopted to deal with this new world formed around the "long telegram" written on February 22, 1946, by George F. Kennan, chargé at the Moscow embassy. Kennan held that the Soviet Union and its satellites could be "contained" within their present boundaries and that, over time, internal and external stress would sap Russia's strength and end Russia's aggressive ambitions.

Kennan believed that the Soviet leaders were obligated to depict the United States as menacing in order to give them an excuse to rule their people by repression, the only method they understood. This inherent conflict between Moscow and the West meant that the two sides could never permanently resolve their differences. That is why the West could only contain Soviet expansionist efforts.

Besides the United States, Kennan saw just four centers of industrial and military power of importance to national security—the Soviet Union, Britain, Germany and Western Europe, and Japan. If all but Russia could be kept in the Western camp by building up their strength, then the Soviet Union would decline in power and capability over time. The West would further weaken the Soviets, Kennan predicted, by exploiting tensions between the Kremlin and Communist movements in other countries.

In the new orthodoxy of containment, the United States would resist all future Soviet expansion but not liberate areas already under Kremlin control. Kennan recommended applying counterforce to the Russians at every point. For example, the United States should set up bases at strategic points around the peripheries of the Soviet Empire. These would protect sea lanes and provide stations for long-range bombers. Surrounding the Soviet Union, Kennan wrote, would incite "the traditional and instinctive Russian sense of insecurity," the root of the "Kremlin's neurotic view of world affairs." This paranoia would induce the leaders to concentrate more and more resources on nonproductive military forces and less on better living standards for the people.[9]

Kennan's plan was remarkably sensible. It avoided direct challenges to the Soviet army and required the Kremlin, in order to expand, to initiate aggressive moves on its own. Such moves would isolate Russia in world opinion, confine conflicts to relatively small areas, and give the United States great strategic advantages, since the U.S. Navy ruled the seas and could deposit superior forces everywhere on earth except directly adjacent to the Soviet land mass.

Winston Churchill launched the containment strategy on March 5, 1946, in a speech orchestrated by Truman at Westminster College, Fulton, Missouri. "From Stettin in the Baltic to Trieste in the Adriatic an iron curtain has descended across the Continent," Churchill announced. A year later, on March 12, 1947, Truman went before Congress and asked for massive aid for Greece and Turkey. Since 1945 Greece had been fighting Communist forces infiltrating from Russian satellites to the north, while Turkey was under pressure from Stalin to give up the Dardanelles and territory adjacent to the Russian Caucasus. Truman was spurred to action when, in February 1947, Britain informed the United States that it could no longer assist Greece and Turkey as it had been doing. Truman told Congress that "it must be the policy of the United States to support free peoples who are resisting attempted subjugation by armed minorities or by outside pressures." This was the Truman Doctrine.[10]

Congress empowered the president to send aid and military and civilian experts to help Greece and Turkey. The cold war had begun.

To gird for the trial ahead, Truman signed the National Security Act on July 26, 1947. This act unified command of the armed forces—including a now independent air force—within a new Department of Defense, and it established the National Security Council (NSC) and the Central Intelligence Agency (CIA) as secret institutions responsible only to the president. The NSC was to refine foreign policy, while the CIA was to gather intelligence information worldwide.[11] Soon thereafter Truman opted for an "air-atomic" plan that made strategic bombing—which might include nuclear weapons—the primary military force. Since the United States at the moment possessed a monopoly on atomic bombs, this strategy seemed to make sense. But it was soon apparent that U.S. leaders could use the A-bomb *only* to meet challenges that threatened the very existence of the United States. And when the Soviet Union got the bomb in 1949, the pattern shifted to mutual deterrence—neither side could use the bomb for fear of a retaliatory atomic strike.[12]

The great danger in Western Europe came not from outside infiltrators, as in Greece, but from economic stagnation in the wake of the wartime destruction of factories, homes, railroads, other infrastructure, and markets. Communist parties were trying to exploit unemployment, poverty, and a deep sense of malaise and discouragement that was sweeping over Western Europe. Kennan had called for the economic rebirth of Western Europe, and on June 5, 1947, at Harvard University's commencement, Secretary of State Marshall proposed that European countries get together and see what they could do for themselves and then submit concrete proposals of what they needed from the United States.

Although Marshall made the offer to the Soviet Union and its satellites as well, it was obvious that the concept directly challenged Communism. The United States developed the plan to show Europe that a market economy and private enterprise could produce prosperity far more easily than could the Marxist command economy that the Soviet Union operated under and was pressing on its satellites. Communism required collectivization—state ownership of factories, farmland, and other productive resources. It squelched private initiative and creativity. Central bureaucrats determined what materials factories and collective farms would be allotted and what they would produce, ignoring the wishes of consumers and forbidding innovation, ingenuity, and imagination. In the Marxist utopia, only those in charge had any right to make plans. Everyone else had to follow them. That's why Marxism led only to tyranny, not prosperity.

The Kremlin spurned the Marshall Plan as "American imperialism." Neither Russia nor its satellites shared in it. Nor did Finland and Czechoslovakia, who dared not offend the Soviet giant. The only other European countries not involved were Fascist Spain, which was not invited to participate, and Britain, which opted out of the plan voluntarily. West Germany would join in 1949, when its government was formally established.

For the sixteen European nations involved, the Marshall Plan proved spectacularly successful. Each year for five years, about 1 percent of the U.S. gross national product flowed into Europe to restore railways, build hydroelectric and other power plants, rebuild factories, construct housing, provide agricultural machinery, and carry out many other projects. The United States had committed itself to a worldwide system of free trade, and Western Europe was quickly integrated into a

North Atlantic trading network.[13] In 1949 production reached the level it had attained in 1939, and it continued to rise. France and Italy eliminated Communists from their governments. Belgium, the Netherlands, and Luxembourg formed a single economic unit, Benelux. The cooperation engendered by the Marshall Plan led to a common market of six Western European states; ultimately it would lead, decades later, to the European Union, which covered much of the continent.[14]

By September 1947 it was plain that the Soviet Union was going to obstruct every effort to establish a coherent, peaceful order in Europe. That month Stalin set up the Communist Information Bureau (Cominform), designed to produce one Communist world, with every other form of government marked for destruction. In this atmosphere, it was hopeless to expect the Kremlin to agree to the unification of Germany, and the Western powers set about to join their three occupation zones into a viable state.

This was precisely what the Soviet Union did *not* want. In February 1948 a coup overthrew the democratic government of Czechoslovakia and installed a regime attached to Moscow. In June the Russians closed off all Western road and rail access to Berlin, located in the midst of the Soviet zone but occupied, like Germany as a whole, by the four powers. The Soviets wanted to oust the West from Berlin by threatening to starve the 2 million people living in the city's Western zones. Such a move would solidify Soviet control of Eastern Europe, and by proving their potency, the Soviets might halt efforts to unify the three Western zones of Germany.

In the crisis President Truman did not hesitate for a second. Since the air lanes to Berlin were still open, American and British transport planes immediately airlifted food and fuel to the city. Within days a highly efficient system had been set up. Hundreds of two-engine C-47s and four-engine C-54s were brought over from the United States to fly in supplies. Truman ordered B-29 bombers to England in July. These, the Russians knew, were the only aircraft capable of reaching Russia with atomic bombs. Truman's challenge was clear: permit the airlift to continue or risk atomic attack.[15]

By September 1, transports were flying in 4,000 tons of supplies every day. Month after month, in good weather and bad, the airlift continued. Eventually it was bringing in more freight than the railroads had done before. The airlift dealt a serious blow to the Soviets' reputation and brought Europe—especially Germany—closer to the United States. Now assured that they would not be abandoned, Europeans lined up solidly with the United States against the Soviet Union. West Germans went promptly to work to write a democratic constitution for the new state. The West German government was established in September 1949 and began to receive Marshall Plan aid.

That May Soviet leaders had already lifted their land blockade, seeing that the West had thoroughly bested them with the airlift. But in October the Kremlin responded to the creation of the West German state by establishing a totalitarian government in its zone, East Germany. Still, because of the airlift, Berlin remained an island of freedom within this dictatorship.

Also in 1949, Truman brought about the North Atlantic Treaty Organization (NATO), which, under U.S. leadership, provided for a collective defense against the Soviets. In September 1949, when Truman announced that the Russians had exploded an atomic bomb, Congress rapidly provided funding for NATO.[16] In 1953 a rearmed West Germany was admitted.

★   ★   ★

AT THE END of World War II, the primary American anxiety in the Far East was not Korea and not Japan but China. This immense civilization, possessing a fifth of the people on earth, had been in the throes of a continuing revolution ever since the last emperor had been ousted in 1912. By 1945 two completely inimical forces—the right-wing Nationalists under Chiang Kai-shek and the Communists under Mao Zedong—were on the verge of civil war to determine who at last would rule the ancient Middle Kingdom.

Despite having played almost no role in the defeat of Japan, China was listed as a great power and the Chinese Nationalists had a permanent seat on the U.N. Security Council with the same veto power as the

United States and Russia. China owed its exalted position almost entirely to Franklin D. Roosevelt. Till the time of his death in 1945, FDR possessed an idealistic, naive hope that China would become a great stabilizing force in East Asia, countering not only the Soviet Union and Japan but also the European colonial empires that still ringed Southeast Asia.

In fact, neither the Nationalists nor their Communist opponents had shown any interest in taking on a great-power role. They were almost completely absorbed in their internal struggle. Both had largely sat out the war, waiting for the United States to win it and free China from the threat of Japan. During the war the United States had laboriously delivered weapons and military supplies to China—first airlifting them over "the Hump" of the Himalayas, and later transporting them over the Ledo Road through the jungles of northern Burma. But Chiang squirreled them away to use against the Reds.

In 1945 the United States aligned itself solidly behind Chiang Kaishek because his opponent, Mao Zedong, was Communist and Americans believed all Communists were being directed by the Kremlin. Therefore, if Mao won, he would simply deliver the Middle Kingdom as a satellite to Joseph Stalin.

This was an altogether erroneous judgment, one that ignored not only the history of the Communist movement in China but also the solid advice of George Kennan, who otherwise was regarded in Washington as an oracle. Kennan wrote that the Chinese Communists "have little reason to be grateful to the Soviet Union. They have survived and grown not because of but despite relations with Moscow."

Communism succeeded in China by turning orthodox Marxist theory on its head. Karl Marx held that the urban industrial worker, the proletariat, was the key to revolution. Mao Zedong, seeing that this proletariat amounted to less than 1 percent of China's population, concentrated instead on the Chinese peasant, who made up 80 percent of the population. These peasants had been exploited for two thousand years by the propertied gentry that charged exorbitant rates to rent land, borrow money, and provide food in times of famine. The Nationalists represented this exploitive class and thus were the natural enemy of the oppressed peasant majority, whom Mao was rallying to a peculiar Chinese form of Communism. If Mao won, China would never be a satellite of Russia. It would go its own way.

One of the few great mistakes that Harry Truman made was to believe, like most other American leaders, that all Communists were alike, and to see in Mao Zedong the specter of Russian domination of China. This misapprehension resulted in tragedy.[17]

President Truman named George C. Marshall as ambassador to China on November 27, 1945, the very day Marshall retired after six years as army chief of staff and principal military adviser to Roosevelt and Truman. Marshall's assignment was to bring the two sides together in a democratically elected parliament with free political parties. This, Truman thought, would dilute the Communist influence and bring peace and harmony. But it was a hopeless illusion. Neither the Nationalists nor the Communists wanted a democracy. Each wanted to rule as a single-party dictatorship. Furthermore, the Chinese Communists could not trust Chiang, for they recognized (accurately) that the United States, because of its fear of Communism, supported Chiang all along.[18]

Marshall attempted to carry out his impossible job until January 8, 1947, when Truman called him home to become secretary of state. By that time a great civil war was raging in China. Chiang Kai-shek was one of the worst generals in the twentieth century. He placed huge armies in the cities of Manchuria, which the Reds simply surrounded and starved into surrender. By October 1949 Chiang's armies had melted away, and he and his closest cronies had fled to the Chinese island of Taiwan, where the Nationalists maintained a precarious existence.

The victory of the Chinese Reds left the Truman Doctrine seemingly in tatters, since Communism had not been contained in China but had advanced. This, of course, was based on the American misconception that made no distinction between Soviet Communists and Chinese Communists. It raised a huge cry that the United States had "lost" China. But Chiang Kai-shek represented reactionary forces with little popular support that could survive *only* if propped up by American military power. No one in authority in Washington was willing to commit a great land army to the continent of Asia for this purpose. By the fall of 1949, the Truman administration had decided to wash its hands of China.[19]

Early in 1950 the administration made two pronouncements that led North Korea and Red China to believe they had nothing to fear from America. These statements profoundly affected the course of history, because they turned out to be directly opposite to how the United States actually responded.

On January 5, 1950, President Truman announced that the United States had no intention of interfering in the situation in Taiwan, which was girding for a Communist invasion. On January 12, Secretary of State Dean Acheson, who had replaced Marshall a year earlier, outlined an American "defensive perimeter" in the Far East that included Japan, the Ryukyus (Okinawa), and the Philippines, but excluded Korea and Taiwan.[20]

On the early morning of June 25, 1950, the North Korean army launched a surprise invasion of South Korea. The North Koreans had about 90,000 men, more than twice as many as the South Koreans facing them along the thirty-eighth parallel. But the key to North Korean success was the 150 Russian T-34 tanks they sent down the narrow Korean roads. The South Koreans had nothing to stop a tank—not a single tank of their own, nor armor-piercing artillery shells, nor combat aircraft, nor antitank land mines.

Within days the North Koreans had captured the South Korean capital of Seoul and flung the disorganized South Korean army into retreat. President Truman decided at once to defend South Korea—notwithstanding the "defensive perimeter" line—and General Douglas MacArthur, the Far East commander, franticly moved elements of the four American divisions occupying Japan to Korea to set up a solid defensive line. The United States obtained the support of the United Nations, but little help.[21] Americans suffered many defeats and much loss before we, with the assistance of the South Koreans and a small British brigade, stopped the North Koreans around the "Pusan perimeter" in the extreme south of Korea.

On September 15, 1950, MacArthur—taking advantage of American command of the sea—launched a surprise invasion of Inchon, drove quickly to nearby Seoul, and sealed off the North Korean army in the south. This army disintegrated, and only individual soldiers made it back into North Korea. The Inchon invasion was in the finest tradition of American military imagination, because it took full advantage of our naval and air strength and completely negated North Korean ground strength. The United States had defended South Korea in spectacular fashion and had driven out the invaders. The war should have ended right then. But it didn't.

The reason it didn't was that the American leaders believed the invasion of South Korea was the first move in a general *Soviet* attack on the West, carried out in this case by surrogate troops. Since Washington also held that Communist China was a satellite of the Kremlin and a party to the invasion, Truman had blocked Taiwan with the American fleet in the first days of the war, in order to prevent the Chinese Reds from capturing the island and destroying the last remnants of the Nationalist regime.

But China had played no part in the invasion of South Korea and was irate at the intervention in its civil war. From this moment the Reds feared an American plot to use Chiang Kai-shek's Nationalists to invade mainland China.

The Soviet Union most definitely was implicated in the attack on South Korea. It had supplied the North Koreans with offensive weapons, especially T-34 tanks. Even so, there is no evidence that the Soviet government actually instigated the invasion. Rather, the preponderance of evidence shows that the extremely aggressive North Korean leader, Kim Il Sung, planned it, and that the Russians, when informed, went along, hoping the Americans would stay out. Kim Il Sung broached the idea to Stalin in the fall of 1949, saying that South Korea would collapse "at the first poke of a bayonet." Apparently this and Acheson's January 12, 1950, statement convinced Stalin, and he agreed, sending the North Koreans much offensive war material in early 1950. But the Soviets never took part in the fighting, and in fact they distanced themselves from the war once the battle began.[22]

All the major American leaders, especially General MacArthur, agreed that the United States should invade North Korea, eliminate the Communist regime there, and unify the peninsula under the South Korean government of Syngman Rhee. This was *not* the containment policy that had been enunciated in 1947 in the Truman Doctrine. It was an effort to push back the frontiers of Communism. And the decision came despite Red China's feverish attempt to prevent it. The Communist leaders were convinced that eliminating the North Korean buffer would lead to a joint Nationalist Chinese–American invasion across the Yalu River frontier, into Manchuria, and on to the Chinese capital of Beijing. On October 2, 1950, Zhou Enlai, the Red premier, informed the Indian ambassador (since the United States had no diplomatic relations with Beijing) that China would intervene if American troops crossed the thirty-eighth parallel but would not do so if South Koreans went alone.[23]

Washington got the warning within hours, but rejected it, calling it a bluff. The invasion went ahead. In response, the Red Chinese secretly moved hundreds of thousands of troops into North Korea and attacked the U.N. advance on November 25. The Chinese offensive drove back U.N. forces, with great losses, all the way to the thirty-eighth parallel by Christmas, and into South Korea in the new year. The Chinese offensive shocked American leaders, but they saw it as a stroke dictated by the Kremlin, not what it was—a wholly Chinese effort to protect their buffer in front of the Yalu River.

By March 1951 the two sides were deadlocked around the thirty-eighth parallel. Truman decided to seize the opportunity and propose a cease-fire, whereupon both sides could sit down and negotiate. The bellicose MacArthur, however, wanted to continue the war against China, even to the extent of invading the country. Informed of Truman's plan, MacArthur, without notifying Washington, on March 24 issued a virtual ultimatum; he threatened to extend the war unless Red China sued for peace. MacArthur announced, "The enemy must now be painfully aware that a decision of the United Nations to depart from its tolerant effort to contain the war to the area of Korea through expansion of our military operations to his coastal areas and interior bases would doom Red China to the risks of imminent military collapse."

MacArthur had torpedoed Truman's peace initiative. He had openly defied the president as commander in chief. On April 9, with the backing of Secretary of State Acheson and the Joint Chiefs of Staff, Truman dismissed MacArthur and replaced him with General Matthew B. Ridgway.

The Chinese tried one more offensive into the south, but it went only a few miles before American forces stopped it. Thereupon the Chinese withdrew to a line generally above the thirty-eighth parallel and dug in. By June 1951, deadlock again had descended on the Korean Peninsula. Since both sides were weary of war, this was another chance to end the fighting. On July 1 the Chinese accepted a simple cease-fire, leaving all political decisions to negotiations after both sides laid down their arms. But Ridgway, speaking for a group of combative leaders— the Joint Chiefs of Staff, the State Department, and President Truman—who distrusted the Chinese, destroyed the possibility of ending the war by mutual agreement.

Ridgway protested that a cease-fire might endanger the safety and security of Americans, saying that the Chinese might use it to strengthen their forces in the peninsula and maybe even launch another offensive. This was highly unlikely, but the Truman administration, while it agreed to start peace talks at Kaesong (later Panmunjom), refused to stop fighting. As a result, two more years of bloody war ensued. The United States would not end the war until July 27, 1953—when it accepted terms identical to those offered on July 1, 1951.

Truman got hung up on an issue tangential to the war. He refused to return Communist prisoners of war who didn't want to go home. Although the United States had signed the 1949 Geneva Convention, which stated that "prisoners of war shall be repatriated without delay after cessation of hostilities," Truman used the POW issue as propaganda to show that soldiers would resist returning to Communist rule. The U.S. position delayed the armistice at least a year. During this period the U.N. command suffered far more casualties in battle than there were POWs. The total number of prisoners on both sides, those who wanted to be sent home and those who did not, was 118,917. But in the last four months of the war alone, the U.N. and Communist forces suffered 200,000 battle casualties. Thus a moral issue was posed: should troops fight and some die to give former enemies freedom of choice? Besides, the U.S. position ensured that *all* POWs, U.N. and Communist, had to endure additional months of captivity. In the end, an Indian proposal broke the impasse. It called for a five-nation Repatriation Commission to take charge of all prisoners who refused repatriation. After interviews, the prisoners who did not want to return home were released.[24]

The refusal to accept a cease-fire and the POW issue were terrible blunders, attributable to Truman's deep suspicion of the Communists. Any cease-fire depends on the goodwill of both parties. And there was every reason to believe the Chinese were earnest. They had secured a buffer in front of the Yalu River and had nothing to gain by continued fighting. The proof of China's sincerity came from the fact the Chinese never attempted another offensive in Korea. From the moment they announced a willingness to cease military operations, they adopted a defensive military posture, protecting the existing line.

In 1952 Dwight Eisenhower became the Republican candidate for president. With no end to the war in sight, Eisenhower said, "I shall go to Korea." This helped him to win the election in November, but his visit to Korea in December 1952 gave him no insights. He accepted a straightforward armistice in July 1953.

★   ★   ★

AMERICAN ACCOMPLISHMENTS WERE magnificent from the end of World War II up to the invasion of North Korea in October 1950. Though the unnecessary continuation of the war in Korea tarnished the glory, U.S. leaders had stopped the advance of Communism in its tracks and had thrown the Soviet Union on the defensive.

And how they did it is telling. Though the United Nations had backed the response to North Korea's invasion of South Korea, the United States provided the military force and leadership to achieve victory. Indeed, in 1956 Henry Kissinger, later to become American secretary of state, concluded that American allies had been as much of a hindrance as a help in the Korean War. He argued that in light of the Korean experience, the United States must be able to go it alone when necessary: "Either the alliances add little to our effective strength or they do not reflect a common purpose, or both. . . . We have to face the fact that only the United States is strong enough domestically and economically to assume worldwide responsibilities and that the attempt to obtain the prior approval by our allies of our every step will lead not to common action but inaction. . . . We must reserve the right to act alone, or with a regional grouping of powers, if our strategic interest so dictates." Such arguments would gain supporters as the years went by, and they would be central to future challenges that the United States faced.[25]

Those challenges were far off, however. For the time being, the Soviet Union remained the central focus of American foreign policy. And the Korean War had done real damage to the Soviets, damage from which they only slowly recovered. The Soviet bloc's command economy, flawed because it took little notice of consumer needs, fell further behind the West's market economy every day. Maintaining a huge army and an industrial system geared to meeting the U.S. military challenge was overburdening the economy and slowly grinding it to collapse. The death of Joseph Stalin on March 5, 1953, led to years of intrigue and clashes among successors vying for power, and this further distracted and weakened the country.

But the Soviet Union's inevitable decline was still invisible to most observers. In 1953 there was little sense of victory. Rather, uneasiness and insecurity spread over American spirits. The mood was akin to the feelings of the traveler who gained refuge in one of the "cold harbors" along ill-traveled roads in the antebellum South. In such a bleak harbor the wayfarer found shelter from the storm, but he got no warmth, no hot food, and no comfort.

★ ★ ★

DOMINOS, ROCKETS, AND CUBA

For two decades, from 1953 to 1973, the United States was consumed with two foreign concerns—the presumed danger of Communist aggression in East Asia, and actual Soviet intimidation that culminated in the threat of nuclear-armed rockets launched from Cuba. During this same period the nation finally brought within the scope of its laws the truth proclaimed in the Declaration of Independence that all people are created equal.

From 1965 to 1973 President Lyndon B. Johnson and his successor, Richard M. Nixon, pursued an unwinnable war in Vietnam. This was one of the greatest mistakes in American history. It was directed at a target that presented no danger. The enemy was unbeatable because he was fighting a guerrilla war, while we were trying to fight a conventional war. America's inability to achieve victory led some leaders to insist on pursuing the war even harder and others to demand that we withdraw. This divided the nation to a degree it had not been split since the Civil War. It happened because Johnson and Nixon refused to examine the real situation they were facing and doggedly continued on a course that could only end in failure.

Nevertheless, by the spring of 1973 the United States was no longer directly involved in Indochina, had achieved near tranquility in East

Asia, and had reached a state of peaceful coexistence with the Soviet Union.

These astonishing successes came about because public pressure forced America to get it right at last and back out of Vietnam, while three presidents got it right in three other matters that saved the world from calamity. In 1955 President Dwight D. Eisenhower rebuffed an effort by his secretary of state, John Foster Dulles, to commence a nuclear war to hold two tiny islands off the coast of China. In 1962 President John F. Kennedy forced the Kremlin to remove missiles it had installed in Cuba. And in 1972 President Nixon, though blind about Vietnam, ended America's long, arid attempt to keep China as a pariah outside the world community of nations.

During this period the Soviet Union's economic structure declined markedly as its leaders failed to meet consumers' needs while devoting most discretionary resources to the impossible task of matching American production of intercontinental ballistic missiles, nuclear bombs, and a vast, sophisticated array of new aircraft, submarines, aircraft carriers, and other weapons. In this unequal struggle, the silhouette of the Soviet Union's ultimate crackup was already visible in 1973.

Although the United States made errors during the two decades after the end of the Korean War, the only ruinous one was the insistence on achieving a victory in Vietnam. There the enemy was a virtually invisible force that struck hard and fast at vulnerable targets and disappeared as quickly back into the population. With no enemy who could be "found, fought, and finished," the war could not be won, but President Johnson refused to recognize the truth, and neither did President Nixon, who extended the war to Cambodia in 1970 in a foolish, costly, and doomed attempt to avert misfortune.

President Kennedy made another proposal in this period that could have resulted in a disaster even worse than the Vietnam War. He failed to take advantage of the great schism between China and Russia revealed in the late 1950s. This fracture proved beyond all doubt that Communist states acted in their *own* interests, not to further some universal Marxist purpose. The United States could have played one side against the other quite effectively. Instead, Kennedy bought the erroneous idea of Chinese belligerence and sided with the *real* threat, the Soviet Union, to try to destroy Chinese nuclear-test facilities at Lop Nur in Xinjiang Province. The Kremlin refused to participate in the air strikes Kennedy proposed, knowing they would bring on a war of unmeasurable dimensions. In this regard, Moscow's leadership showed better judgment than Kennedy.

★   ★   ★

AT THE END of the Korean War on July 27, 1953, our leaders advertised the armistice as an American victory. But in private they knew this was not the case. The United States, with the most advanced military technology on earth, had been stopped by a bunch of Chinese peasants with no air force, no tanks, and few vehicles of any sort and armed mainly with a hodgepodge of old rifles, machine guns, and mortars. American leaders had ceased talking about the now-vanished resolve to conquer North Korea, but they found it difficult to accept the fact that they had been pushed out of North Korea and that thereafter the Chinese had maintained themselves solidly in numerous bloody battles along the Korean ridgelines.

The country that had successfully defied the United States now became a mortal enemy. American leaders nurtured a fierce hate that took on the irrational fervor of a blood feud. This alone explains the bizarre intensity by which American leaders pursued a vendetta against China for most of the next two decades, a vendetta they did *not* pursue against the real danger, the Soviet Union. For example, in September 1952, during the Korean War, the United States prohibited a long list of strategic goods from being sold to Red China and North Korea. This list, "the China differential," was much broader than the prohibited list for the Soviet Union, and the United States got its allies to agree to the embargo. When the war ended, the China differential continued.

American domestic opinion generally accepted claims out of Washington that Beijing had held up peace in Korea. In fact, U.S. refusal to settle the POW issue is what delayed the armistice. Not knowing this, most Americans supported official policy treating Red China as an outcast. We largely endorsed the administration's efforts to maintain Nationalist China in the U.N. Security Council and to exclude Red China, although Red China represented 96 percent of the people of China.

The United States had decided to support Chiang Kai-shek and his Nationalists on Taiwan, even if this meant war. To justify this policy, the Eisenhower administration accused China of a conspiracy to conquer all of East Asia. The only evidence it could find to support this charge was Beijing's insistence on capturing Taiwan. The island, however, was Chinese territory—even Chiang Kai-shek insisted on that—and an attempt to capture it could scarcely be viewed as an effort to seize East Asia. The only way out of this logical trap was to claim that Red China was really an agent of the Kremlin, not an independent power. This was manifestly foolish, yet the fiction continued for a long time.

The only other examples the Eisenhower administration could come up with to show Chinese aggression were the intervention in Korea and Beijing's recognition of the Ho Chi Minh regime in Vietnam. But Red China had moved into Korea *only* after the United States announced that it was going to conquer North Korea, and it made no real effort to drive American forces out of South Korea.[1] As for recognizing the Communist Ho Chi Minh, this was no more evidence of aggression than the American recognition of the French-supported regime of emperor Bao Dai in Vietnam.

In January 1954 Secretary of State Dulles added to the tension by announcing the doctrine of "massive retaliation." This meant that the United States, in crises with Communist states, might defend itself with nuclear weapons. The doctrine displeased President Eisenhower, because it implied an almost instantaneous escalation to nuclear warfare whenever the United States was blocked. The concept not only was unreasonable, it was extremely dangerous, since the Soviet Union now also had the hydrogen bomb. Dulles soon modified the policy to permit "flexible" responses when atomic strikes were not called for. Even so, America's stated readiness to accept nuclear war as a solution to conflicts frightened world leaders—and, as events were to show, frightened President Eisenhower as well.

By early 1954 the central point of dispute in the Far East was Indochina. There the French had been engaged since 1946 in a deadly, losing war with the Vietminh (Vietnamese Independence League) under Ho Chi Minh. French generals had sent 13,000 men to Dien Bien Phu in extreme northwestern Vietnam near the Laotian border. The aim was to break Vietminh supply lines. But the French army itself was isolated after the Vietnamese general Vo Nyugen Giap surrounded the army, blocked its road access to Hanoi, dragged artillery over the mountains, shot down relief aircraft, and commenced a siege.

Military defeat was now all but certain. France, seeking to preserve some of its "prestige," engineered a peace conference at Geneva. The United States went along with the conference, but it opposed a non-military solution in Indochina, because that flew in the face of Dulles's domino theory. The Vietminh, Dulles announced on March 29, 1954, took their orders from Moscow and Beijing. If they gained any substantial part of Indochina, "they would surely resume the same pattern of aggression against other free peoples in the area."

To put themselves in the best possible position at Geneva, the Vietminh captured Dien Bien Phu on May 7, the day before the conference opened. France, its hopes of keeping Indochina dashed, decided to get out, leaving the United States as the only power opposed to the creation of a Communist state in Vietnam.

At the same time, it became clear to close observers—though not to Dulles—that the falling-domino theory was false. Both the Soviet Union and China showed they were willing to sacrifice their supposed ally Ho Chi Minh and any advances in Southeast Asia in order to achieve goals elsewhere. The Soviets encouraged ending the war on terms acceptable to France in order to get Paris to reject the European Defense Community (EDC) and a supranational European army (which the French ultimately did reject). Red China wanted peace to prevent an American presence on its southern border.

In the war, the Vietminh had overrun most of Vietnam and expected to get the support of the Soviet Union and China to gain control of the whole country. But those governments agreed to a "temporary" partition of Vietnam along the seventeenth parallel, with a Communist state in the north and France's puppet Bao Dai ruling in the south. Both Russia and China knew the seventeenth parallel would be a permanent boundary, but neither had any interest in getting involved in Vietnam.

It is a measure of Dulles's obsession with falling dominos that he did not recognize that Red China had been remarkably consistent: it had gone to war to preserve a buffer state in North Korea, and now it required nothing more than a buffer state in North Vietnam. These positions clearly signaled that China had no plans to expand into Southeast Asia and was not operating as part of a Communist conspiracy. But Dulles refused to see the evidence.[2]

Vietnam was in the midst of a violent *nationalist* revolution to throw off years of French colonial exploitation and to rectify severe social inequities. Moderate Vietnamese had been forced to move to the left to join the Communists, the only force strong enough to resist French power, or to the right to cleave to the small, native privileged elite who shared dominion with the French. No middle ground was possible. The existing native power structure was unwilling to distribute land, wealth, and political rights more fairly. In this atmosphere the Communist movement thrived because it promised to remedy abuses.

Having been abandoned by China and the Soviet Union, Ho Chi Minh accepted the seventeenth parallel border, along with a promise to hold nationwide elections on July 1, 1956, which the Communists were certain they would win. The Communists withdrew into North Vietnam, but the United States, now protector of South Vietnam, had no intention of actually holding an all-Vietnam election. Washington did not sign the Geneva accord, and just as the Chinese and Soviets expected, it moved to transform the temporary division into a permanent partition. The U.S. government persuaded the sybaritic Bao Dai to remain in European spas and to appoint Ngo Dinh Diem—a wealthy, American-educated Roman Catholic, in a land overwhelmingly Buddhist—

to form a new government. American advisers began to train a new South Vietnamese army, and the United States sent massive amounts of weapons and money to arm it. In 1955 Diem rejected an all-Vietnam election, and Eisenhower backed him. Over the next seven years the United States supplied most of Diem's expenses, allowing Diem to suppress political rivals, Communist and non-Communist alike. By 1959 Diem's repressions triggered a guerrilla revolt, which was soon taken over by Communists, the Vietcong.

Meanwhile Dulles tried to create a security pact similar to Western Europe's North Atlantic Treaty Organization (NATO). At Manila in September 1954, the United States, Britain, France, Australia, New Zealand, Pakistan, the Philippines, and Thailand formed the Southeast Asia Treaty Organization (SEATO). But India, Burma, Ceylon (Sri Lanka), and Indonesia refused, and SEATO did not become a solid alliance like NATO. In response to any attack, a member would merely act "in accordance with its constitutional processes."

★   ★   ★

WITH INDOCHINA TEMPORARILY quiescent, America's attention shifted back to China. In March 1954 the National Security Council endorsed continuing trade embargoes — the China differential — to delay Red Chinese efforts to achieve large-scale industrialization.

But a real crisis was building around two groups of tiny islands the Nationalist Chinese still occupied near the coast of mainland China — Jinmen (Quemoy) off Xiamen, and Mazu (Matsu), twenty miles off the coast opposite Fuzhou. Preoccupied with the Korean War, China had allowed these tiny outposts to remain in Nationalist hands. But now Beijing was moving to seize them. Chiang Kai-shek had stationed a third of his army on these islands, mainly as a gesture of defiance. But they were indefensible, and the Reds could capture them easily unless the United States intervened.

Dulles pushed hard to guard the islands, arguing that they were strategically important to protect Taiwan. He enlisted the support of Admiral Arthur W. Radford, chairman of the Joint Chiefs of Staff, but not General Matthew B. Ridgway, army chief of staff, who said that loss of the islands would not affect the defense of Taiwan one iota.[3]

Defense of the islands could lead to war with China. In September 1954 President Eisenhower said that if the United States went to war, he was opposed to "any holding back like in Korea." Thus, defense of Quemoy and Matsu would probably lead to the use of nuclear weapons. This was sobering beyond measure. Since the Chinese Reds were making no overt moves, the administration decided to back off. But by March 1955 Dulles had emerged as a war hawk. Having convinced himself that the Chinese Reds were about to attack Taiwan, he told Eisenhower the United States should help Chiang Kai-shek and defend the offshore islands. This, he said, "would require the use of atomic weapons."

For the moment Eisenhower agreed. But General Nathan F. Twining, the air force chief of staff, told the president that the Communists were not going to attack Taiwan soon because they had not built up airfields sufficiently. A 1955 national intelligence estimate stated flatly that Red China did not have the capability to attack Taiwan. General Ridgway reiterated that he did not consider the offshore islands important, and he made it clear that he didn't want to risk atomic war over them.

In April 1955 Chinese premier Zhou Enlai opened a peace offensive at an Afro-Asian conference at Bandung, Indonesia. There Zhou presented "five principles of peaceful coexistence" that China was going to follow—respect for a nation's territorial integrity, nonaggression, noninterference in another's affairs, equality and mutual benefit, and peaceful coexistence.

Zhou's demarche caused Eisenhower to reassess the situation. The president had become increasingly reluctant to use atomic weapons against the densely populated Chinese mainland, because such a move would arouse intense world revulsion. He climbed down off his war horse—and pulled Dulles off his.

In July 1955 Zhou announced that Red China was ready to liberate Taiwan by peaceful means. Dulles remained as hostile as ever. But the rest of the world breathed easier, recognizing that China had turned away from confrontation with the United States. In the years to come there were a few more alarms about Quemoy and Matsu, but they finally subsided, and the islands remain in Taiwanese hands to this day.[4]

★ ★ ★

DURING THE EISENHOWER administration a revolution commenced that finally made the constitutional principle of equal protection of the law a reality for all people. Here at last the American people got it right. The revolution began on May 17, 1954, when the Supreme Court in the case of *Brown v. Board of Education* ruled that segregating public school children by race was unconstitutional. This set off an agonizing process of delays, evasions, and some violence to end segregated schools in the seventeen states where black and white children were taught separately. By the 1970s legal desegregation had been achieved everywhere, though "white flight" to the suburbs left de facto segregation in many central cities. But a new moral crusade developed against the entire concept of separation of the races in December 1955, when Rosa Parks, a black woman, refused to obey a law requiring segregated seating in buses in Montgomery, Alabama. After February 1960, when African American college students staged "sit-ins" at lunch counters in Greensboro, North Carolina, white Americans everywhere began to see plainly how demeaning and unjust segregation was. Thus only die-hard segregationists objected when President Johnson pushed through the Civil Rights Act in 1964. And on March 7, 1965, when state troopers used tear gas and clubs to break up a peaceful march for voter registration at Selma, Alabama, the entire nation was outraged. That outrage spurred passage of the Voting Rights Act of 1965.[5] These two laws transformed the nation, turning African Americans into a powerful voting bloc and bringing much fairer opportunities for African Americans in all fields.

During this same period, the United States also accorded women equal status. In the book *Beyond Terror,* Ralph Peters writes, "America accomplished a peaceful revolution whose reverberations will be felt far longer than those of a violent change. The introduction of a vast pool of female talent and energy into the workplace supercharged economic development even as it altered traditional roles."[6]

★   ★   ★

ALTHOUGH PRESIDENT EISENHOWER was uncomfortable with Dulles's "massive retaliation" policy, he was a cold warrior who saw Communism as a dangerous enemy that had to be restrained. In his inaugural address in January 1953 Eisenhower said, "Forces of good and evil are massed and armed and opposed as rarely before in history. Freedom is pitted against slavery, lightness against the dark. In the final choice, a soldier's pack is not so heavy a burden as a prisoner's chains."[7]

But Eisenhower continued Truman's containment policy. When Poland and Hungary tried to establish more liberal Communist governments in 1956, the United States offered nothing but moral support, even when Soviet tanks crushed an uprising in Budapest.[8]

Eisenhower did take decisive action in the Middle East, however. In 1956 Egyptian dictator Gamal Abdel Nasser nationalized the Suez Canal, thereby shutting off Israel's use of it and jeopardizing Western Europe's access to the region's oil. In October 1956 Israel launched a surprise attack against Egypt that quickly overran the Sinai Peninsula. Britain and France intervened against Egypt, using the excuse that they needed "to protect the Suez Canal." It was a bald-faced effort to reassert colonial power over Egypt, and Eisenhower would have none of it. He demanded that the Europeans and the Israelis withdraw, which they did. This effectively ended France's and Britain's influence in the region.

The world changed abruptly on October 4, 1957, when the Soviets launched the world's first earth-orbiting artificial satellite, the 184-pound Sputnik. A month later they launched a second Sputnik, six times larger, and carrying a live dog. It was a public-relations disaster for the United States. The Soviets gloated that here was evidence that their scientists had far outstripped American technology. Sputnik set off a frenetic U.S. program to match and exceed the Soviet space program, not only because American prestige had been wounded, but also because rockets used to throw satellites into orbit could also send nuclear bombs from one continent to another.

On January 31, 1958, the United States sent up its own, much-smaller, satellite, the 31-pound Explorer I. But this satellite's instruments discovered the Van Allen radiation belt around the earth, a find of great significance. The same year the United States established the National Aeronautics and Space Administration (NASA) to direct the space program. The Soviet lead continued for some time, however. Russian satellites were the first to orbit the moon, first to hit the moon, first to launch a probe toward Venus. But the United States soon went far beyond, sending John Glenn in orbit around the earth in 1962, and landing men on the moon in 1969.

Parallel with space exploration came the development of nuclear-armed missiles. On August 26, 1957, Soviet premier Nikita Khrushchev announced his country had tested an intercontinental ballistic missile (ICBM). By 1959 the Soviets had these missiles in mass production. American competitors matched Soviet advances—the intermediate-range Thor, Jupiter, and Polaris for launching from submarines, and the ICBM Minuteman, Titan, and Atlas. The "balance of terror" had been attained—any nuclear strike by one country would be answered by a retaliatory strike by the other.

Less than two weeks after the first Sputnik orbited, Khrushchev agreed to provide China with atomic bomb technology, giving the Chinese the head start they needed. A gaseous diffusion plant near Lanzhou in Gansu Province duplicated Soviet facilities, and at the Lop Nur nuclear-test site in Xinjiang Province the infrastructure followed Soviet designs. But this was virtually the last example of Soviet-Chinese cooperation.

Khrushchev undertook a celebrated tour of the United States in September 1959. During his visit Khrushchev appealed for peaceful coexistence between the Soviet Union and the United States, spoke darkly of the danger of nuclear war, and paid high tribute to President Eisenhower for his efforts to improve relations with the Soviet Union.

Immediately afterward, Khrushchev flew to Beijing to take part in the tenth-anniversary celebrations of the founding of the People's Republic. There he told Mao Zedong that Chinese interests would best be served by accepting a "two-Chinas" formula, a U.S. plan by which Red China would give up its claim to Taiwan and the United States would continue to recognize the Nationalists as the "official" government of China with a seat on the U.N. Security Council. This was wholly unacceptable to Beijing. At the same time, to curry favor with the United States, Khrushchev reneged on assisting in A-bomb development. These two actions broke the last ties between China and the Soviet Union. Russia withdrew all its aid and technicians in 1959 and 1960.

Khrushchev's tour of the United States pointed toward a thaw in East-West relations. But in May 1960, on the eve of a summit conference to discuss arms control, Khrushchev announced that the Soviet Union had shot down an American U-2 spy plane. The United States eventually admitted that it had been using U-2s to fly over Russia at high altitudes and gather information. Thus the cold war continued when John F. Kennedy became president in 1961.

The schism that developed between China and Russia presented the United States with a dazzling opportunity to reach an understanding with Red China and isolate the Soviet Union, the principal American antagonist. Instead, Kennedy took the opposite tack, seeking an understanding with Russia at the expense of China.

America's vendetta against China lay at the core of this irrational policy. While the United States had reacted warmly to Russia's efforts at peaceful coexistence, it rejected China's virtually identical five principles of peaceful coexistence. Washington insisted that Beijing was demonstrating aggression by refusing to accept as permanent the Nationalist regime on Taiwan and by supporting North Vietnam. This position required the United States to downplay the fact that the Soviets also supported North Vietnam, and to maintain that Taiwan was an issue of international concern rather than an internal Chinese matter. Since Chiang Kai-shek held with Beijing that Taiwan was a part of China, the United States had to assert that the Chinese Communists were agents of a conspiracy of world conquest directed by the Kremlin, the very agent Washington was trying to befriend! The idea had become ludicrous by 1961, but Kennedy still accepted it.

★   ★   ★

CUBA, HOWEVER, BECAME the defining factor in Kennedy's presidency. In 1959 a Communist leader, Fidel Castro, overthrew Cuba's corrupt and murderous dictator, Fulgencio Batista; nationalized private U.S. holdings; and, as relations with Washington worsened, turned to the Soviet Union for assistance. In his last days as president, Eisenhower ordered the CIA to plan a military coup to overthrow Castro. By the time Kennedy became president, the CIA had organized 1,400 Cuban exiles and, with Kennedy's authorization, attempted the operation in April 1961. But the CIA, which had planned badly, sent in the invaders at an indefensible site in the Bay of Pigs and gave them little air cover. Castro's tanks and jet aircraft quickly overcame the invaders and captured the survivors.

The fiasco humiliated Kennedy. It gave Castro the opening he wanted to announce that Cuba was a Communist state and to claim that other Latin American countries would follow his lead. Soon he was receiving substantial aid from the Soviet Union. The United States cut off all trade with the island, but Kennedy refused to intervene directly.

Meantime, at a meeting with Kennedy in Vienna in June 1961, Khrushchev demanded that the United States recognize the two German states as wholly separate and terminate the Allied occupation of Berlin. Kennedy refused, but he came back sobered by Khrushchev's hostility. He was even more disturbed in August, when Khrushchev ordered a wall to be built between East and West Berlin. The wall stopped the flow of refugees from Eastern Europe who had been streaming into the West through this opening at the rate of 20,000 a month.

The move signaled Soviet acceptance of failure—not only the failure of a totalitarian state to gain the loyalty of its people, but also the failure to bully the United States into abandoning Berlin. Nevertheless, the Soviets, in their frustration, might repeat the folly of 1948 and close off road and rail access to Berlin. To test whether this was indeed in Khrushchev's mind, Kennedy decided to send 1,500 battle-ready troops by road from West Germany to West Berlin. Khrushchev, seeing American resolve, made no move to stop them. The immediate crisis passed, but shutting off the relief valve that Berlin had offered increased frustration for people under Soviet control. The Berlin Wall became a symbol of Soviet oppression. It proved that everyone in the Soviet empire lived in a slave state. The Berlin Wall held back freedom for a few decades. But the pressure it built up contributed greatly to the raging flood that ultimately washed Soviet Communism away.

During the summer of 1962, Soviets began building sites in Cuba that could fire missiles with a range of 2,000 miles, enough to reach the Panama Canal and most cities in the United States. Overflights by U-2s confirmed the Soviet missile sites, and in October 1962 Kennedy summoned his top officials to determine how the United States would respond. Kennedy at once restated the Monroe Doctrine—Soviet power in the Western Hemisphere was not negotiable. The survival of the United States was at stake. Kennedy resolved to get the missiles removed peacefully, if possible, but if negotiations failed, they would be removed by force—whether or not this brought on nuclear war.

In a televised speech on October 22, 1962, Kennedy announced that he had ordered a "quarantine," or naval blockade, to exclude offensive weapons from Cuba. He warned that if any Cuban-based missiles were launched, the United States would regard the weapons as coming from the Soviet Union and would instantly retaliate—against the Soviet Union, not Cuba. Meanwhile, a massive, round-the-clock buildup of American air and naval power in and around Florida left no doubt that the United States was prepared, at a moment's notice, to destroy the missile sites by direct attack.

Khrushchev did not comprehend how Americans feel about the Western Hemisphere, and he had thoroughly underestimated the U.S. response. He protested that Soviet ships in the mid-Atlantic carried nonmilitary goods and that the missiles had already arrived in Cuba. He offered to remove the weapons if the United States would end the blockade and respect Cuban independence. The next day Kennedy received a more belligerent note from Khrushchev, demanding that the United States also withdraw missiles it had in Turkey in exchange for Soviet withdrawal of missiles from Cuba. Kennedy decided to pretend that this second message had not been received, but he told Moscow privately (but not publicly) that he would dismantle the missiles in Turkey and accepted Khrushchev's "offer" to withdraw Soviet missiles from Cuba. Khrushchev, handed a face-saving way out of by far the most dangerous confrontation of the cold war, retreated. The ships on the way to Cuba turned around. Khrushchev promised inspections in Cuba to prove that the missiles were gone. But Castro balked, and the United States determined by overflights that the Russians had indeed dismantled the missiles and evacuated Cuba.

The Cuban missile crisis was the closest we ever came to nuclear war. Yet the fact that Khrushchev blinked rather than challenge the United States was a wondrous, comforting outcome. Khrushchev saw that he had three choices, and three choices only: remove the missiles and back down in defeat, stand aside passively while the United States blew up the missiles, or resist and watch his nation be destroyed by thermonuclear bombs. Kennedy, getting it absolutely right, drew the matter down to these three essential facts. Neither the United States nor any other democracy could survive under the threat of a nuclear attack. The challenge was clear—the United States *had* to accept the chance that Russia would refuse to dismantle the missiles. Otherwise the United States would be conquered. Kennedy saved the world from Communism. He also showed the world that no responsible leader— even the leader of a dictatorial regime like Russia's—will willingly and knowingly risk the obliteration of his own country in order to blackmail another power.

A profound, less obvious consequence of the Cuban missile crisis was this: it showed that the Soviet Union was bound to die. The Soviet Union relied only on *force* to expand. It kept a huge, heavily equipped army whose thousands of tanks seemed capable of overrunning Europe within days. If such an event actually occurred, it would fatally weaken the United States. If the United States could not keep the Russians out of Western Europe, it could not stop them from seizing the rest of the world. Cuba demonstrated, however, that if faced with a crisis like the overrunning of Western Europe—which would threaten the very existence of the United States—Washington would respond with nuclear strikes directly against the cities of Russia. As the leaders in the Kremlin absorbed this reality, they comprehended they could *not* use brute force to achieve their goals. Cuba had erased that possibility.

The Soviet Union could challenge the United States *only* on economic and political grounds, and on these it was hopelessly inferior. The sole hope lay in "peaceful coexistence." But even this gave no guarantee, because the Soviet Union's noncompetitive economy offered no model for the world, and this in turn eliminated its political influence over any country not already under its heel. Consequently, the Soviet Union inevitably would succumb to free markets.

The Cuban missile crisis also proved that nuclear powers could not use force against other nuclear powers—even *conventional* force, for a nonnuclear attack might prompt a retaliatory nuclear strike. This applied not just to the United States and the Soviet Union but to *any* nuclear power. In other words, atomic and hydrogen bombs imposed a momentous peace between the nuclear nations of the world. At the same time, a nuclear power could not use nuclear weapons against a nonnuclear state, because this would arouse universal loathing and unite the world against it. A nuclear state could, however, attack a nonnuclear state with *conventional* weapons. These factors pushed all nations *not* possessing nuclear weapons to seek to acquire them, in order to gain insurance against attack by conventional forces. The world was henceforth divided between nuclear powers immune from attack, and nonnuclear powers in danger of attack.

Although great power blocs may still exist in the world, the missile crisis proved that they no longer can fight one another. They can compete only by economic and political pressure. Another great military conflict, like the First or Second World War, is impossible.

While the Cuban missile crisis stopped the use of nuclear weapons by any *responsible* power, the danger still exists that an underhanded leader of a nuclear rogue state might *sell* a nuclear device to a terrorist group, which would have no compunctions against detonating it. The only hope in this situation is for the United States to inform any rogue state that acquires nuclear weapons that a nuclear strike by any terrorist group *anywhere* would automatically mean that this rogue state would be destroyed by a nuclear counterstrike.

★   ★   ★

ON JULY 25, 1963, President Kennedy signed a nuclear test ban treaty with the Soviet Union, prohibiting tests in the atmosphere.[9] One of the principal reasons Kennedy worked for this treaty was to get the assistance of the Soviet Union in preventing China from developing its own nuclear deterrent. He envisioned a "stable world order" dominated by the two superpowers. Khrushchev never showed interest in such an unholy alliance and refused either to pressure China to halt its nuclear development or to join with the United States in making a preemptive strike on the Chinese test facilities at Lop Nur in Xinjiang Province. Kennedy was unwilling to launch a strike on his own for fear it might reunite China with the Soviet Union.[10]

By trying to enlist Soviet support for such an attack, Kennedy showed that he no longer regarded China as a satellite of the Soviet Union. But he did not take the next logical step and realize that Russia and China were natural rivals. This was an enormous mistake. The Kremlin's efforts to advance the Soviet Union were practically indistinguishable from the empire-building pursuits of the Russian Romanov imperial dynasty that was ousted in 1917. Its ambitions were directed as much against China as against Western Europe. China was extremely sensitive to dangers along its immense land frontier with Siberia and would have welcomed an accommodation with the United States. Yet Kennedy rejected any dealings with Red China. He lost the opportunity to drive the two great Eurasian land powers further apart.[11]

★   ★   ★

BY 1963 THE U.S.-backed regime in South Vietnam, led by Ngo Dinh Diem, was rapidly losing support to the Vietcong, a Communist insurgent movement supported by North Vietnam, and to non-Communist

dissidents, especially the Buddhists, by far the largest religious group in
the country. Diem refused to institute political and economic reforms,
staffed his government with members of his own family, and showed a
preference for fellow Catholics. This led to demonstrations, retaliatory
imprisonment and killing of hundreds of Buddhists, troops firing on
demonstrators, and Buddhist priests who set themselves on fire in
protest.

Convinced that Diem would do nothing to stop the growing chaos,
the American ambassador to Vietnam, Henry Cabot Lodge, began
pressing Washington almost immediately after his appointment in August 1963 to support a coup against Diem. He got results. On November 1 a cabal of dissident generals, encouraged by the CIA, seized the
government, and the next day the group murdered Diem and his
brother, Ngo Dinh Nhu.[12]

An assassin shot and killed President Kennedy on November 22,
1963, in Dallas, Texas. The new president, Lyndon B. Johnson, continued Kennedy's policy of hostility to Red China, claiming that Communist China had embarked on a drive to dominate Asia.

In Vietnam, the Kennedy administration had hoped, by ousting
Diem, to get a more efficient leadership that could destroy the Communist Vietcong. The opposite occurred. In the two years after Diem's
death, there were nine regimes in Saigon. They represented no popular
forces and depended entirely on American support. Secretary of Defense Robert S. McNamara visited Vietnam in December 1963 and
reported that the Communists would probably take over unless American troops forcefully intervened. This led President Johnson to esca-
late American involvement.

In early 1964 Johnson authorized a vastly expanded program of
covert actions against North Vietnam, including parachuting sabotage
teams into the north, bombarding coastal installations with torpedo
boats, and sending in commandos to blow up bridges. U.S. destroyers
gathered intelligence information on radar warning and coastal defenses. The destroyers ran as close as four miles off the North Vietnamese coast.

On August 2, 1964, two American destroyers on a spy mission in the

Gulf of Tonkin were fired on by two North Vietnamese torpedo boats. The U.S. ships suffered no damage, but two nights later American destroyers returned to the Gulf and reported that they, too, came under attack. Though these reports later were found to have been in error, President Johnson immediately seized on them to order air strikes against six North Vietnamese naval bases and to request congressional support for his action. Congress, which did not know that the destroyers had been on an intelligence mission, passed the fateful "Gulf of Tonkin resolution" on August 7, 1964. This gave Johnson virtually a blank check, authorizing him to take "all necessary measures in support of freedom in southeast Asia," including sending U.S. military forces.

The harsh American action roused a storm of protest from the Communist world, but it prompted no threat of intervention. Beijing informed Washington privately that, short of a full-scale invasion of North Vietnam that threatened China's frontiers, it would not go beyond material aid.[13] The United States, therefore, could move into South Vietnam and into the air over North Vietnam, but an invasion of North Vietnam would bring on another war like in Korea.[14] Despite President Johnson's arrogance, he did not want a direct military confrontation with Red China. That much, at least, he had learned from the Korean War.[15]

Nikita Khrushchev fell from power in a virtual coup on October 14, 1964, with Leonid Brezhnev and Alexei Kosygin succeeding him. Two days later, China exploded its first atomic bomb, thus joining the "nuclear club." China now stepped on the world stage as a great power, but the event brought no change in American policy.

★   ★   ★

UNTIL THIS POINT, the United States had intervened only tentatively in the Vietnam War. American leaders had hoped to train the South Vietnamese army to defeat the Vietcong. But the army reflected the corruption that permeated the government. It was unable to win because it was structured to attack internal opponents of the regime, not Communists. Promotion depended on loyalty to Diem or, later, to the current military coup leader. Competence or resolve to defeat the

Vietcong played little role in selecting commanders. Also, venality led many officers and soldiers to exploit the peasants and other vulnerable people.

Seeing that the South Vietnamese army was incapable of defeating the Communists, Johnson in 1965 launched a massive bombing campaign of North Vietnam. It caused tremendous damage to Hanoi and other cities but did not change North Korea's resolve to pursue the war. Johnson also sent American troops into South Vietnam to do the fighting—100,000 in 1965, rising to 385,000 in 1966, and more than 500,000 in 1968.

But Johnson and other U.S. leaders did not understand that the key to defeating the Vietcong was not battle at all. It was removing the elite's abuses of power and ending their exploitation of the common people, thereby undermining support for the Communists. American leaders were wrong in committing an army to solve a political problem.

The Vietcong refused to conduct a conventional war with battle lines and defended positions, the kind of war the American army, with its massive firepower, was designed to fight. The Vietcong rarely defended battle positions, and never for any length of time. Instead they struck anywhere in the country, usually with small forces. This obligated the United States to disperse its power widely and to employ large numbers of combat troops (never below 40 percent of total strength) to defend American bases, airfields, and supply points against assault, while reserving other forces to search out the enemy.

The process reduced the conflict to a war of attrition, which exacted a steady penalty of American killed and wounded, but offered no victory, and no foreseeable end. The elusiveness of the Communist enemy greatly frustrated American commanders, leading army lieutenant colonel John Paul Vann to complain that the Vietcong could be whipped "if they would only stand and fight." Since Americans could not determine where, when, or in what strength the enemy would attack, they were forced to assume a largely passive role.

There was an inexorable logic to the Vietcong strategy. The lesson from the Cuban missile crisis was clear: nuclear states cannot use nuclear weapons against nonnuclear states. Knowing this, the North

Vietnamese could resist the United States without fear of nuclear an-
nihilation. But since America's *conventional* forces were vastly superior
to those of North Vietnam, the only way the Communists could fight
was by adopting guerrilla warfare. This situation can be stated as an
axiom: any state attacked by a more powerful state will *always* move to
guerrilla warfare, since it can hide its soldiers among the people,
whereas an invading state cannot hide its soldiers, who then become
vulnerable to debilitating surprise attacks. (The relevance of this
axiom has been proven in recent years as well.)

American commanders did not understand this kind of war; they
wanted to carry out conventional search-and-destroy missions. They
maintained the belief, articulated by Lieutenant General Lionel C.
McGarr, chief of the U.S. Army's advisory group from 1960 to 1962,
that the objective was to "find, fix, fight, and finish the enemy." American commanders clung to this conviction despite the fact that the
Communists, even when found, seldom stood to fight.

The search-and-destroy system was immensely counterproductive.
The plan was to make contact with the enemy, then withdraw, so that
bombers, attack helicopters, and artillery could blast the enemy. As one
American general described the procedure, "You don't fight this fellow
rifle to rifle. You locate him and back away. Blow hell out of him, and
then police up." But because the Vietcong did not wait around to be
pounded by American shells, missiles, and bombs—they usually provoked action, fought long enough to inflict casualties, and then disen-
gaged—U.S. forces might "find" Communist units, but they rarely
could "fix, fight, and finish" them.[16]

Aside from being inefficient, the bombing campaigns were extremely expensive. American forces used twice as many tons of explosives in Vietnam as in all of the campaigns in World War II.

The Vietcong and the North Vietnamese forces who joined them
challenged American forces head-on only a few times. The last occa-
sion came on January 31, 1968, when 70,000 Communist soldiers
surged into a hundred South Vietnamese cities, including Saigon, the
capital. Though this effort—known as the Tet offensive—failed, it
demonstrated that the Communists had not been defeated.

America's military commanders were not the only ones who failed to understand the situation in Vietnam; the civilian leadership got it wrong as well. President Johnson never understood guerrilla war and therefore did not comprehend that he could not win. Enemy soldiers struck hard and fast at vulnerable American targets—often bases and supply depots, and convoys—and then disappeared, usually melting back into the population where they could not be picked out. So long as a substantial portion of a civilian population harbors guerrilla fighters, a conventional army cannot succeed. The Vietcong did not "stand and fight," because this was not the way to victory. They only had to *endure*. In the words of Henry Kissinger, President Nixon's national security adviser and later secretary of state, "The conventional army loses if it does not win. The guerrilla wins if he does not lose." In time opposition to the war at home would become so overwhelming that the United States would have to withdraw. This is the crisis President Johnson faced after the Tet offensive. A growing antiwar movement in the United States turned into a rage after Tet; there was no hope of victory; the American death toll passed 30,000. Finally, Johnson decided he could not stand for reelection in 1968.

Lyndon Johnson was a consummate politician who learned how to exercise power in Congress. There he became legendary. By threats or promises, he wheedled recalcitrant politicians into following his lead. The historian Theodore H. White wrote that "Johnson's instinct for power is as primordial as a salmon's going upstream to spawn." Johnson believed that by using force he could induce the Communists to back out of South Vietnam. Johnson possessed immense arrogance, referring to Vietnam as a "piss-ant third-rate country" and implying that it had no right to stand up to the United States, the top nation in the world. Johnson never understood that the methods he employed to pull senators into line in Washington did not work in a life-and-death civil war in Indochina.

His successor, Richard M. Nixon, also possessed stupendous arrogance. Although he knew he had been elected to bring the war to a close, he refused to withdraw, saying that defeat would bring the "collapse of confidence in American leadership"—when in fact it would have brought tremendous relief to the world. Nixon did reduce American ground forces by 25,000 in May 1969, but by January 1970 troop strength had only fallen to 474,000. In the interim, Nixon recommenced the massive bombing of North Vietnam, which Johnson had halted in October 1968. He also increased aid to South Vietnam in a program he called "Vietnamization."

The results greatly displeased most Americans, and 250,000 war protestors marched on Washington in November 1969. Instead of withdrawing from Vietnam, Nixon promised to end the draft and move to an all-volunteer army (these changes took place in 1973). But the nation was scandalized when it learned that U.S. troops under the command of Lieutenant William Calley at Mai Lai in 1968 had massacred 347 unarmed South Vietnamese peasants—mostly women, children, and old people. That revelation eroded most of the remaining support for the war.

A more sensitive president would have seen the chaos erupting on American streets as a signal to get out of Indochina. But Nixon did precisely the opposite: on April 30, 1970, he sent 74,000 U.S. and South Vietnamese troops into neighboring Cambodia to "clean out" Vietcong supply sanctuaries and to destroy North Vietnamese troops lurking in the country. The incursion gained little militarily. North Vietnamese troops retreated, spreading the war into central Cambodia. Nixon had supported a rightist coup by Prime Minister Lon Nol on March 18, 1970, but the new pro-American regime showed little strength. Cambodia soon became embroiled in a five-year civil war between the corrupt and repressive Lon Nol regime and murderous Communist revolutionaries known as the Khmer Rouge. Ultimately more than a million Cambodians died.[17]

The Cambodian invasion precipitated tremendous protests in the United States, especially on college campuses. The governor of Ohio called out the National Guard to protect property at Kent State University. On May 4, 1970, when campus demonstrators who had been ordered to disperse failed to do so, guardsmen, feeling they were surrounded, fired into the crowd. They wounded nine and killed four, including two students leaving class. The Kent State deaths electrified the nation. Strikes closed 350 universities and colleges and mobilized millions of demonstrators. Congress set a summer deadline on the Cambodian deployment, and the Pentagon withdrew more ground troops.

Even so, Nixon ignored public protests, and on February 8, 1971, South Vietnamese troops, supported by American aircraft and helicopters, crossed into Laos with the aim of cutting the Ho Chi Minh supply line that ran from North Vietnam through Laos and Cambodia into South Vietnam. Communist forces badly mauled the South Vietnamese troops, and in March they hurried out of Laos. This time Nixon did not send in American troops. He allowed the Communist victory to stand and continued to withdraw forces from Indochina.[18]

The Laos escalation generated marches involving hundreds of thousands of protestors. In May 1971, 30,000 activists blocked Washington traffic, leading to the arrest of 12,000 people, the largest mass arrest in U.S. history. In June 1971 the New York Times began to publish the Pentagon Papers, a secret history of the war commissioned by Robert McNamara when he was defense secretary. These papers showed duplicity during the Kennedy and Johnson administrations. Nixon tried to get a court order to stop publication, but the Supreme Court ruled that the government had no grounds for preemptive censorship.[19]

★   ★   ★

DURING THIS PERIOD of mounting anger over America's continued presence in Vietnam, President Nixon made a remarkable move that led to a settlement with China—though not to peace in Indochina.

In April 1971 a Chinese table-tennis team at an international tournament in Nagoya, Japan, invited the American team, also at the games, to visit China to play other Chinese Ping-Pong teams. This had clearly been set up as a demarche by Beijing. Washington at once approved, and the fifteen Americans arrived in China on April 10 and received enthusiastic welcomes everywhere they played. Zhou Enlai met the American players and said their trip had "opened a new page in the relations of the Chinese and American people." It was an astute psychological approach—a people-to-people event, ignoring decades of official hostility. With the approval of Washington, the American team invited the Chinese to the United States in 1972.

"Ping-Pong diplomacy" brought the breakthrough Nixon was waiting for. He relaxed the twenty-year embargo on trade with China and secretly sent National Security Adviser Henry Kissinger to Beijing to ask whether the government would welcome a visit by Nixon himself. On July 15, 1971, Nixon stunned the world with the announcement that Zhou Enlai had invited him to visit Beijing in 1972, and that he had accepted.

On October 25, 1971, the United States supported a motion in the United Nations to assign China's seat on the Security Council to Beijing, removing Nationalist China. The U.S. effort to retain Nationalist China as a member of the U.N. General Assembly was made only for show—and was rejected by a two-to-one vote. The Communist government became China's sole representative in the United Nations. Kissinger had obviously worked out this change in his July talks with Zhou Enlai; the move marked the end of two decades of American intransigence.

On February 21, 1972, President Nixon, wife Pat, Kissinger, and Secretary of State William P. Rogers arrived in Beijing for a week's visit. At the end the two sides did not agree on all subjects, notably Taiwan, but the great powers were at last reconciled.

By the time Nixon returned to the United States, the American people had overwhelmingly endorsed Nixon's trip. The only heated argument that broke out revolved around which American city would get the two giant pandas that Red China presented as a gift to the United States. President Nixon finally gave the pandas to the National Zoo in Washington. Somehow, a great national debate about pandas seemed an eminently sensible way to lay to rest a generation of hostility toward China.

★   ★   ★

AFTER HIS VISIT to China, Nixon flew to Moscow and signed the Strategic Arms Limitation Treaty (SALT I), the first reduction of missiles and missile sites. Nixon won a landslide victory over Democratic presidential candidate George McGovern in 1972. This led him to be even more intransigent with the North Vietnamese. In the "Christmas bombing" of 1972, one of the most intensive air attacks in history, B-52s targeted populated areas and destroyed a children's hospital.

Yet in January 1973 Kissinger in effect took the United States out of the war. He brokered an agreement to withdraw the 25,000 remaining U.S. troops from South Vietnam in exchange for the release of 587 American prisoners of war. Washington recognized the Vietcong and accepted the seventeenth parallel as a provisional boundary, not a political frontier. In March 1973 the last American combat troops went home. The North Vietnamese and the Vietcong faced little resistance from the South Vietnamese and took over the entire country in 1975. On April 29, 1975, military helicopters evacuated 1,000 citizens from the U.S. embassy in Saigon. The next day North Vietnamese troops marched in and renamed it Ho Chi Minh City.

The war in Vietnam cost 1.5 million Vietnamese dead and left 10 million homeless. More than 56,000 Americans died in Vietnam, and more than 300,000 were wounded. Vietnam was a great, unnecessary tragedy, and it left wounds that took decades to heal. Kenneth Quinn, an Indochina analyst for the National Security Council just after the war ended, wrote, "The country was in a state of shock. Vietnam had been such an emotional, wrenching, painful experience that there was just a huge national relief and a sense the country needed to be put back together. *Our* country."[20]

The experience had indeed been wrenching, and America's political and military leaders had of course made grave mistakes by allowing the United States to become embroiled in the Vietnam conflict. Still, even after fighting this long, unwinnable war, America remained the world's leading power. The Vietnamese conflict had not antagonized our true rival, the Soviet Union. In fact, since the high tensions of the 1960s, the Americans and the Soviets had settled into a more manageable coexistence. And in due time it would become clear that our longtime Communist rival simply could not endure.

FOURTEEN

★ ★ ★

THE SOVIETS FALL

The last quarter of the twentieth century witnessed two immense international movements—the disintegration of Communism, and the emergence of militant Islam. The United States was the catalyst for the collapse of Communism, but it was mainly a victim in the surge of anti-Western forces in the Middle East.

During this period the Soviet Union disappeared, Germany reunited, the Soviet satellites rushed into a market economy, Red China transformed itself into a mutant form of capitalism, and even Vietnam became less Red and more an emerging third world economy. Only one Stalinist state remained—North Korea, a hermit kingdom saddled with a deranged dictator, an oversized military, and an outdated industry producing goods no one wanted.[1]

Radical Islamist forces arose throughout the Middle East. There were two main reasons—frustration over the Arabs' inability to defeat Israel, and the efforts of a militant fundamentalist minority to turn Islam into a bigoted, fanatical theocracy to disguise its centuries-long incapacity to build a successful civilization. The militants wished to drive the United States out of the Middle East, because its model of progress, success, and tolerance was a constant reminder of the failure of Islam.

The irrational hatred that this movement spawned was expressed in 1998 by Osama bin Laden, leader of the al Qaeda terrorist network.

He railed against America's "occupation" of the holy land of Arabia, its "aggression" against Iraq, and its support of "the petty state of the Jews." He called for the killing of Americans until their armies, "broken-winged, depart from all the lands of Islam."[2]

Despite such explicit warnings, the United States would not recognize the severity of this threat until it struck directly on our shores.

★   ★   ★

IMMENSE ECONOMIC PRESSURE from the United States pushed the Soviet Union to early collapse. But Communism would have failed in time under any circumstances. A command economy controlled by central bureaucrats who direct factories and farms to produce what the bureaucrats think is needed cannot survive except by brute force in competition with an economy that produces what customers want and will pay for.[3] Communism also operates directly contrary to human nature. Where property belongs to all, it belongs to no one. If people cannot own property, they no longer value or protect it. Jobs that offer no incentives for advancement or creativity become onerous labor without purpose. Such jobs are performed grudgingly and with little concern for quality or results.[4]

The Soviet Union collapsed in 1991 rather than later because the United States got it right in a series of decisions stretching back before the end of World War II. Every American president challenged every aggressive move the Soviet Union attempted to make. This forced the Kremlin to match the military power of the United States and then to sustain this level year after year and decade after decade. No economy on earth could endure such a confrontation, and the Soviet command economy was notably unable to respond.

The Soviet system had worked well during the war to produce the tanks, guns, ammunition, and other war material needed to fight the Nazis. In this case there was a ready market—the front line—for the factories' goods. The concentration on heavy industry seemed to offer a model for postwar expansion as well. But war material contributes *nothing* to the economy. War goods are designed to be destroyed or to block enemy weapons. Unlike a grain combine or a machine tool—so-called capital goods, which can produce other goods that people want—no tank, gun, or rocket launcher has any constructive purpose whatsoever. At the end of World War II the Soviet Union was manufacturing few capital goods and even fewer consumer goods, which satisfy the needs of the people.

Instead of moving toward a consumer economy to supply the products the exhausted and deprived people of Russia wanted so desperately, Joseph Stalin crippled the Soviet Union by continuing to concentrate on heavy industry and nonproductive military hardware. Furthermore, the Soviet Union had been gravely wounded in the war. Vast portions of the country had been devastated, its buildings and fields shattered. Perhaps 25 million Russians had died, and many more millions had been maimed. And these were largely the youngest, most active elements of the population.

The proper course for the Soviet Union in 1945 would have been to forget about aggression and instead work to make the people happy and prosperous. But Stalin and those who followed him made exactly the opposite decision, aiming to expand the Soviet empire throughout the world. In doing so, they presented a direct challenge to the United States. This was economic madness. In 1945 the United States produced one-half of all the goods made on earth. The proportion declined in the years following, but, compared to Soviet capacity, American production was enormous, and it was growing every year. The United States matched every weapon the Soviets could make and more, and still had ample productive capacity left over for the nation's economy to produce all the consumer goods its people wanted.

Nixon's presidency did not survive the fallout from his criminal behavior, which involved covering up the June 1972 burglary of the Democratic Party's headquarters in Washington's Watergate complex. The covert "plumbers" who carried out the burglary were seeking information on Lawrence O'Brien, Democratic national chairman. Nixon's part in the cover-up was not discovered until two years later, although Nixon had long been derisively known as "Tricky Dick" because he often manipulated the truth. Mort Sahl, a nightclub comic, joked about the Nixons sitting home at night, wife Pat knitting the American flag and Dick carefully reading the Constitution, "looking," Sahl said after pausing for effect, "for loopholes."[5] Faced with impeachment, Nixon resigned on August 9, 1974, and was replaced by Gerald Ford. But Ford was tainted as a Republican, and a Democrat, Jimmy Carter, was elected president in November 1976.

After taking office, Carter sought rapprochement with the Soviet Union. He tried to reduce tensions, proposing to withdraw troops from South Korea and signing a second strategic-arms limitation treaty (SALT II) with the Soviet Union in 1979. This accord limited long-range missiles, bombers, and nuclear warheads. He also agreed to cede the Panama Canal to Panama in 2000. But in 1979 Carter was devastated when the Soviet Union invaded Afghanistan in an effort to contain Islamic fundamentalism, which was influencing Muslim populations in the Soviet Union. Carter boycotted the 1980 Olympic Games in Moscow and asked the Senate to shelve ratification of SALT II, but he continued to seek détente with the Soviet Union.

Ronald Reagan defeated Carter in the 1980 presidential election by questioning détente, demanding a strong defense, and attacking government bureaucracy and social spending that contributed to raging inflation in the 1970s. The country had been reeling from the Vietnam War and the Watergate conspiracy, and Reagan promised to restore U.S. global power and respect.

Reagan held that high taxes and government regulations inhibited production and caused inflated prices. He reduced government spending, increased outlays for defense, lowered taxes, and balanced the federal budget. Reagan also pushed deregulation of telephones, banks, airlines, and oil drilling. He cut social spending, confining safety-net protection for citizens to the Social Security system. These factors helped to restore economic prosperity.

Reagan initiated the largest peacetime military buildup in U.S. history, embracing production of the B-1 bomber—which Carter had canceled—and creating a rapid-deployment force. He also proposed a strategic-defense initiative (SDI) that would use space satellites and laser weapons to ward off missile attacks. This "Star Wars" program was extremely theoretical, but it frightened the Soviet Union. If SDI was deployed successfully and could intercept missiles, the United States would neutralize the Soviet Union's principal weapon. Even so, in 1983 Reagan committed the nation to SALT II.

Reagan's buildup of U.S. military power put an intolerable strain on the Soviet Union. In order to compete, the Kremlin devoted 35 percent of Soviet gross domestic product (GDP) to its military. This left far too little to satisfy even the minimum consumer needs of the people or to create capital goods that could raise production. Thus the Soviet economy was spiraling rapidly down to destruction. Underground (and illegal) firms arose to satisfy to a limited degree the tremendous shortages caused by the command economy. In the book *World on Fire,* Amy Chua quotes an émigré to the United States describing her uncle in Russia during this period: "He manufactured shoes on his own. Later he sold the shoes either at the weekend flea market or through an 'off-the-books' arrangement with a state-owned shoe store. . . . There would have been no shoes on the shelves without people like my uncle."[6] Winston Churchill understood well the fallacy of socialism. "If you destroy a free market," he wrote, "you create a black market. . . . The vice of capitalism is that it stands for the unequal sharing of blessing, whereas the virtue of socialism is that it stands for the equal sharing of misery."

Unfortunately the CIA kept believing false Soviet statistics, which claimed at most 9 percent of Soviet GDP was going to military expenditures. As David Frum and Richard Perle write, the CIA missed "entirely the sounds of the cracking and the crumbling of the whole Soviet system."[7]

Reagan saw far better that the end was coming, so he increased his pressure on the Kremlin to match our weapons. He contrasted the "evil empire" of the Soviet Union with the moral superiority of the United States, and he drew the distinction even more clearly by cooling relations with military governments of countries like Chile and Paraguay that, though anti-Communist, oppressed their people. In like fashion, Reagan occupied the tiny Caribbean island republic of Grenada when Fidel Castro of Cuba opened ties with a new Marxist government there in 1983. And although he supported a right-wing military government that killed thousands of people in a civil war in El Salvador from 1980 to 1983, he also supported a centrist leader who won election in 1984 and ended the war. Reagan used covert CIA action to oppose a Sandinista government in Nicaragua, which he saw as a front for Cuban and Soviet expansion. When Congress prohibited use of public funds for Nicaragua, Reagan raised $36 million from wealthy U.S. donors and from allies like Saudi Arabia and Taiwan. He also diverted profits from illegal arms sales to Iran, which created a huge controversy when discovered. But the controversy subsided in 1988, when the Nicaraguan government agreed to peace talks with its domestic rivals, the "contras."[8]

Despite presenting a renewed military challenge to the Soviet Union, Reagan approved wheat sales to Russia and met with the new Soviet leader, Mikhail Gorbachev, in Geneva in 1985. There Gorbachev expressed a desire for *glasnost* (openness) at home and abroad. The government admitted the brutality of the Stalin era and criticized the corruption and stagnation of the Leonid Brezhnev era. *Glasnost* also led to some democratic political reforms, reduced censorship, and allowed Russians more freedom to travel. Coupled with *glasnost* was a domestic program called *perestroika* (restructuring). Its aim was to transform the Soviet Union's centralized command economy into a decentralized market economy. Gorbachev granted industrial managers, local government, and party officials greater autonomy, and he instituted open elections within the Communist Party.

Gorbachev's efforts represented a desperate attempt to save the Soviet Union. He was trying to revolutionize his country without bringing on a revolution. But every effort to produce orderly change in a repressed society opens the floodgates to complete reform, as seen in the French Revolution of 1789 and in the Russian Revolution of 1917. *Glasnost* and *perestroika* actually precipitated the collapse of the Soviet Union.

Reformation was long overdue. The economy had failed to provide for even the basic needs of the people, like adequate food, and Reagan's military buildup was putting intolerable pressure on the Kremlin to increase military expenditures. The satellites in Eastern Europe were becoming restive because their people were learning through radio and television signals from the West how inadequate and incompetent their own economies were compared to the prosperous economies of Western Europe.

In 1986 Reagan met with Gorbachev again, this time in Iceland, where they nearly reached an agreement on major arms reduction. But progress halted when the Soviets insisted that the United States confine SDI to laboratory development only. Even so, the summit led to mutual dismantling of 2,600 medium- and short-range missiles in Europe and to an extensive system of weapons surveillance involving both superpowers.

But things were falling to pieces in the Soviet Union. *Glasnost* and *perestroika* loosened the tight social controls on the people, while the government granted limited private ownership of business and land, and let prices rise in accordance with market forces. All these factors created immense instability and pressure for even more change.

The crisis finally centered on the place where the cold war had actually ignited — Berlin. This was where Stalin had instituted a land blockade in 1948 in a failed attempt to drive the West out of the city. It was where Khrushchev built the Berlin Wall in 1961 to keep the people of the East in captivity. The Wall had become the abiding symbol of the cold war. On one side was slavery, on the other freedom.

Things came to a head on June 12, 1987, at the Brandenburg Gate, right on the dividing line. To wild applause, President Reagan said, "Mr. Gorbachev, tear down this wall!" Nothing was the same after that. *Glasnost* and *perestroika* were undermining the Soviet state. On March 29, 1989, Gorbachev told the premier of Hungary that the Brezhnev Doctrine had been abandoned. Brezhnev had pronounced this dogma in November 1968, saying that when internal developments in a Communist country "endangered the socialist community as a whole," the Soviet Union was justified in intervening. Gorbachev said the Soviet Union was no longer willing to use force to prevent the democratic transformation of its satellites.

This was the kiss of death for all the satellite governments. On May 2, 1989, Hungary announced that it was dismantling its barriers along the Austrian frontier, the first breach in the iron curtain, and on

September 11 it opened its border with Austria. Germans poured out of East Germany through now-seething Czechoslovakia and Poland. Within a few months 220,000 had passed over to the west.

On October 7, 1989, East Germany celebrated its fortieth anniversary, but the celebration turned into a protest. As guest of honor, Gorbachev was welcomed with pleas from the demonstrators, "Gorbi, help us!" He told the people, "Whoever arrives [at reality] too late is punished by life." ("*Wer zu spät kommt, den bestrafft das Leben.*") This was a clear warning that the end was near. Communist leaders in East Germany immediately ousted dictator Erich Honecker.

Then it happened. On November 9, 1989, at the end of a rambling press conference, a senior East German official said that people could cross at will into West Berlin. Wildly enthusiastic crowds massed at the crossing points. At 11 P.M. the gates were opened. Hundreds of thousands of Germans moved through the openings in a giant national celebration. That night and for days to come, citizens tore down portions of the wall with sledgehammers, one concrete block at a time.

Premier Gorbachev announced from Moscow his support for the German people's action. As Germany rushed toward reunification (which occurred on October 3, 1990), the Soviet Union rushed toward collapse. Having renounced the use of force to hold the empire together, Gorbachev could do nothing to keep it from flying apart.

Gorbachev was successful in dismantling the totalitarian aspects of the Soviet state and in moving his country toward representative democracy. He was less willing to release the Soviet economy from the grip of centralized state direction. Gorbachev refused to use force to keep the Soviet economy functioning, but he resisted any decisive shift to private ownership and a free market. Gorbachev sought in vain a compromise between these two diametrically opposed alternatives. The centrally planned economy crumbled with no private enterprise to replace it. Gorbachev remained master of the Communist Party, but his attempts to augment his powers through decrees and administrative reshufflings proved fruitless, and his government's authority collapsed on December 25, 1991, when the Soviet Union ceased to be.

The Eastern European satellites regained their independence. Each of the Soviet Union's constituent republics became a separate state in 1991. Everywhere Communism died, and it was replaced by the beginnings of a market system. Economic chaos reigned, joyous people celebrated, and the Soviet Union was buried with few regrets. It was a magnificent victory for freedom and a tribute to the determination of the United States.

In the last great crisis of the twentieth century, America had got it right for itself, and for the world.[9]

As the political scientist Walter Russell Mead writes, "The United States is not only the sole global power, its values inform a global consensus, and it dominates to an unprecedented degree the formation of the first truly global civilization our planet has known."[10]

FIFTEEN

★ ★ ★

THE TERRORISTS RISE

Had it not been for two major developments—the discovery of vast reservoirs of oil beneath its sands, and the founding of the state of Israel—the Middle East might have drifted along indefinitely, largely ignored by the rest of the world, and continuing to live in poverty within its static, backward-looking Islamic civilization that rejects most elements of modern Western life and denies rights to half its population, its women.[1]

But the world's need for oil and the West's resolve to reconstitute Israel inserted Western ideas into the Middle East and demonstrated to the Muslims their abysmal economic, social, and political failure. Frustrated and humiliated, radical Muslims reacted violently, mainly against Israel and the United States, the most successful and visible of the Western powers. In the resulting crises, the United States always exhibited the best motives and got it right in most cases. In a couple of the most critical crises, however, Presidents Jimmy Carter and Bill Clinton got it absolutely wrong.

In 1979 President Carter refused to take any positive action when Iran invaded the U.S. embassy and seized fifty-two Americans as hostages. This convinced Islamic terrorists that the United States was impotent, which emboldened them to commit further attacks on Americans. In 1993 President Clinton wrongly undertook a nation-building program in anarchic Muslim Somalia. He ignored the fact that this "peacekeeping" effort was arousing great opposition, and he refused to arm American troops with heavy weapons. Nation-building led to an ill-conceived raid against a renegade warlord in Mogadishu, in which the inadequately protected American troops fell into a trap set by guerrilla fighters. Eighteen Americans died and seventy-three were wounded.

There were other mistakes, most notably President Ronald Reagan's sending U.S. Marines into Beirut, Lebanon, where 241 had been killed in a car-bombing in 1983, and the naive U.S. belief that Palestinian leader Yasser Arafat, although a congenital liar, was telling the truth in 1988 when he announced that he no longer wanted to destroy Israel.

Nevertheless, correct decisions far outweighed the bad ones. Every American president supported Israel even as Arab states attempted to eliminate it. President Nixon correctly stopped the Israelis from over-running all of Egypt and Syria in 1973 and upsetting the entire political balance in the Middle East. President Carter engineered a peace treaty between Egypt and Israel in 1979. President George H. W. Bush, by means of a swift and overwhelming campaign in 1991, drove Iraq out of Kuwait after Iraqi dictator Saddam Hussein had seized the oil-rich state. And President Clinton made a sincere effort to work out an agreement in 2000 to partition the Holy Land between the Palestinians and Israel. The demarche came to naught because Arafat, despite getting nearly everything he asked for, refused to agree, showing that he was interested only in the destruction of Israel.

★   ★   ★

ALTHOUGH THE MUSLIM world made great contributions to art, learning, and industry in the early centuries of Islam, it turned its back on liberty and progress, adopted repressive governments, and fell hopelessly behind Europe as early as the fifteenth century. Today, other than oil, the total exports of the 280 million Arabs amount to less than the exports of Finland, a country of 5 million people. A July 2003 United Nations report showed that over a twenty-year period, annual income growth per head was lower (0.5 percent) in the twenty-two Arab countries than anywhere else in the world except sub-Saharan Africa.[2]

Bernard Lewis, an eminent authority on the Middle East, summarizes the problem as follows: "To a Western observer, schooled in the theory and practice of Western freedom, it is precisely the lack of freedom — freedom of the mind from constraint and indoctrination, to question and inquire and speak; freedom of the economy from corrupt and pervasive mismanagement; freedom of women from male oppression; freedom of citizens from tyranny — that underlies so many of the troubles of the Muslim world."[3]

No Arab country possesses the legal, financial, and political institutions necessary for prosperity in the modern world. None provides what David Landes, in his book *The Wealth and Poverty of Nations,* says are mandatory: rights to private property; personal liberty; contract rights that are enforced; and a stable, responsive, honest, efficient, and ungreedy government.[4]

The most striking difference between the Middle East and the West is Muslim misogyny. Over the centuries, Muslim visitors to the West condemned the freedom granted to European women, how those women disobeyed men, and how European men had failed to curb what the Muslims saw as the inherent immorality and promiscuity of women.

For a thousand years, the *mutawaeen,* or religious police, have stalked the streets of Muslim towns in search of "immodest" women. Today women are treated better in parts of the Muslim world, but in other parts the environment remains as repressive as ever. In Saudi Arabia, for example, a woman cannot drive a car, cannot walk the streets unveiled or unchaperoned, and cannot travel abroad without a *mahram,* a male guardian from her immediate family.[5]

Saudi Arabia spreads far beyond its borders the puritanical and often anti-Western doctrine preached in the eighteenth century by Muhammad ibn Abd al-Wahhab, who advocated purging Islam of all modern ways and relying strictly on the Koran and the *hadith,* or the record of the words and deeds of the prophet Muhammad. Muslims take the Koran to be the word of God dictated directly to Muhammad. Wahhab was a Sunni, the largest branch of Islam.[6] But the smaller

Shiite branch also is exposed to anti-Western ideas, which are spewed out every Friday from mosques in Iran.

The Muslim world's inability to compete with the West has led some Muslims, reflecting the teaching of Wahhab, to demand a return to the harsh *sharia,* or the laws of God.[7] Osama bin Laden, a Saudi Arabian, became the loudest voice calling for this retreat into the past. He preached a *jihad,* or armed struggle, against both the distant enemy — the United States, Israel, and the West in general — and the closer enemy, the impious secular regimes of the Muslim world.

The modern West began to intervene directly in the Middle East in 1798, when Napoleon Bonaparte occupied Egypt in an attempt to get at his main enemy, Britain. This effort failed, but European advances, mostly British and French, continued. By 1919, European powers dominated the entire Middle East except Turkey. The British created Iraq around the oil fields of Mosul and Kirkuk, and Kuwait likewise around its oil fields. Egypt was structured to protect the Suez Canal. Lebanon was carved out of Syria to give French protection to the Maronite Christians of the region. Transjordan (now Jordan) became a British military outpost to guard against the Arabian Peninsula. Each new state was built around an army created by the colonial power for police purposes.[8]

A great change came with World War II. Although the world became increasingly dependent on Middle Eastern oil, all the states of the region gained independence. The military elites seized power to protect their position and privilege, redefining their states as standard bearers of Arab nationalism in the face of Israel, which had been placed right in their midst.

Not only did Israel represent the Western elements of progress, commerce, industrialization, freedom, democracy, and the rule of law that were conspicuously lacking in the Muslim world, but Israelis were a standing rebuke to Arab pretensions because they were eminently *successful*—especially in military matters. This was particularly true because the Arab military regimes concentrated not on defeating the alien presence of Israel but on waging war on their societies, with the aim of destroying all alternative sources of authority. The Arab armies were superb in oppressing their own people but incompetent in fighting the Israelis.

The great Middle Eastern watershed event was the Six-Day War (June 5–11, 1967). In whirlwind campaigns, Israel humiliated Egypt, Syria, and Jordan; occupied the entire Sinai Peninsula, the West Bank of Palestine, and the Golan Heights of Syria; and demonstrated that the Arabs' claim that they could drive the Jews into the sea was a fantasy.[9]

The war showed the Palestinians that the Arab states could not help them regain their homeland. This disillusionment prompted the new Palestine Liberation Organization (PLO) under Yasser Arafat, as well as the rising Islamic fundamentalist movement, to search for ways other than conventional warfare between nation-states to drive the Jews and other infidels out of the Middle East.

Their answer was terrorism. It was a logical decision. The secular Arab states had abandoned the PLO. To the Islamic fundamentalists, these same states—since they refused to set up a theocratic dictatorship—were as much the enemy as Israel and America. Like its related species, guerrilla warfare, terrorism gave both the weak Palestinians and the weak fundamentalists a means to influence powerful states. Terrorism had one further benefit: the PLO and the fundamentalists could recruit and train gullible zealots in clandestine groups, but if they were ever accused of instigating terrorist acts, they could deny any connection. Yasser Arafat turned this act of deceitful disavowal into an art form.

Three months after the end of the Six-Day War, the PLO formed the autonomous Popular Front for the Liberation of Palestine (PFLP). Over the next year the PFLP hijacked fourteen foreign airliners and destroyed four planes at once in Jordan. Exasperated, and under pressure from Israel, King Hussein of Jordan expelled the PLO, causing Arafat to move to Lebanon in 1970. From there terrorists crossed the frontier and committed many atrocities against civilians in Israel. The PFLP and other Palestinian groups linked up with anti-Semitic conspiracies in Europe, leading to random violence that culminated in the deaths of nine Israeli athletes taken hostage at the Olympic Games in

Munich in September 1972. Five terrorists also were killed in a gun battle with police.

Anwar el-Sadat, successor to Egyptian dictator Gamal Abdel Nasser, who died in 1970, joined with Syria in one more try to destroy Israel. On October 6, 1973, the date of Yom Kippur, the Jewish Day of Atonement, Egyptian and Syrian forces launched a surprise attack across the Suez Canal and on the Golan Heights. The outnumbered Israelis fought back in fierce battles, and as soon as President Nixon set up an emergency supply line, they advanced on both fronts. On the Golan, Israelis struck out on the road to Damascus, while other Israelis crossed the Suez Canal and began to destroy an entire Egyptian army. Israel now was on the verge of conquering both Syria and Egypt. Nixon brought about a cease-fire by threatening to cut off supplies.

Although Nixon had stopped Israel from shattering the Middle East's political order, he got no credit from the Arabs. Led by Saudi Arabia, the Arab oil-producing states instituted a five-month oil embargo on the United States that caused great economic upheaval, endless lines at gas pumps, and a fourfold increase in the cost of crude oil.[10]

The Yom Kippur War nevertheless convinced Sadat that he could never defeat Israel. In order to get back the Sinai, Sadat entered into negotiations with Menachem Begin, the Israeli prime minister, and President Jimmy Carter, and signed a peace treaty in the White House on March 29, 1979. The historic settlement dismayed the other Arab states and caused violent outbursts. In December 1979, for example, 300 Islamic fundamentalists briefly seized the holiest of all Islamic shrines, in Mecca; on October 6, 1981, extremists assassinated Sadat himself. Sadat's successor, Hosni Mubarak, was prepared only for a "cold" peace with Israel.

★   ★   ★

PRESIDENT CARTER HAD won the 1976 presidential election by capitalizing on Americans' disgust with Vietnam and Watergate, but he was inept in international affairs, lacking both resolve and judgment. And he indeed faced severe challenges, particularly after February 11, 1979, when a Shiite fundamentalist, the Ayatollah Ruholla

Khomeini, ousted the shah of Iran, Reza Shah Pahlavi, and installed himself as the supreme ruler of a theocratic state.[11] This marked the first time an Islamic fundamentalist movement had captured a Muslim state, and the extreme anti-Western propaganda that the ayatollah unleashed provided a clear warning of the danger the United States faced.[12]

Carter granted the shah's request to come to the United States for medical treatment. This outraged the fundamentalists, who demanded that the shah—and his fortune—be returned to Iran. The ayatollah, who denounced the United States as the "great Satan," authorized Iranians to seize the American embassy in Tehran on November 4, 1979; they imprisoned fifty-two Americans as hostages.[13] This clearly violated diplomatic immunity and international law, but Carter refused to take any positive action to free the American citizens. Refusing to negotiate with the fundamentalists, he merely severed diplomatic relations and froze Iranian assets in the United States. In other words, the president did not respond to a direct challenge to the honor and integrity of the United States. The people in the embassy were official representatives of the nation, and the United States was obligated to insist that Iran protect them—or, if this proved impossible, to exact a terrible vengeance.

Once diplomacy failed to free the hostages, Carter should have at once closed the Strait of Hormuz with the U.S. Navy and ended all Iranian oil shipments. This would have cost no lives and would have shown Khomeini that if he continued to hold Americans in captivity, Iran's economy would be shattered. In addition to a naval blockade, Carter should have warned Khomeini that if any of the American hostages were harmed, the United States would bomb Iran's oil-shipment ports at Abadan and Kharg Island.

Instead, Carter made almost the worst possible decision. He opted for an extremely difficult and highly complex military rescue mission in April 1980. Carter was attempting to duplicate the brilliant Israeli commando raid of July 1976 that rescued Israeli hostages at the airport in Entebbe, Uganda. German and Palestinian terrorists had hijacked an Air France airliner, and four Israeli aircraft landed at the Entebbe airport in the dead of night, taking the hijackers completely by surprise.

But the U.S. effort involved far more aircraft—six C-130 transport planes, plus eight RH-53 helicopters—and demanded a complicated rendezvous at Posht-e Badam in central Iran, as the helicopters arrived from the aircraft carrier *Nimitz* in the Arabian Sea and the C-130s came from Egypt. Two of the helicopters developed mechanical troubles; one had to be left in the desert, and the other returned to the *Nimitz*. At Posht-e Badam a third helicopter's hydraulic system failed, leaving only five in operation. Carter then canceled the mission. During takeoff, one helicopter crashed into a C-130, and both burst into flames. The remaining helicopters were abandoned, and the survivors returned in the C-130s. In this horribly bungled operation, eight commandos were killed.

The hostage crisis fatally crippled Carter's reelection bid in 1980. He won only 49 electoral votes against Ronald Reagan's 489. The Iranians held the Americans for 444 days, releasing them only hours before Reagan became president on January 20, 1981.

But Carter's failure to act decisively damaged far more than his own political career. It convinced many potential terrorists in the Middle East that the United States was a paper tiger that would endure almost any insult. We are living with the consequences of that misjudgment to this day.

Israel, by contrast, presented a model of how a nation *should* act to protect its vital interests. In June 1981, in a daring preemptive strike, Israeli aircraft destroyed a nuclear reactor at Osirak, Iraq, that could produce weapons-grade plutonium for Iraqi dictator Saddam Hussein. France was building the reactor for Iraq, oblivious to the dangers to Israel and to the West if Iraq possessed the A-bomb. Getting nowhere diplomatically, Israel took the matter into its own hands and solved the problem. The Israeli action set off a storm in the United Nations, but Israel had done precisely the right thing, and all peace-loving people on earth knew it.

★   ★   ★

EVEN BEFORE THE AYATOLLAH'S forces overthrew the shah in Iran, Islamic fundamentalists in Afghanistan, Iran's neighbor to the east, launched an insurrection of their own, in 1975. The Kremlin wanted to stamp out the movement, because the Muslim majority populations in the Soviet Union's republics just north of Afghanistan were vulnerable to fundamentalism. Accordingly, in April 1978 the Kremlin—in its usual heavy-handed fashion, and without talking the matter over with the United States—arranged for the tiny local Communist Party to take over Afghanistan. President Carter made almost no response, even after the murder of the U.S. ambassador in Kabul in February 1979. The Afghan Reds, however, fell into a bloody intramural squabble, and the resulting chaos strengthened the fundamentalist elements the Kremlin was trying to suppress.

This was exactly the time when the Ayatollah Khomeini was turning neighboring Iran into a repressive theocratic state. With a similar fundamentalist state in Afghanistan becoming a dangerous possibility, the situation cried out for dialogue between Moscow and Washington. But Carter did not see the connection. He didn't respond—perhaps because of the distraction of the hostage crisis—even when the Kremlin hinted in the fall of 1979 that it might have to intervene.

Carter therefore was bewildered when the Soviet army invaded Afghanistan on December 25, 1979, and installed as premier Babrak Karmal, a creature of the Soviet KGB, or Secret Service. The Kremlin had tried to make clear that it was opposing Afghan fundamentalists, not seeking a path to a warm-water port on the Arabian Sea, as some doomsayers believed. But in the absence of discussions between the two superpowers, Carter saw the invasion as an application of the Brezhnev Doctrine—that the Soviet Union could intervene when internal developments in a Communist state endangered the socialist community.

As a result, Carter suspended grain sales to the Soviet Union, ordered a boycott of the Moscow Olympics, and shelved ratification of SALT II. Over the next ten years covert U.S. assistance allowed rebels to turn Afghanistan into rubble. In the war, 2 million Afghans fled the country, and both sides committed atrocities. The Soviets withdrew in 1989, leaving anarchy. That opened a path for a horribly repressive fundamentalist movement, the Taliban, to take over and give refuge to Osama bin Laden's al Qaeda terrorist network.

★   ★   ★

BY 1982 THE FOCAL point in the Middle Eastern crisis was Lebanon. This tiny country (four-fifths the size of Connecticut) just north of Israel contained both Muslim and Christian populations. After Yasser Arafat's PLO moved in, the country descended into civil war in 1975. Syria occupied northern Lebanon, while the PLO took control of southern Lebanon, whence it launched terror attacks into Israel. Israeli forces invaded southern Lebanon in March 1978 to drive the PLO away from the border, but they had to withdraw in June as a result of international pressure.

The untenable situation came to a head in June 1982, when a PLO group tried to assassinate Israel's ambassador to Britain. Prime Minister Menachem Begin ordered the bombing of PLO positions in Lebanon, the PLO retaliated with a rocket barrage on northern Israeli towns, and Israel invaded Lebanon, quickly reaching the capital, Beirut, and besieging Arafat and his PLO units. President Reagan's secretary of state, George Shultz, inserted a multinational peacekeeping force into Lebanon, including 1,200 U.S. Marines, allowing Arafat and his group to evacuate Beirut in August 1982 and move to Tunisia. In retrospect, this was a great mistake. The United States should have stood aside and allowed Israel to destroy Arafat and the PLO, because they were violently opposed to any settlement and wanted to eliminate the Jewish state. With an intractable Arafat, there was no hope for a settlement.[14]

Reagan kept the Marines in Beirut, seeing them as a peacekeeping force. But they actually served as a lightning rod for Islamic terrorists, who increasingly regarded the United States as a partner of Israel, not as a force trying to reach an equitable settlement in the Middle East. The first blow came on April 18, 1983, when a suicide bomber struck the U.S. embassy in Beirut, killing sixty-three people, including the CIA's entire Middle Eastern team.[15] A greater disaster struck on October 23, 1983, when another suicide bomber from the radical Iran-supported Shiite Muslim organization Hezbollah blew up the Marine headquarters at Beirut airport, killing 241.[16] Reagan soon withdrew American forces. But Americans continued to be the target of violent attacks, kidnappings, and hijackings.[17]

In December 1988 a new stage in the Israeli-Palestinian tragedy opened when Yasser Arafat announced that he was ready to recognize Israel and suspend terrorism provided that the Palestinians obtained a state.[18] This turned out to be a lie, but the United States, hopeful for a solution, promptly recognized the PLO and opened a discourse. Arafat's demarche came a year after a PLO-inspired rebellion opened on the West Bank and in Gaza that became known as the *intifada* ("shaking off"). The uprising was distinguished by street violence in which children and teenagers battled Israeli troops with rocks and stones.

After secret negotiations in Oslo, Norway, Arafat decided to gamble, accepting the idea of an authority to rule parts of the occupied territories in order to obtain a foothold in Palestine. The two sides signed accords in 1993 and 1994, which gave Arafat control first of Gaza and Jericho, with the Palestinian Authority's rule to extend over time to other parts of the territories.[19] The resulting thaw induced Jordan to sign a peace treaty with Israel on October 26, 1994. But Hamas, an Islamic group especially strong in Gaza, opposed the agreement, and its terrorists killed scores of Israeli civilians between 1993 and 1997.[20] Arafat refused to repress Hamas, and the Israelis closed borders that prevented thousands of Palestinians from commuting to jobs in Israel.[21]

Hoping to break the deadlock, in July 2000 President Bill Clinton called a meeting with Arafat and Israeli prime minister Ehud Barak. At the meeting, held at Camp David in Maryland, Barak conceded to Arafat more than any Israeli leader had been willing to grant—he agreed to a sovereign state of Palestine and to sharing the holy city of Jerusalem. But Arafat, having been offered what he had said he wanted, refused to accept, indicating that he had always been dishonest about his professed willingness to divide the Holy Land with Israel and that in fact he wanted only to destroy the Jewish state. A second *intifada* resulted, as suicide bombers from Hamas and other terrorist groups killed hundreds of Israeli civilians. Arafat talked a great game of cooperation publicly, but he did nothing to stop the killings.[22]

★   ★   ★

ON AUGUST 2, 1990, the world came face-to-face with Saddam Hussein of Iraq, a monster as horrible as Adolf Hitler or Joseph Stalin. Saddam had already used poison gas against Kurdish civilians in northern Iraq, and in his ten-year war of aggression against Iran. He routinely murdered anyone in Iraq who voiced the slightest opposition to him. On this day he occupied Kuwait. His intention was to seize its oil, along with that of the Persian Gulf emirates and Saudi Arabia, which among them held one-third of the world's oil reserves.

Saddam Hussein was a villainous dictator who deluded himself into believing he was a military genius. He wanted to unify the Arabs and defy the West. Although not an Islamic fundamentalist, Saddam had the same ambition as did the fundamentalists: to drive the United States and other Western states out of the Middle East. In seizing Kuwait, however, Saddam aroused intense opposition in the Arab world and also came up against a solid wall in President George H. W. Bush. Bush got the U.N. Security Council to vote economic sanctions against Iraq, and when King Fahd of Saudi Arabia requested help, he deployed 200,000 American troops into the kingdom, along with British and French forces.

Bush built a world coalition to oppose Iraq, and he remained unmoved when Saddam tried to break the alliance by beginning to release foreigners he had taken hostage when he entered Kuwait. Unlike Bush, however, the French and Soviet governments were deceived, and they began frantic efforts to head off a military operation. Bush rejected an offer Saddam made to "negotiate" if he could keep the huge Ar-Rumaylah oil fields of Kuwait and two strategic islands offshore. Saddam was not going to be rewarded for aggression, Bush insisted. The president doubled the size of American forces to 400,000. On November 29, 1990, the Security Council authorized the use of force if Iraq failed to withdraw.

In the United States, liberals and peace activists were chanting "no blood for oil" while neoisolationist conservatives wanted the United States to pull behind its oceans and forget the rest of the world. In the January 1991 congressional debate, the pro-war and antiwar sides proved to be fairly evenly matched: the Senate voted 52–47 and the House 250–183 to authorize the president to use force.

The United Nations had set a deadline of January 15, 1991, for Saddam to withdraw from Kuwait. The day after this deadline passed, Bush launched a huge aerial attack against targets in Kuwait and Iraq. After bombs, rockets, and missiles knocked out Iraq's radar and air-defense network in hours, U.S. F-15 air-superiority fighters rose to challenge the Iraqi air force. But this force fled to Iran without firing a shot. Now in command of the skies, U.S. and allied aircraft launched a powerful bombing campaign. In this campaign the United States used its new satellite-guided global positioning system (GPS), which delivered bombs and cruise missiles precisely on targets. In 1991 only a fraction of American bombs and missiles were precision directed, but they pointed to the shape of American-style warfare to come. They demonstrated that the old American combination of massive power and military imagination had entered a revolutionary new phase, one that would separate the United States even more from the rest of the world. The 1991 air bombardment of Iraq and Kuwait showed the world that the United States reigned supreme in military power, and that no other country had the slightest chance of countering it.

Saddam Hussein tried to pull Arab states away from the coalition by firing thirty-nine Russian-made surface-to-surface Scud missiles against Israel, hoping to draw Israel into the war. But the Israelis held firm, despite great anger, and made no countermove. Most of the Scuds fell harmlessly, and others were shot down by U.S.-supplied Patriot missiles.

Saddam also opened Kuwaiti oil pipelines into the Persian Gulf to create a huge oil slick in hopes of clogging Saudi freshwater plants and creating terrible environmental damage. This only proved that Saddam was a madman and reinforced resolve to defeat him.

On February 23, 1991, the ground war commenced. U.S. Marines on board ships feinted at making an amphibious landing directly on Kuwait, while other Marines punched through the main Iraqi defenses on the southern Kuwaiti frontier. This two-front action locked the Iraqi army in place. Meanwhile the main attack, by U.S. Army forces with British and French allies, swept through the desert far around the western flank and pressed the Iraqi army into a corner at Basra on the Euphrates River and against the advancing Marines on the other side. This brilliant campaign cost few lives and was all over in a matter of hours. The Iraqi army put up no effective resistance and collapsed in ignominy. The only damage the Iraqis could do was to set fire to the Kuwaiti oil wells, an act wholly without military significance and designed simply to cause harm.

President Bush made a great mistake by not continuing on to Baghdad and destroying Saddam Hussein's regime. His answer to complaints after the war was that the coalition had been formed to drive the Iraqis out of Kuwait, not to destroy the Iraqi regime. But it was a huge blunder not to rid the world of Saddam Hussein then and there, as time was to show.

★   ★   ★

THE FIRST TERRORIST blow on American soil occurred on February 26, 1993, when a device packed in the cargo space of a Ford van, and composed mostly of 1,500 pounds of urea nitrate fertilizer, exploded in the parking basement of the World Trade Center in lower Manhattan, New York. The blast produced a crater 150 feet wide and five floors deep. It killed six people and injured a thousand. On March 3, 1993, a typed letter to the *New York Times* claimed that the bombing had been carried out "in the name of Allah." The FBI and other authorities found the conspirators after one of them made the unbelievably stupid mistake of returning to collect the security deposit on the truck they had just exploded. Four Muslim extremists were convicted in March 1994.

Meanwhile, a tragic situation was developing in Somalia. This Muslim country on the Horn of Africa had degenerated into anarchy caused by internecine conflict among warlords. Hundreds of thousands of people were dying in the fighting and in the resulting famine. In the last days of his term, President Bush dispatched American troops to restore order and distribute food to the people. Marines landed at Mogadishu in December 1992, planning to turn over the operation to the United Nations as soon as possible. Other U.N. member countries also sent troops.

The new administration, led by Bill Clinton, endorsed a March 1993 U.N. resolution that called for "the rehabilitation of the political institutions and economy of Somalia"—in other words, building a nation in the ravaged land. Clinton's U.N. ambassador, Madeleine Albright, who defined American policy as "assertive multilateralism," praised the Somalia plan as "an unprecedented enterprise aimed at nothing less than the restoration of an entire country."[23] Unfortunately it was pie-in-the-sky reasoning, since neither Clinton nor Albright consulted the Somali people, who were not interested in creating a country in the image of the United States.

The United Nations took over responsibility for the Somali operation, recruiting a force of 28,000 peacekeeping troops. The United States agreed to keep about 4,000 troops in the area, including a 1,300-member quick-reaction force under U.S. command.

On June 5, 1993, gunmen of the renegade Somali warlord, Muhammad Farah Aydid, ambushed Pakistani peacekeepers, killing and mutilating more than two dozen. The U.N. Security Council ordered the killers captured. The American quick-reaction force led several raids on Aydid's weapons caches, but U.N. peacekeepers did not operate as a coherent military force and therefore could not seize Aydid. In response to U.N. pressure, the United States sent a 400-man Army Rangers unit, plus a Special Forces contingent, but did not provide heavy weapons. If tanks and armored personnel carriers had been on hand, the disaster that came to pass might have been prevented.

On October 3, 1993, Rangers and Delta Force members embarked on a mission to capture Aydid in the midst of Mogadishu. As depicted in the motion picture *Black Hawk Down,* American forces approached in only thinly armored vehicles along narrow streets in the heavily built-up city. There they encountered close-in attacks from rocket-propelled grenades and other weapons fired from adjoining buildings and roof-tops. In the resulting chaos, two American helicopters were shot down. The U.N. command responded slowly to the crisis, so the Rangers and Delta force tried to rescue the downed helicopter crewmen. Eighteen Americans were killed and seventy-three wounded in the desperate ef-fort. An American soldier's body was dragged through the streets in full view of television cameras.

The killings so soured American opinion that, after forcing the So-malis to release a wounded American pilot they had captured, the United States pulled out of Somalia, abandoning the nation-building effort.

The Black Hawk Down episode represented an atrocious failure of leadership and prior planning by Clinton and his secretary of defense, Les Aspin. All the elements of danger were present—Somali resis-tance, inadequate weapons, inadequate command structure, and a fool-ish tactical plan that ignored the possibility of Somali counteraction, though it could easily have been anticipated. The Somali fiasco left lasting harm in its wake. Osama bin Laden maintained that members of his al Qaeda network had engineered the ambush in Mogadishu. Whether this was true or not, it encouraged terrorists to believe that Americans were especially vulnerable to attack.

The next blow came on November 13, 1995. Two terrorist bombs killed six people, five of them Americans, and wounded sixty others at a military training facility outside Riyadh, Saudi Arabia. Seven months later, on June 25, 1996, a terrorist bomb exploded outside the northern perimeter of the U.S. portion of the Khobar Towers housing complex in Dhahran, Saudi Arabia, killing 19 American servicemen and wound-ing 250 others.[24]

Two more blows came on August 7, 1998. Bin Laden's network engi-neered a devastating attack on American embassies in Nairobi, Kenya, and Dar es Salaam, Tanzania. A massive truck-bomb blast killed 257 people, 12 of them Americans, and left more than 5,000 wounded in Nairobi, while an almost simultaneous blast killed 11 and injured hun-dreds in Dar es Salaam. The attacks proved how vulnerable American property and people were to sneak attacks of this type. Clinton launched a retaliatory cruise-missile raid on August 20 against a number of al Qaeda training sites in Afghanistan, and on an alleged chemical weapons factory in Khartoum, Sudan. The attacks apparently did little damage. Worse, President Clinton did not follow up with further action against the terrorist network.

A little more than two years later, al Qaeda struck again. On October 12, 2000, as the guided-missile destroyer USS *Cole* put into the port of Aden, Yemen, for refueling, terrorists drew a small boat laden with explosives alongside the ship and detonated it. The explosives blew a massive hole in the *Cole*'s side, killing seventeen and wounding thirty-nine. The terrorists clearly knew the *Cole* was arriving that day and had prepared in advance to attack it. This demonstrated a high level of planning and preparation.

The terrorist war against the United States was fully under way. More was to come.

★ ★ ★

GENOCIDE IN THE BALKANS

Although the main themes of the last quarter of the twentieth century were the fall of Communism and the rise of Islamic terrorism, another evil reappeared during the last decade of the century. This abomination was extreme nationalism. It was the same potion that Adolf Hitler had induced the Germans to swallow. Hitler had told the Germans that nationalism would transform them into the master race, when in fact it was a poison that nearly destroyed their nation. In the 1990s, another madman, the Serbian leader Slobodan Milošević, induced his small Balkan nation to drink the same nationalist toxin. It brought in its wake the identical horrors that the extreme nationalism of Nazi Germany had spawned—deadly concentration camps, mass evictions of peoples from their homes, rape, maiming, murder, torture, and genocide. In the Balkans, genocide became an attempt to destroy a people merely because they were Muslims, and not Eastern Orthodox Christians like the Serbs. Milošević invented a chilling term, "ethnic cleansing," to describe the process by which his willing Serbian executioners evicted Muslims, occupied their lands, and killed and raped helpless victims.[1]

President George H. W. Bush and especially President Bill Clinton handled the crisis badly. Clinton solved the problem only after hundreds of thousands had died and millions had been displaced. The United Nations and the countries of Western Europe handled it even worse, waiting until the United States took charge. All the West should have heeded Elie Wiesel, a survivor of the Holocaust. On accepting the Nobel Peace Price in 1986, he said, "Take sides. Neutrality helps the oppressor, never the victim. Silence encourages the tormentor, never the tormented."

The inaction of the United Nations and Europe demonstrated that the leadership of the world has fallen on American shoulders. In crises when other countries do not face imminent danger, nothing is going to be done unless and until the United States acts.[2] This raises moral questions: When monstrous events occur, is the United States obligated to intervene? And if it intervenes in one place, is it then compelled to intervene in the next place an atrocity occurs?

The answer given by champions of one extreme is the old doctrine of *Realpolitik:* to step in only where American interests are at stake. The answer by champions of the other extreme is to take up the role of world policeman and try to stop all atrocities, wherever they occur.

For most of American history, this moral dilemma weighed very lightly on our consciences. Until we entered World War I, we left broad solutions to moral questions outside our country to the other great powers to solve, if they were to be dealt with at all. Even in World War I the clear and present danger of Germany far overrode the "make-the-world-safe-for-democracy" multilateralist idealism of Woodrow Wilson. We embarked on the job of destroying Nazi Germany and imperial Japan in 1941 only after we were attacked directly. And the entire story of the cold war can be written as a way of protecting vital American interests. Hence, the American people entered a new world when the Soviet Union died in 1991. We were left as the only superpower, and, by implication, as the only moral arbiter.[3]

Our leaders recoiled from this implication. George H. W. Bush's administration adhered to the approach of General Colin Powell, chairman of the Joint Chiefs of Staff. The Powell Doctrine, as it came to be known, held that the United States should intervene only to protect the vital interests of America or its allies. Such intervention should carry out a clearly defined political and military objective, should use decisive force, and should have a clear exit strategy. When Yugoslavia (which included Serbia) broke apart in June 1991, the situation appeared to threaten no obvious U.S. national interests and to meet few criteria for intervention.[4] Thus the administration was delighted when European leaders claimed they had the will to manage the Yugoslavian conflict. Secretary of State James Baker said "it was time to make the Europeans step up to the plate and show that they could act as a unified power." But by the time Bosnia, one part of Yugoslavia, degenerated into bloody chaos in April 1992, it was clear that there was no "European" diplomacy to speak of.[5]

American inaction continued under Bill Clinton's administration, which took office in January 1993 (and retained Colin Powell as chairman of the Joint Chiefs). The shibboleth of the Clinton administration was Wilsonian "multilateralism"—or the idea that well-meaning countries will work in concert to solve international problems.[6] But Yugoslavia showed it to be a sham. Multilateralism succeeds only when one powerful country takes the lead and brings along other states. Clinton's multilateralism revealed his paralyzing aversion to risk.

Since the United States refused to lead, nothing decisive occurred.[7] Symptomatic of this lack of leadership was the international arms embargo established in September 1991 to keep weapons away from both sides. The embargo did not damage the Serbs, the perpetrators of genocide, since the former Yugoslav army supplied them with weapons. It hurt only the victims, the Bosnian Muslims, who were prevented from arming themselves to fight Serbians. This stacked the deck against them and contributed to the killings in Bosnia from 1993 through 1995.

Multilateralism also failed because the modern democracies of Western Europe were wrapped up in their own affairs. They would not undertake dangerous, difficult, and expensive operations, and risk the lives of their soldiers, unless their own interests were directly involved. Thus, in Bosnia, Britain and France did not challenge Serbia militarily, fearing that the U.N. peacekeeper troops ("blue helmets") they provided for humanitarian purposes would be harmed by the Serbs.

The conclusion must be that only the United States will intervene when evil leaders begin killing people, because no one else will do so. Yet as plain as this obligation is, it is impossible for the United States to intercede everywhere and in every horrible situation.

We stayed out of the killing fields of Cambodia right after the Vietnam War because we did not want to get enmeshed again in Indochina. We avoided the murders of the military regime in Myanmar (Burma) because it was too distant. We did intervene in Somalia in 1992, but when our nation-building crashed after the killing of our soldiers, we pulled out. We might have done something in Rwanda when genocidal killings erupted there in 1994, but central Africa also was far away, and Clinton—after the fiasco in Somalia—did not want to send in American troops. (Moreover, the United Nations had peacekeepers on the ground when the genocide broke out in Rwanda. But it did nothing, refusing again to "take sides," in Wiesel's phrase.) It has never occurred to us to intercede in the long bloodlettings between Catholics and Protestants in Northern Ireland, the Basques and Spaniards in northern Spain, the Tamils and the Ceylonese in Sri Lanka, or the Indians and the Pakistanis in Kashmir. And in addition to Rwanda, we have assiduously avoided the many internecine and interstate conflicts in sub-Saharan Africa.

So where does this leave us? It leaves us focusing on our primary *Realpolitik* job of looking after the essential interests of our nation, and it tells us to step into nonessential regions only when we *can* do so. This, of course, puts the United States in an equivocal moral position. We choose some places to go into, ignore others. It is ethically better than the selfish do-nothing policies of Western Europe, but it by no means is a universal resolve to stop beastly behavior everywhere on earth. Americans also are more likely to respond to atrocities within Western civilization than outside it. We are a part of this civilization. When something diminishes Western civilization, it also diminishes us.

★   ★   ★

WE COULD AND SHOULD have intervened in the Balkans when Slobodan Milošević commenced his killings. In the end, the United States did act decisively, and in the end we got it right. But many died before we did so. Bosnia, with the later, related crisis in the Serbian province of Kosovo, is a lesson we should remember. It shows that the United States needs to examine every developing situation at once, and to move quickly when it can do so—because other nations are almost certain *not* to act.

Yugoslavia was an artificial country cobbled together after World War I. It consisted mostly of Slavic speakers of the Serbo-Croatian language, but also Slavic Slovenes and Macedonians, as well as a number of Muslim Albanians in Kosovo, descendants of the ancient inhabitants of the Balkan Peninsula. The Serbo-Croat speakers were divided into Serbs, who adhere to Eastern Orthodox Christianity; Croats, who are Roman Catholics; and Bosniaks, who are Muslims.

Not all the Serbs resided within the republic of Serbia. When Yugoslavia came apart in 1991, Milošević sought to annex all the Serbian regions of neighboring Croatia and Bosnia, and, in addition, to kill as many Muslims in Bosnia as possible and steal their land. It was this aim that led to war, murder, deportations, and genocide.

In 1991 Slovenia in the north and Macedonia in the south withdrew from Yugoslavia without much difficulty. But in June 1991, when Croatia did likewise, the Serbs who lived in a third of the country declared their own separate independence. This led to a civil war that ended in January 1992, when the United Nations brokered a cease-fire and sent 14,000 U.N. peacekeepers into Croatia.

In Bosnia, a country three-quarters the size of West Virginia, Serbs made up about 31 percent of the population, Croats 17 percent, and Bosniak Muslims nearly all the rest. In March 1992, when Bosnia cut its ties with Yugoslavia, the Serbs and Croats there set up "autonomous regions" in the areas they lived. But the Serbs were not satisfied. They commenced ethnic cleansing, driving Muslims out of their homes and lands, and bombarding the Bosnian capital of Sarajevo with heavy artillery. Within weeks, the Serbs occupied more than two-thirds of Bosnia. The Muslims who survived the murders and forcible evictions were crowded into a small region in the center of the country, and into five small enclaves surrounded by Serb-held territory.

The United Nations refused to intervene, but sent peacekeeping troops (mostly French, British, and Dutch) to facilitate delivery of food and other aid to the Muslim refugees.

By the summer of 1992, reports of Serbian atrocities and horrors in prisoner-of-war camps were flooding the media. In August, reporters finally gained access to the Serb-operated POW camp of Omarska, in northern Bosnia. They found emaciated men who were clearly being starved. When pictures of these men were broadcast, President Bush was forced to speak out. He said the pictures were stark evidence of the need to deal with the problem. His solution, however, was to push through a U.N. Security Council resolution that dispatched a hundred U.N. monitors and 6,000 additional peacekeepers to ensure that humanitarian aid was delivered; he sent no American forces. Deputy Secretary of State Lawrence Eagleburger announced, "Until the Bosnians, Serbs, and Croats decide to stop killing each other, there is nothing the outside world can do about it."

The Bush administration refused to see that Bosnia was not a war between equals. It was a land grab by Serbia, and in the process of seizing the land the Serbs were killing as many Muslims as possible. It was genocide and flagrant aggression. But Bush was unwilling to risk troops with the presidential election coming in November.

When Clinton took over the White House in January 1993, he was equally unwilling to act. Even so, pressure had built up by May. To relieve it, Clinton worked through the U.N. Security Council to create "safe areas" for Muslims—in Sarajevo, and in the five Muslim-held enclaves under Serb siege. The United States refused to send peacekeepers to protect these areas, and other countries provided only a few. Thus the so-called safe areas remained extremely vulnerable.

Bob Dole, Republican of Kansas and Senate minority leader, protested this do-nothing approach. American interests were under attack, Dole proclaimed. If Clinton refused to act, Milošević would soon turn on the Albanians in Kosovo. Islamic fundamentalists were using Western indifference to Muslim suffering as a recruiting device. Dole urged Clinton to demand that the Serbs adhere to a cease-fire, permit free passage of humanitarian convoys, place heavy weapons under U.N.

control, and disband the many paramilitary forces that were carrying out atrocities. If the Serbs disregarded the ultimatum, air strikes should commence, and the embargo against the Muslims be lifted.

Clinton ignored Dole. The president's reluctance to act reflected several influences. First was Powell, who stayed on as chairman of the Joint Chiefs of Staff until the end of September, and who spoke out against humanitarian missions without vital U.S. interests. (Madeleine Albright, Clinton's ambassador to the United Nations and later secretary of state, once asked Powell, "What's the point of having this superb military that you're always talking about if we can't use it?" He responded, "American GIs are not toy soldiers to be moved around on some sort of global game board.") Just as influential were the president's foreign policy advisers, committed multilateralists who would act only with the consent and participation of European partners. Deputy Secretary of State Strobe Talbott articulated the one-world ideal that liberals of the Clinton administration pursued when he described "pooled sovereignty"—the concept that America must give up some of its freedom of action to the emerging international community.[8] In this case, France and Britain feared Serb retaliation against them if they made any decisive move beyond deploying troops for humanitarian missions. Also, with Serbs controlling 70 percent of Bosnia by 1993, many European leaders privately urged partition as the way to achieve peace. A final factor was Clinton's fear of the political fallout at home if Americans began suffering battle casualties.

On February 6, 1994, however, a monstrous act occurred: sixty-eight Muslim civilians were killed in the shelling of a Sarajevo marketplace. Clinton denounced the "murder of innocents" and issued a NATO ultimatum that banned Serb heavy weapons around Sarajevo. For several months Sarajevans lived free of artillery and sniper fire. But when the Serbs resumed shelling, NATO did nothing.

The Western European powers were waiting for American leadership. The U.N. Security Council passed resolutions deploring the conduct of the perpetrators, created a channel for negotiations, called on states and organizations to document human rights violations, deployed peacekeepers, funded a humanitarian airlift of food and other supplies, and set up an international criminal tribunal at The Hague to try crimes against humanity and genocide. But these measures were meaningless in stopping the killing and the ethnic cleansing. What was lacking was American willingness to risk its own soldiers, or to convince the Europeans to support NATO bombing.

In July 1995, an atrocity occurred in the safe area of Srebrenica in eastern Bosnia that at last forced Clinton to take action. Bosnian Serbs under Ratko Mladic seized Srebrenica, where 40,000 Muslim refugees lived. The enclave was protected by 600 lightly armed Dutch peacekeepers, who required NATO air strikes to fend off the attack.[9] Although the Dutch commander repeatedly called for air strikes, the U.N. force commander, French general Bernard Janvier, refused to sanction them. On July 11, the day the Serbs actually occupied the town, he acquiesced and eighteen jets arrived, but their attacks were poorly planned, came too late, and had little effect. Meantime, the Serbs had captured several dozen Dutch peacekeepers and now threatened to kill them if air attacks continued. The Dutch government and the U.N. commanders opted to surrender Srebrenica to get the hostages released.

Mladic, left entirely unmolested, slaughtered 7,000 Muslim men and boys over the next week. A fortnight after seizing Srebrenica, he also took over Zepa, another safe area nearby, with 16,000 Muslim refugees. Here, as well, he killed men and boys.

Grisly stories began to come out of Srebrenica. Women, children, and elderly men were forced onto buses and taken on a ghastly journey to Tuzla, another Muslim town declared "safe" in 1993. Bodies were strewn along the roadside. Some were mutilated, many with their throats cut. Witnesses saw large clusters of men and boys with their hands tied behind backs, heads between knees. Buses frequently stopped along the way so Serb gunmen could select young women for roadside rape. The first evidence of summary executions came on July 14, 1995, when reliable reports told that men held in the town's stadium had been killed en masse. On the evening of July 12, a teenage girl watched the Serbs take twenty young men she knew. The next morning before her bus left for Tuzla, she found her friends stacked in a pile, dead, hands tied behind their backs. Others described rapes and throat slittings carried out before their eyes. Survivors told of hundreds of Muslim men who were herded into a large warehouse. Serb soldiers stood in doorways and windows and threw grenades and fired rifles and rocket-propelled grenades into the massed men. Only a few survived by hiding among the corpses. There were many other eyewitness reports of horrors.

Congressional criticism of Clinton rose to fever pitch, as Senator Bob Dole began pushing a bill to lift the arms embargo. European leaders began publicly slamming the Clinton administration for failing to lead. They told Washington that they would withdraw their peacekeepers if Congress lifted the embargo. If this happened, Clinton would have to follow through on a prior commitment to help the allies extract the blue helmets. Clinton would do everything possible to avoid a humiliating extraction mission that could hurt his bid for reelection.[10]

Meanwhile, Senator Dole made many television appearances to push for the embargo bill, which was cosponsored by Joseph Lieberman, Democrat of Connecticut. Periodicals of all political stripes joined in the attack. The literary editor of the liberal *New Republic* magazine, Leon Wieseltier, wrote, "You Americanize the war or you Americanize the genocide."

Clinton recognized that he was in danger of paying a political price for nonintervention. At a White House meeting on July 14, 1995, he stormed, "This can't continue. . . . We have to seize control of this. . . . I'm getting creamed!"[11] On July 17, National Security Adviser Anthony Lake unveiled Clinton's new strategy: the United States would take over the diplomatic show, and back its diplomacy by threatening to bomb the Serbs and lift the embargo. Time was short. On July 26, the Senate passed the Dole-Lieberman bill to end the arms embargo. On August 1, the House followed by a veto-proof margin. The Serbs began massing troops around the safe area of Bihac.

In a conference with Western leaders immediately thereafter, the United States secured a commitment to bomb Serbs if they attacked the Goradze safe area. This was enough to prevent a congressional override when Clinton vetoed the bill to lift the arms embargo. In the coming weeks, American representatives extended NATO's umbrella to three other safe areas, Bihac, Tuzla, and Sarajevo. More important, Washington made it plain that next time air strikes would not be pinpricks, but devastating blows. Meanwhile, U.N. peacekeepers were withdrawn from Serb-occupied territory, to avoid being taken as hostages.

While the West at last was taking decisive action, Croatia was conducting offensives that regained all the territory lost to the Serbs since 1991. In May 1995 the Croatian army swept through Serb-held territory in eastern Croatia, and in August it recovered in days the Krajina region in central and western Croatia.

On August 14, Secretary of State Warren Christopher gave Assistant Secretary of State Richard Holbrooke command over U.S. diplomacy in Bosnia. Two weeks later a shell landed near the same Markale market in Sarajevo where sixty-eight people had been killed in February 1994. This time thirty-seven died and eighty-five were wounded. Holbrooke called the White House: "We've got to bomb."

NATO acted quickly and decisively. Beginning on August 30 and continuing for the next three weeks, NATO planes flew 3,400 sorties against fifty-six Serb targets, concentrating on ammunition bunkers, surface-to-air missile sites, and communications centers. The attacks threw the Bosnian Serb army into chaos. Muslim and Croat soldiers now launched a new offensive and retook a fifth of Bosnian territory captured and cleansed in 1992.

In November 1995 Holbrooke brokered a peace accord in Dayton, Ohio. Three now ethnically pure blocks of territory—Muslim, Croat, and Serb—were kept together in a single country, but under a weak central government. More than 200,000 had been killed since the war began in April 1992. One out of two persons had lost their homes. In December 1995 Clinton deployed 25,000 troops in Bosnia as part of a NATO-led Implementation Force (IFOR) to keep the peace.[12]

★   ★   ★

THE WARS ORCHESTRATED by Slobodan Milošević had left Serbia ravaged. Stringent economic sanctions had brought high unemployment and inflation. In the two years after the Dayton accords, the Serbian population staged massive demonstrations, demanding the end of Milošević's corrupt rule. Milošević responded with more oppression and more control, by suppressing dissent, and by diverting attention to the only other significant ethnic minority in Serbia, the Albanians of Kosovo.

Albanians made up more than 90 percent of the population of this province, four-fifths the size of Connecticut. Milošević had set his sights on eliminating the Albanians in 1989, when he stripped Kosovo of its autonomy, fired Albanians from their jobs, closed their schools, and increased the Serb police presence.

The Kosovars had hoped that the Dayton conference would restore their autonomy, but the subject had not come up. Embittered, some Albanians formed the Kosovo Liberation Army (KLA) to protect the people and force the West to intervene. The group attracted little attention until March 1998, when it gunned down several Serbian policemen. Milošević struck back violently. Serbian troops murdered fifty-eight relatives of a KLA leader, Adem Jashari, including women and children. The attack brought KLA reprisals. With every Albanian attack, Serbian responses intensified. Serb soldiers and police killed 3,000 people and expelled 300,000 from their homes, which they then burned.

In October 1998 Richard Holbrooke got Milošević's agreement to pull back some of his forces in exchange for avoiding NATO air strikes and for allowing 2,000 unarmed international verifiers to go into the province. But the Serbs ignored the verifiers' presence. After bombarding the small town of Racak with artillery, they executed forty-five civilians, including three women, a twelve-year-old boy, and several elderly men, on January 15, 1999. The Serbs left the bodies facedown in an icy ravine.

Madeleine Albright, who had succeeded Warren Christopher as secretary of state, feared that Racak was the beginning of another Srebrenica. She and Tony Blair, the new British prime minister, were intent on stopping Milošević and engineered a conference of Western powers at the French chateau of Rambouillet, outside Paris. They told Milošević to remove most of his troops from Kosovo, grant the province autonomy, and allow in 25,000 armed European and American troops to keep the peace. Milošević refused, and beginning March 22, 1999, jets under the command of U.S. General Wesley Clark, NATO supreme commander, began a bombing campaign.

Milošević now did something wholly unexpected and unprecedented. He sent in troops and police and expelled virtually the entire remaining Kosovar population at gunpoint, some 1.3 million people, 740,000 of whom fled into neighboring Macedonia and Albania. Serbian troops surrounded Kosovo towns and villages and used artillery barrages to frighten the people into flight. In many areas, Serb police separated women, children, and old men from men of fighting age. They killed some 4,000 people, tore up identification papers, birth certificates, and property deeds, looted everything in sight, and burned houses.

The NATO jets did little to deter the ethnic cleansing. They flew at 15,000 feet to elude Serbian air defenses. The Serbs ignored the air strikes, which hit nothing vital, and continued to drive out the Albanians.

General Clark proposed a ground invasion and deployment of Apache attack helicopters that could fly close to the ground and target individual Serb units and vehicles. But Defense Secretary William Cohen and the Joint Chiefs of Staff rebuffed him. The senior military brass and Cohen were suspicious of Clark's hawkishness. President Clinton did not want to commit ground forces because he did not want to incur casualties. The Kosovo campaign was going to be fought at a distance — at 15,000 feet, in fact.

The efforts were not stopping Milošević. Senior American and European policymakers began to sense the possibility of defeat. They intensified air attacks. Aircraft committed rose from 400 to 1,000. On April 3, 1999, attacks commenced directly on the Serbian capital of Belgrade. NATO also announced that it was sending a 5,000-man task force to neighboring Albania, including twenty-four Apache helicopters. It was a propaganda device to frighten Milošević into believing a ground attack was about to be launched.

Even this did not end the Kosovo tragedy, however. In fact, a traditional ally of Serbia — Russia — had to step in at last to halt the conflict. Russian president Boris Yeltsin sent former Russian prime minister Viktor Chernomyrdin to Belgrade to tell Milošević, "I don't care what you do, just end it. It's ruining everything." Meantime, on May 24, the U.N. war crimes tribunal indicted Milošević for crimes against humanity and war crimes committed in Kosovo. Milošević, having lost the support of Russia, was afraid that if a ground invasion came, he'd be arrested for war crimes.

Milošević capitulated on June 3, 1999, agreeing to take Serbian troops and police out of Kosovo, and allowing 30,000 NATO peace-keepers to enter. Although Kosovo officially remained a part of Serbia, Albanians would govern themselves. The Albanians returned and slowly began rebuilding their lives.

Clinton's refusal to employ troops seemingly had paid off. But the real reason the crisis ended was that Russia had withdrawn its support for Milošević. The Serbian leader was now doomed. In fact, he was roundly defeated in a September 2000 election by an economics pro-fessor, Vojislav Kostunica. When Milošević tried to contest the results, miners, workers, police, and soldiers joined with intellectuals and stu-dents to end his deadly thirteen-year reign. In March 2001 the Kostu-nica government arrested Milošević, and in June 2001, in return for $40 million of urgently needed U.S. aid, it delivered him to The Hague, where a seemingly interminable trial commenced.

The long, harrowing conflict in the former Yugoslavia served as a powerful reminder of two truths. First, it showed that aggressors and tyrants will always be with us. Second, it emphasized that America's leadership remains more important than ever. In the 1990s America's risk-averse leaders tried an arm's-length approach to a crisis that de-manded decisive and forceful intervention. Genocide, concentration camps, murder, torture, and mass displacement of peoples resulted, since no other nation stepped in to deal with the conflict.

After the Berlin Wall crumbled and the Soviet Union collapsed, a period of heady optimism ensued, in which many believed that the United States could step back from its role as dominant global power. But reality soon intervened, just as it had done after World War I— indeed, just as it always does.

And America would soon receive an even more startling reminder of the need to step up to global challenges, when terrorist war against the West was brought directly to our shores.

SEVENTEEN

★ ★ ★

WITH US OR AGAINST US

More than any other people, Americans see issues in black and white terms. Many of us judge a matter in contention as right or wrong, good or evil. We are impatient with the infinite shades of gray that the peoples and nations of Western Europe use to paint over their failures to take decisive action, and to justify positions that to us are plainly wrong.

The American habit of polarizing issues grew out of the individualism and self-reliance imposed by the frontier. From our earliest days, individuals and families learned by hard experience that success largely depended on what they themselves accomplished—and failure came when they themselves did not meet the tests and challenges they encountered. For us, self-sufficiency has always been a virtue, and we expect individuals to take responsibility for what they do.

We extend to other peoples this tendency to decide on the evidence at hand, not to accept excuses or to condone wrongful acts by explaining them away. What finally motivated us to end the carnage in Bosnia, for example, was the firing of a shell onto innocent people in the Sarajevo marketplace on August 28, 1995. This wanton act of villainy was the last straw. We overrode Western Europe's years-long, passive acceptance of such iniquity. And the atrocity forced our timid president,

Bill Clinton, to respond because he saw that inaction would lower his numbers in the next poll.

It was natural, therefore, for Americans to see the al Qaeda terrorist attacks on the World Trade Center and on the Pentagon on September 11, 2001, as pure evil, with no mitigating circumstances. The vast majority of us resolved then and there to destroy the people and the groups that had brought on this travesty and killed 3,000 of our fellow citizens.[1] President George W. Bush reflected the will of the American people exactly when he vowed revenge, and when he toppled the repressive Taliban regime in Afghanistan in the fall of 2001, scattering the al Qaeda cells that the Taliban were protecting.

But President Bush also reinforced the intense resolve that seized the American people to root out and destroy *all* terrorist elements, wherever they exist, and to drive out the governments of all countries that threaten to harm the United States or that harbor terrorists. The world after 9/11 became *entirely* black and white. President Bush spoke for the great preponderance of the American people when he said, "Either you are with us, or you are with the terrorists."

The decision to remove Saddam Hussein in the spring of 2003 was completely justified, and the logic of the move, simplicity itself. He represented as severe a threat to the safety of the United States as the al Qaeda terrorists, and he had to be eliminated. To be sure, Saddam was no friend of the terrorists. They want to abolish all secular governments in the Middle East and establish a theocratic dictatorship. But Saddam saw a temporary community of interest with them. Both wanted to drive the West out of the Middle East and both wanted to destroy Israel. The danger was too great that Saddam would provide the terrorists with arms and protection. With an oil-rich state behind him, Saddam could have done great damage himself and could have given tremendous assistance to terrorists.

The Bush administration erred when it justified the war in Iraq by emphasizing one aspect of the case against Saddam—his apparent possession of weapons of mass destruction (WMD). When inspectors could not locate any such weapons, liberal Democrats found an excuse to attack the administration and the war. David A. Kay, director of the

Iraq Survey Group, which was charged with searching for WMD, found that Saddam had all but abandoned efforts to produce biological and chemical weapons after the Persian Gulf War of 1991. Kay also concluded that American intelligence agencies had failed to detect the facts primarily because the CIA lacked its own spies in Iraq and relied on satellites to survey Iraq's activities. Even CIA director George J. Tenet, who defended his agency's intelligence-gathering, admitted that U.S. spy agencies may have overestimated Iraq's illicit weapons capabilities.[2]

Opponents of the war seized on these discoveries to mount new attacks on the Bush administration. But many of Bush's critics ignored or downplayed a more disturbing discovery Kay made: Saddam was trying to revive his quest for an atomic bomb in 2000–01. And despite the media firestorm over President Bush's statement in his 2003 State of the Union address that "the British government has learned that Saddam Hussein recently sought significant quantities of uranium from Africa," as it turned out the evidence showed not only that British intelligence had actually reached this conclusion, but also that Saddam had in fact tried to get uranium ore from Niger.[3]

Charles L. Duelfer, who replaced Kay as the top U.S. weapons inspector in Iraq, made the point even more clearly in his fall 2004 report, stating that Saddam clearly intended to produce nuclear, chemical, and biological weapons if U.N. sanctions were lifted. In other words, Saddam was merely biding his time until he could reconstitute his weapons program. Duelfer's finding refutes the liberal view that the U.S. attack on Iraq was a mistake.[4]

In any case, Iraq's weapons capabilities, and the dictator's plan to ramp up those capabilities once the weapons inspectors left, only partially explain why the United States had to go into Iraq and remove Saddam and his regime. Indeed, the military actions in Iraq had far greater significance than eliminating Saddam Hussein, just as the Afghanistan campaign involved far more than ousting the Taliban. These moves signaled to the leaders of all Islamic states that they cannot assist terrorists publicly. If they do, the United States will oust them. Yale historian John Lewis Gaddis made this point precisely when he said we went into Iraq "quite simply, to frighten any state that might in the future be harboring terrorists. It's like the parking signs that Mayor [Ed] Koch used to put up around New York. Remember those? 'Don't even think of parking here.' Don't even think of harboring terrorists."[5]

Osama bin Laden understood the significance of what the United States was doing. In a frantic effort to keep Iraq as a terrorist haven and to warn other Islamic states against cracking down on terrorists, he proclaimed in a December 2004 audiotape that any Iraqis who voted in democratic elections would be "infidels."[6]

That is why the United States got it right when it set out to neutralize terrorism and tyrants. Together these two constitute a single malady threatening the world's body politic. The two are connected because the only major support for terrorism comes from rogue Islamic states and from North Korea. There can be no compromise with this dual danger, no business-as-usual dealings with anyone who harbors or supports terrorists. The argument made by John Kerry during the 2004 presidential campaign that the war in Iraq diverted us from the "real" war on terror is false. Terrorists and rogue rulers are part and parcel of the same threat.[7]

★   ★   ★

MANY OTHER COUNTRIES, especially our equivocal allies in Western Europe, refuse to confront the peril solidly. They have tried not to get involved very deeply, and they were happy to let the United States take responsibility in Afghanistan and Iraq. In this way they hoped to avoid making their countries targets for terrorist attacks, and they could criticize the United States for what it did. Envy plays a role here, because these countries no longer can dictate policies to the world. Malice is another factor. Author Robert Kagan writes that Europeans "fear that they have lost control over the United States and, by extension, over the direction of world affairs."[8] Dominique Moïsi, a senior adviser of the Institut Français des Relations Internationales, claims that Europe "feels that it must exist as an alternative to the United States—a different and better West."[9]

Accommodation or compromise, even at the expense of principle, is another European excuse for inaction. Whereas Americans see the world as divided between good and evil, Europeans "generally favor peaceful responses to problems, preferring negotiation, diplomacy, and persuasion to coercion," Kagan writes.[10]

Former Swedish prime minister Carl Bildt has emphasized this divide between Europeans and Americans. The central date for Europeans is November 9, 1989, when the Berlin Wall fell, he said. The central date for Americans is September 11, 2001, when America was attacked. Every European minister wakes up in the morning thinking about how to consolidate the Continent into one big family, Bildt asserted. The U.S. president wakes up thinking about where the next terror attack might come from. "While we talk about sharing sovereignty," Bildt said, "they [the Americans] talk about exercising sovereign power."[11]

President Bush told Congress on September 20, 2002, that the United States "will not hesitate to act alone" and, if necessary, will act preemptively or preventively.[12] This decision aroused a flurry of opposition among leftists who claimed we never should strike first. But America's leaders never contemplated a true preemptive attack—such as the one the Japanese launched on us at Pearl Harbor on December 7, 1941—except against terrorist groups that have to be hit quickly, before they will disappear.

Opponents maintain that the United States has no right to act without international consent. For example, in 2004 Samuel (Sandy) R. Berger, who served as President Clinton's national security adviser from 1997 to 2001, wrote that if there were a "Democratic administration," it should "act in concert with its allies in meeting global threats as a first, not last, resort. When we ask our allies to join us . . . we should be ready to share not just the risks but also the decision-making."[13] Such a policy would give *a single foreign power* a veto over any military action we might feel obligated to take. If the Bush administration had allowed France and Germany a "share" in the decision making on war with Saddam Hussein in 2003, we would not have acted, because they opposed any attack. Handing over to allies the authority to decide matters affecting the vital interests of the United States is another way of saying we are *surrendering* our sovereignty to foreign countries. This is not going to happen. Despite the "one-world" view of some liberals, the vast majority of the American people will *not* accept abandoning our most vital national treasure—our independence.

President Bush was entirely right in his 2004 State of the Union address when he announced that "America will never seek a permission slip to defend the security of our country."

Our task is *not* to join in an international group that requires a majority, much less a unanimous, vote in order to proceed. We saw in Iraq in 2003 that such a group is an illusion, and a search for international consensus is simply a device for doing nothing. Our task, instead, is to show hesitant nations that it is in *their* interests to fight terrorists and rogue states, and to induce these nations to join us in the war terrorists and rogues are waging against civilization.

Some observers claim that we are not looking at the world realistically. They say that although we live today in a unipolar world, the global stability that comes with unipolarity will not last. They envision a coming multipolar world—a united Europe, a resurgent Russia, a revived Japan, and a growing China, all future counterweights to American strength.[14] These critics claim that our tendency today is to act alone and that we seek our *own* interests, not a global good or a universal tranquility. America's movement away from multilateralism, they assert, raises the chances of making opponents out of the new centers of power.

But there is little evidence that this charge is true, because competing power centers are seeking influence and accommodation *within* the existing order. They are not trying to overturn it. Besides, no reasonable person can believe that the war on terror is serving only American interests. The entire civilized world benefits. And we have always sought allies in our actions. Nevertheless, the opposition to ousting Saddam Hussein shows that many people in Western Europe don't appreciate what the United States is doing for their own safety. This requires us to modify our approach. As John Lewis Gaddis writes, "Influence, to be sustained, requires not just power but also the absence of resistance, or, to use Clausewitz's term, 'friction'. . . . This is what was missing during the first Bush administration: a proper amount of attention to the equivalent of lubrication in strategy, which is persuasion."[15]

At the moment, however, we have a world that is being defended by only one of its elements, the United States, with limited help from Britain, Australia, Italy, and a few others.

The West is being assailed by religious fanatics who represent only a tiny minority of Muslims from a technologically backward part of the world. In any balance of power test, the Islamic fundamentalists come off as overwhelmingly inferior. But these inferior fundamentalists managed to kill 3,000 of our citizens in a matter of minutes because they attacked our weakness—the manifold places in our land that we cannot defend but where a terrorist can strike. Such a world is profoundly unsafe and anxiety-ridden, and it cannot be tolerated. Terrorists represent a clear and present danger to the world, and rogue states are their principal sources of supply and sustenance. At some placid time in the future we can think great thoughts about creating a multilateral utopia. But right now we must deal with murderers who are stalking our cities.

Countries unwilling to take up the challenge of terrorism are like British prime minister Neville Chamberlain, who appeased Adolf Hitler, wishing the danger of Nazi Germany would go away. The majority of nations today keep a low profile and simply hope that the United States will take care of the terrorists, or that the terrorists will just go away on their own. But as Winston Churchill warned Chamberlain when he returned from Munich in 1938 after selling out Czechoslovakia to Hitler, "You were given the choice between war and dishonor. You chose dishonor, and you will have war."

Only the extreme Left in the United States has, like Chamberlain, chosen dishonor. It supported France's and Germany's do-nothing position on Iraq, hunted for any reason to condemn the action, and used the limited guerrilla war that developed in the Saddam-friendly "Sunni triangle" around Baghdad to demand our withdrawal from Iraq.

★   ★   ★

THERE HAS BEEN much talk about the United States becoming an imperial power, especially since 9/11. A Scot, Niall Ferguson, traces the rise and fall of the British Empire, and writes that the United States has taken over Britain's old role of world hegemon "without yet facing the fact that an empire comes with it." Historian Chalmers Johnson claims that the United States has consolidated global imperial rule.[16]

Although some conservatives have espoused an imperialist worldview, the vast majority of Americans want nothing to do with it. We believe in a world in which countries, especially democracies, work together wherever possible. Our goal in the Middle East is to stop terror and oppression. Our goal in East Asia is a nuclear-free Korean Peninsula. If, after achieving these goals, either evil returns, we'll go back in. That's been the American pattern in the unstable countries of the Caribbean for a century. That's how we went into World War I and World War II. We solved clear and present problems in foreign lands, then got out as fast as we could. An empire requires an enduring hierarchical system, in which control resides at the center. We lack any interest in building such a structure. Imperialism implies subordination, democracy implies freedom. In any vote, we opt for freedom.

★   ★   ★

THE MILITARY CAMPAIGN against Iraq in March–April 2003 demonstrated the overwhelming military superiority of the United States. The Iraqi army was incapable of challenging U.S. power in any way.[17] This easy victory disguised the real military problem the United States will face for the foreseeable future: since no other country can challenge us to a standup fight, any opponent we invade will automatically resort to guerrilla warfare. Partisan fighting is the only way an enemy can neutralize America's vast technical supremacy to some degree.

The process began with the Taliban fundamentalists and al Qaeda terrorists in Afghanistan in 2001–02. Neither possessed regular military forces that could stand toe to toe against American power. The Taliban and al Qaeda forces could strike only at isolated American elements and then disappear into the population.

A similar guerrilla war erupted in Iraq soon after Saddam Hussein's government collapsed in spring 2003. In the Sunni triangle (Baghdad-Falluja-Tikrit) enough supporters of Saddam lived to shelter guerrilla elements, permitting those guerrillas to emerge to do their damage and then slip back into the populace with some assurance of safety. The Sunni members of Saddam's Baathist party were trying to prevent a stable successor government from being established, for they were certain to be excluded from it.

Thus, in Afghanistan and Iraq, the axiom confirmed in the Vietnam War was reasserted: any state attacked by a more powerful state will *always* move to guerrilla warfare, since it can hide its soldiers among the people, whereas an invading state cannot hide its soldiers, who then become vulnerable to debilitating surprise attacks. Just as in Vietnam, then, we came in unprepared for the reality of guerrilla warfare that met us in Iraq. This failure to anticipate and plan for an entirely predictable development represents the most damaging error on the part of the intelligence community and the military.[18]

The guerrilla outbreak in Iraq drew in a few al Qaeda and other terrorists to cooperate with the Baathists. The Pentagon designated Ansar al-Islam as the key terrorist threat in Iraq in 2003. This Taliban-like organization has ties with al Qaeda and was established just prior to 9/11 in a mountainous region of Kurdish northern Iraq near the Iranian border. U.S. and Kurdish forces destroyed this base in the spring of 2003 and later captured some of the movement's top leaders.[19] The terrorists and the guerrillas shared a common goal—to strike at the Americans, and at anyone helping to build a new Iraq.

No guerrilla uprising occurred in the Kurdish regions in northern Iraq or in Shiite southern Iraq. The lack of an uprising in these regions demonstrated how guerrillas can exist only if they have active leadership and if a substantial portion of the population supports them. While guerrillas in Iraq had strong leadership, they could not rely on the population to support them in these regions, since the people in both areas had long been oppressed by Saddam's Sunni Baathists. Guerrillas did move into these areas temporarily to carry out isolated strikes against forces allied with the United States, but on the whole guerrilla movements did not flourish here. To borrow the language of Chinese Communist leader Mao Zedong, in these areas guerrillas could not "swim" in the "water" of the people and go undetected.

There is little difference in the goals of the various terrorist or extreme religious groups in the Middle East—al Qaeda, Taliban, Hamas, Islamic Jihad, al Aqsa Brigades,[20] Hezbollah, Ansar al-Islam, and others, or the successors to the Shiite fundamentalist Ayatollah Ruholla Khomeini, who have imposed a despotic theocracy on Iran. All hate Israel, all are supporting one form or another of a repressive Islamic state ruled by the *sharia,* or Islamic law, and all are opposed to Westernization, democracy, and modernization. Virulent, nihilistic terrorism is distorting the Middle East. Its victims are any persons, whether Muslim or non-Muslim, who support modernism and pluralism.

The Baathists in Iraq are different. Although they hate democracy as much as the fundamentalists do, they were trying to bring back the secular totalitarian dictatorship that existed under Saddam Hussein, because it gave them great privileges. The Baathists were happy to have the support of the terrorists, but the two groups did not have the same goals.

The guerrillas and terrorists were copying the strategy outlined by Mao Zedong in his victorious war against the Chinese Nationalists in the 1930s and 1940s. Mao, in turn, followed the teachings of the great Chinese strategist Sun Tzu, who lived 2,400 years ago. Sun Tzu held that one should first adopt a successful strategy against one's enemy, then attack the enemy's alliances, and finally attack the enemy's army.[21]

The Sunnis followed Sun Tzu's doctrine precisely. The successful strategy they adopted was to avoid challenging the American military head-on and to switch to guerrilla warfare, in which U.S. weapons and power were least effective. Second, the guerrillas attacked American alliances by striking U.N. headquarters, the Turkish chancery, Red Cross headquarters, an Italian mission, and the bases of troops allied with the United States. They killed civilian workers from many countries in highway ambushes, took others hostage, and killed individual Iraqis supporting the United States. Finally, guerrillas attacked the American army—setting off roadside bombs or firing on soldiers as they went by, bringing down helicopters, and firing mortars and rockets into army bases and the "green zone" headquarters of American forces in central Baghdad. The aim was threefold—to estrange the local population from the Americans, to inflict casualties on Americans, and to reduce the determination of Americans at home to pursue the job of producing a more equitable government in Iraq.

The guerrillas hoped to regain power. They failed, but still they brought the American occupation to an end faster than the Bush administration had planned. In light of intensifying insurgency and rapidly eroding Iraqi support for the occupation, the administration abandoned a deliberate process of writing a constitution, holding elections, and then transferring power to a democratic Iraqi government. Instead, it turned power over to an interim government on June 28, 2004. This government, approved by a unanimous vote of the U.N. Security Council, held elections in January 2005 and aimed to have a popularly chosen permanent legislature and constitution by the end of 2005.

The American-appointed Iraqi Governing Council approved a temporary constitution on March 1, 2004. It designated Islam as "a source" of legislation but did not subordinate all decisions to the *sharia*. The document prohibited any legislation "against" Islam, however.

The ambivalence expressed in the temporary constitution was reflected on the ground. Sunni Baathist radicals and Islamic terrorists unleashed violent attacks in an attempt to undermine the caretaker government. They were joined by the minor radical Shiite faction of Moqtada al-Sadr, whom Iran was using as a stalking horse to impose a Shiite theocratic state in Iraq. Meanwhile the Ayatollah Ali al-Sistani, senior Shiite cleric in Iraq, objected to the provision that authorized Kurds to nullify a permanent constitution if it didn't provide for their self-government.

All these events showed that the creation of a secular, democratic Iraq may be extremely difficult, if not impossible, in the short run. At this writing it appears that without effective American intervention, three separate but equally unacceptable political outcomes are possible: a Shiite dictatorship could take over the whole country; the Kurds could lose the freedoms they have enjoyed since the end of the 1991 Gulf War; or the minority Sunnis could return to absolute power.

Iraqis are wildly divided on how their country should be governed.

All have learned their approach to power from a murderous dictator, Saddam Hussein. Few have had any lessons in compromise. None has had any experience in democracy. We hope the Iraqis will see that the rights of Shiites, Kurds, Sunnis, and minorities must all be protected. We urge them to decide that a power-sharing agreement is better than violence. We wish the Western model of liberty, democracy, self-expression, self-reliance, and the rule of law will find a place. But until the Iraqis learn more tolerance for each other, we must prevent either a Shiite or a Sunni dictatorship from emerging.

We ran into a similar discordant situation in Afghanistan. Much of the country is ruled by local warlords, who function as absolute potentates and have little interest in giving up their power to a unified nation. In addition, the country is deeply divided between modernizers and Islamic conservatives and between majority Pushtuns and ethnic minorities. These conflicts made it difficult for the interim Afghan government to get a *loya jirga,* or grand assembly, to approve a new constitution in January 2004. Although the new basic law states that men and women are to be treated equally, it contains no bill of rights. Moreover, the constitution established the Islamic Republic of Afghanistan, with civil laws "in keeping with Islam." It offers no assurance that an equitable society can be created, much less sustained, in Afghanistan.[22]

★   ★   ★

THE CIRCUMSTANCES IN IRAQ and Afghanistan demonstrated an important truth: it's easy to topple a dictatorship, but it's impossible to impose political solutions by military occupation. Therefore, as soon as we have achieved a military victory in a rogue state, we must launch as equitable a domestic government as we can, bring in the United Nations to handle peacekeeping, and limit our occupation to the shortest time possible.[23]

After the terrible experience of Vietnam, the American public will *not* tolerate an extended guerrilla war with steady, unrelenting casualties and no clear exit strategy. In the face of daily attacks on our troops, the American people will rebel if asked to accept a long-term occupation that requires the painstaking creation of democratic institutions, a constitution, elections, and a government. Such a process is unrealistic.

Although Americans endorse democracy everywhere and want to set up conditions in which it can thrive, few are interested in using military force to create replicas of the American system in other lands. Most Americans realize that aspirations of this sort are futile. Democracy succeeds only when citizens accept it *willingly*. Besides, Americans are primarily concerned with stopping attacks on our people and our country. Our principal aim is to establish governments that are peaceful, both with their own people, and with the world at large.[24]

We should learn from our experiences in Somalia, Afghanistan, and Iraq. Democracy is a frail flower, difficult to grow in uncultivated soil, even more difficult to make flourish. It took the English centuries to work out a democratic system strong enough to withstand the efforts of kings, nobles, bishops, and ostensible reformers like Oliver Cromwell to kill it. We inherited the traditions and institutions of England and were able to establish a democratic government in the United States. But even we had difficulty.

As Yale law professor Amy Chua argues in her 2003 book *World on Fire,* the tremendous increase in market economies and democracy since the fall of the Soviet Union has *not* transformed the world into a community of modern, peace-loving nations. "Adding democracy to markets has been a recipe for instability, upheaval, and ethnic conflagration," she writes. Chua reminds us that democratizing a society is a complex affair, with myriad pitfalls and barriers, and not something that outsiders can impose.[25]

We cannot hope to transfer in a short space of time European or American democracy and the rule of law to countries that have never known either. It could take years to build institutions that can sustain democratic government. An occupying power is an alien presence. No matter how benign our intentions, our soldiers soon become a burden and an enemy. As Charles de Talleyrand, the cynical master diplomat of the Napoleonic era, observed, one can do anything with bayonets except sit on them.

This point was underscored when, in April and May of 2004, reports and pictures emerged of male and female U.S. Army military police tormenting Iraqi prisoners in the Abu Ghraib prison near Baghdad. The pictures provoked outrage both in the United States and throughout the world, and they fed anti-American feelings in all quarters that opposed U.S. intervention in Iraq. Although only a minuscule fraction of American military personnel were involved, investigations showed that their superior officers failed to provide proper leadership, guidelines, and supervision. Bush administration officials acknowledged that the episode made it more difficult for Americans to operate in Iraq and had damaged the nation's image around the world.[26]

But the horrible nature of the terrorist enemy surfaced on May 11, 2004, when the al Qaeda leader in Iraq, Abu Musab al-Zarqawi, released a videotape of the gruesome beheading of Nicolas Berg, an American civilian working in Iraq, ostensibly in revenge for American mistreatment of Arab prisoners. Other beheadings soon followed; the victims included an American civilian worker in Saudi Arabia and a Korean civilian worker in Iraq. These wanton murders showed that the terrorists are savages who will go to any extreme to get their way. The beheadings put the problem of Iraq in perspective. The behavior of a few American guards at Abu Ghraib was gross and unacceptable, and those responsible were punished. The murders for show emphasized what had become evident on 9/11: terrorists are barbarians who reject every tenet of civilization and humanity. They must be hunted down and destroyed. There is no other way.[27]

We are obligated in every country we occupy to restore order, eliminate safe havens for terrorists, and reach political solutions that will prevent chaos from returning. But we cannot hope, in the space of a temporary occupation, to create a government that can meet all the democratic standards of America or Western Europe. In lands where Americans risk being attacked by guerrillas every time they step into the open, we must be satisfied with less—an end to aggression, the elimination of terrorists, but only the first steps toward a democratic state in a peaceful and secure Middle East.[28]

★   ★   ★

WHAT, THEN, ARE THE choices?

The death of Yasser Arafat on November 11, 2004, gives Arabs the opportunity to decide whether they want to live in peace with Israel and the West, or whether they want to support continued terrorism. Violence appears to be the aim of Hamas, Islamic Jihad, and al Aqsa in Palestine, and Hezbollah, Ansar al-Islam, al Qaeda, and other terrorist elements elsewhere. If the terrorists continue killing innocents, and if the people and governments of the Middle East allow the fundamentalist minority to dominate their societies, then tragedy will stretch out far into the future, for Israel will never surrender, and the United States will occupy the lands of Islam until terrorism has ceased.

We and the Israelis will reach solutions whether or not the Arabs and their governments cooperate. By careful, meticulous intelligence-gathering, the United States military has been highly successful in ferreting out and eliminating terrorist cells. One among many examples was finding Saddam Hussein in a hole in the ground in December 2003.[29] In the Holy Land, either the Palestinians will willingly conclude a peace or Israel will impose a peace by separating the two peoples physically. In December 2003 Israeli prime minister Ariel Sharon showed he was willing to do exactly that when he sketched out a plan for an impervious barrier, a "security line," dividing the terrorists from the Israelis. In short, he was proposing a unilateral solution in the event the Palestinians remained locked in their intransigence.[30]

The greatest help Middle Eastern states can provide for themselves is to convince their own people that the terrorists are *their* enemy, not just the enemy of the West. We hope that once Middle Eastern people see that harboring terrorists leads to disorder, death, and destruction within their own societies, they will root out the cells, which will induce the Americans to leave.

But there's little evidence that this is happening. Although a reevaluation of terrorists is taking place, it has not produced a groundswell to destroy them. Rather, the Arabs as a whole are distancing themselves from the violence.[31]

Islamic fundamentalism is eating its own young, turning against the very people it must rely on to gain long-term support. Zarqawi and other Islamic fundamentalists are increasingly targeting Muslims, not Americans. In 2004, suicide bombers killed hundreds of Muslims in Baghdad, Karbala, Basra, and other cities in Iraq and in the Pakistani city of Quetta. These and other bombings mirrored similar strikes that killed mostly Muslims in Casablanca, Morocco; Riyadh, Saudi Arabia; Istanbul, Turkey; Tashkent, Uzbekistan; and Damascus, Syria, in 2003 and 2004.[32]

Such blows are counterproductive. They will not bring about an Islamic theological tyranny. Still, a vast flood of public anger has *not* been unleashed against terrorists. Despite the wanton killings of their own people, the Arabs as a whole remain detached and passive. It's unrealistic to think that they will take up the cause to oust the terrorists soon, if ever. We can't wait for a social transformation in the Muslim world that may or may not come. We must destroy the terrorists ourselves.

CONCLUSION

★ ★ ★

THE TASK AHEAD

The United States has three overriding responsibilities in the
coming years. We must eliminate the threat of a nuclear bomb
being brought into one of our cities by terrorists. We must root out and
destroy all the terrorist networks and cells everywhere on earth. And
we must reorganize our military and intelligence structures to find and
kill terrorists, while also keeping our existing overwhelming military
power to protect us and the rest of the world from any nuclear threat.

All three requirements are interrelated. Insuperable military power
is necessary to prevent all rogue states that do not have nuclear weapons from acquiring them. A restructured intelligence system is necessary to root out terrorist cells and conspiracies in renegade states, and a
restructured military is necessary to create small, rapid-reaction forces
that will meet the challenge of targeting those partisans and terrorists.

The weapons and technology that make the American military in-
comparable in conventional warfare have virtually eliminated the possibility they will be *used* in conventional warfare, except to destroy
rogue governments. We don't need overwhelming military power to
intimidate other great powers like China. Other great powers are not
going to challenge American military strength. They will compete
economically.

For the foreseeable future our peerless military force will be used almost wholly against rogue states that—although lacking conventional

military strength—might be unenlightened enough to confront us. Our greatest weapons against any intractable country are our aircraft carrier groups and our air force because of the great range and the great reach they have. No state that challenges us can win, because our piloted aircraft and our unmanned aerial vehicles (UAVs) can deliver devastating rocket and bomb attacks with pinpoint accuracy on any target anywhere by means of the global positioning system (GPS), as well as by laser, infrared, acoustic, or radar homing signals.

At the same time we are obligated to restructure the army and the Marine Corps to fight a weak enemy armed with relatively unsophisticated weapons. Terrorists can deploy few arms other than what they can bring with them—explosive-laden vehicles, automatic rifles, machine guns, mortars, rocket-propelled grenades, and shoulder-fired missiles. If they by chance could acquire heavy cannons or tanks, they could never use them because our air power would destroy them as soon as they showed themselves. Terrorists, like the guerrillas to whom they are related, can fight only a war in the shadows—hit-and-run attacks, roadside bombs, suicide missions, missiles fired from windows, mortars quickly set up to drop rounds on a military base or position and as quickly taken down and hidden. This is the nature of terrorist warfare, and of all guerrilla-like operations.

To fight these kinds of enemies, we need to reorganize our ground forces to create small, autonomous elements that move so fast and so lethally that they can kill terrorists and partisans before they get away. These small battle groups have already proven their value in Iraq and Afghanistan. They work together in a network—using instantaneous radio, TV, and computer communications—to swarm around an enemy target on all sides, isolating it, and destroying it quickly. Some of these teams are infantry forces, some heavily armored tank elements, some attack helicopter units, some artillery sections, and some AC-130 gunship teams that can fire cannons, rockets, and machine guns directly on enemy targets. Our military must dramatically reorganize existing structures to make possible more flexible teams that coalesce quickly, move within minutes by air or ground to eliminate any danger spot, and as quickly dissolve.

Recognition of this reality is revolutionizing the American military. The highly trained forces will form only a small part of the military, but they will be so fast and so powerful that they can dominate any military situations they encounter. More conventional forces will cooperate with and back up these fast forces.[1] As John Arquilla, an outstanding analyst of future warfare, writes, "The situation is a little like 1940, when the Germans had only ten panzer divisions against the Anglo-French forces, but being thinly mechanized was still good enough, because of the adoption of the right doctrinal and organizational innovations, to win a signal victory."[2]

While creating these small, fast-acting tactical units to deal with terrorists, we must be certain to maintain the planet's most formidable military power. As different as the two missions may be, they are equally important, for heavy forces will be used to support our highly mobile strike forces in specific military challenges, and the possession of supreme military power will prevent any ambitious leader from launching a program to acquire similar power.

Overwhelming bombing strikes against a broad group of targets, like those delivered on Iraq in the 1991 Gulf War, will be rare or nonexistent. Instead, each target will be eliminated by explicit precision strikes, some by air, some on the ground. For example, in the invasion of Iraq in the spring of 2003, Special Forces arriving by air killed Iraqi observers along the Kuwaiti border, while others moving on the ground neutralized the "Scud box" in western Iraq targeted against Israel. The defenders didn't have a lot of time to be caught by surprise because Special Forces killed them. Meanwhile, aircraft using precision munitions destroyed individual military targets that Special Forces could not take out.

The fighting in Iraq in 2003 therefore combined a series of precision strikes on targets—some by aircraft, some by Special Forces teams—with a relatively small conventional ground force of 90,000 troops that moved swiftly from Kuwait to Baghdad and beyond. Iraqi divisions on the flank couldn't get near the speeding Americans because Special Ops forces had blown out bridges. The Iraqi divisions sat in place until they were decimated by air power. The Kuwait-to-Baghdad drive showed that a small conventional force moving rapidly can have the same impact and the same firepower as a large force advancing slowly. And the smaller force can gain a quicker victory with fewer troops and fewer casualties by surprising the enemy.

Since the U.S. military will become more and more focused on high technology and precision operations, it is unrealistic for us to take on the additional burden of fielding peacekeeper forces in any strength. Peacekeepers are by nature garrison troops, more policemen than soldiers; they do not need high-intensity combat training or highly sophisticated weapons. We must rely on our allies to keep the peace, after we have established it.[3]

★   ★   ★

AS A CONSEQUENCE of the Cuban missile crisis in 1962, it became clear that no responsible leader would use nuclear weapons, because to do so would ensure that his own country would be destroyed. The lesson applies even today, though with certain troubling exceptions. Most existing nuclear states are ruled by governments that are responsible and that will guard their nuclear stockpiles with all the strength they possess. But problems emerge because rogue states are actively seeking nuclear weapons, and one such state already has them.

Rogue states have already proven their intention to develop nuclear weapons programs. For all the attention paid to Saddam Hussein's lack of weapons of mass destruction, too little attention has been paid to the stark conclusion drawn by the weapons inspectors who went in after the military campaign of 2003: the Iraqi dictator intended to develop nuclear, chemical, and biological weapons after the United Nations removed sanctions and inspectors. Similarly, in 2003 Libya was discovered trying to import critical components for an atomic bomb; caught red-handed, the Libyans were forced to give up their nuclear weapons program.

Another rogue state, Iran, despite its denials, is apparently trying to build an A-bomb of its own. We can and must monitor problematic states and move against any that contemplates acquiring a nuclear weapon. In other words, we can *prevent*—by the threat of overwhelming conventional military force—any other rogue state from threatening the world with nuclear arms. By this same threat we can prevent Iran from continuing its clandestine nuclear program. Using preemptive air strikes, we can destroy all Iranian installations where bomb-making is under way, if necessary. The Iranians don't have the power to retaliate, and air strikes could do the job without our having to invade the country with ground forces.[4]

Still another rogue state endangers the safety of America and the rest of the world: North Korea. Unlike Iran, North Korea already *has* nuclear bombs. Because of that, we cannot threaten North Korea with military action. The reason is simple: its unstable dictator, Kim Jong Il, might launch an atomic strike against South Korea, even though by doing so he would—like Samson bringing down the temple on his own head—guarantee an almost immediate retaliatory strike that would destroy North Korea.

While the possibility that North Korea might use nuclear weapons to attack South Korea must be considered, the even graver threat is that North Korea might *sell* one or more A-bombs to terrorists. The United States has one potent weapon it can use to prevent this from happening. It can inform North Korea that a nuclear strike by any terrorist group *anywhere* would automatically mean that North Korea would be destroyed by a nuclear counterstrike. This was precisely the threat President Kennedy leveled against Nikita Khrushchev during the Cuban missile crisis—that any use of nuclear-armed missiles in America would mean an American nuclear assault against the Soviet Union. This was the threat that brought Khrushchev to heel.

The United States has already attempted, and failed, to curtail North Korea's nuclear weapons program through negotiation. In 1994 Kim Jong Il agreed to a Clinton administration plan to shut down plutonium-production facilities at Yongbyon in exchange for shipments of fuel oil and assistance in building two light water nuclear reactors to generate electric power. By 2002 North Korea had reneged on the deal and was secretly conducting a new nuclear program using a uranium-enrichment system. After President George W. Bush cut off the oil supplies, North Korea, in a fit of pique, expelled International Atomic

Energy Agency (IAEA) inspectors, restarted the Yongbyon reactor, and became the only country to withdraw from the Nuclear Nonproliferation Treaty, which has been signed by 184 states.

In short, Kim Jong Il is an unpredictable leader, and North Korea cannot be trusted. Although the United States cannot resort to a direct military challenge, in the event that we negotiate with the North Koreans to destroy their nuclear weapons and capability, we must be certain to obtain a *verifiable* and *enforceable* agreement. Kim Jong Il's primary interest is in keeping his tenuous hold on power. The United States should therefore offer to provide substantial economic aid that would keep Kim in place as North Korea's leader; in exchange, Kim would have to give up all nuclear, biological, and chemical weapons, as well as missile programs. Making a pact with the devil is unsavory, but providing aid is preferable to other scenarios. We could never say for sure whether a seemingly unstable leader like Kim would accept such an offer, even if he had no alternative. But to make the offer is the only rational choice *we* have.[5]

Keeping nuclear arms out of rogue states also will minimize the chances that a terrorist group will be able to buy a nuclear device or nuclear materials to build a "dirty bomb." The possibility of that occurring exists even now, with nuclear-armed nations like Russia and Pakistan, but the chances would increase significantly if other states obtained nuclear capabilities.

If we are to prevent other dangerous regimes from joining the nuclear club, we must remain vigilant and stop the kind of proliferation that has gone on for years. The discovery of Libya's clandestine attempt to import nuclear weapons components exposed this sort of proliferation. In August of 2003, American spy satellites watched cranes lifting five giant cargo containers full of specialized centrifuge parts into a nondescript cargo vessel in Malaysia. The ship passed through the Strait of Malacca and docked at the United Emirates port of Dubai, where other cranes transferred the parts, relabeled "used machinery," to a German ship, the BBC *China*. The German vessel passed around the Arabian Peninsula, up the Red Sea, and through the Suez Canal. Trackers now were certain the destination was Libya. The order went out: stop the ship. American naval forces seized the *BBC China* and took it to an Italian port.[6]

American and British intelligence agencies had finally put together an extremely complex jigsaw puzzle. They had figured out that the centrifuges were key components provided by the "nuclear bazaar" run since 1987 by Abdul Qadeer Khan, the father of the Pakistani atomic bomb.[7] Later revelations showed that Khan had a $100 million program to provide Libya with nuclear equipment and technology, and his operatives had been meeting with Libyan officials since 1997. And in May 2004 the IAEA reported that North Korea had provided 1.7 metric tons of uranium hexafluoride, a fuel stock, to Libya in 2001.[8]

Seizure of the *BBC China* had momentous consequences. Pakistani leader Pervez Musharraf pulled the plug on Khan's racket and began a frantic effort to convince a doubting world that the Pakistani government had not been a party to Khan's treachery. And Libyan dictator Muammar al-Qaddafi decided that after years of terrorism, he would now set out on a path of virtue. He gave up his efforts to build an atomic bomb and all other weapons of mass destruction. Qaddafi thereby avoided the fate of Saddam Hussein. He feared that if he had not renounced his evil ways, the United States would have invaded Libya, and his own demise would have followed.[9]

The disclosure that Khan's network had been operating for sixteen years was extremely troubling. During this time, Khan provided A-bomb knowledge and equipment to the renegade states of Iran, North Korea, and Libya, and approached Iraq, Syria, and other states with offers to help them build atomic weapons. Algeria, Egypt, and Saudi Arabia especially are under suspicion.[10] For much of this time, U.S. intelligence services were either ignorant of Khan's activities or baffled by what they were seeing.

In the 1970s Khan, a bright young Pakistani metallurgist, was working in the Netherlands for Uranium Enrichment Company, or Urenco, a European consortium that possessed blueprints of the world's best centrifuges. Khan stole these designs, fled back to Pakistan in 1975, and set up a uranium-enrichment project near Islamabad that reported directly to the Pakistani prime minister. Khan drew on Urenco's network of suppliers to get his parts, including 6,200 rotor tubes, the heart of Urenco's uranium-enrichment centrifuges, and a plant for the recovery of tritium, a volatile gas used to increase the power of nuclear bombs. Khan later said that "Europe was crucial for bringing in high-tech machines and components. Dubai was the place for shipments and for payments."

Around 1987, Khan struck a deal with Iran to build an atomic bomb. He provided Tehran with old Pakistani centrifuges and parts, using the vast logistic system available to him as chief of the Pakistani atomic program, including government cargo planes, to ship components to middlemen, who cloaked the source.

The centrifuges on the *BBC China* meant for Libya were twice as fast as the parts Khan had sold to Iran. When British and American investigators went to Libya, they found that Khan's network had also provided blueprints for a nuclear weapon. These investigators were startled to learn how dangerous the black market had become; most troubling, intelligence agencies knew little about who else was buying and selling atomic technology.

But at least the discovery of Khan's nuclear bazaar provided a wake-up call to the peaceful peoples of the world. Here was an official representative of a sovereign state running a racket to supply atomic bombs to renegade regimes. Every responsible government on earth now knows that it must work with other responsible states to prevent this from happening again.

President Bush proposed that the forty nations that sell most nuclear technology refuse to provide equipment to any country not already producing nuclear fuel. A ban would make it more difficult for other renegades to set up nuclear trading networks. At the same time the United States has led in creating the proliferation security initiative (PSI), an affiliation of sixteen countries that is working to intercept unconventional weapons. The capture of the *BBC China* occurred under this program. PSI also has captured equipment on the way to North Korea and has halted North Korean exports of missiles, drugs, and counterfeit dollars that finance the rogue state's nuclear habit.

The task ahead is crystal clear: we must stop the traffic in nuclear technology, and we must locate and destroy all biological, chemical, and nuclear weapons possessed by rogue states. Otherwise, they could sell them to terrorists. As Harvard scholar Michael Ignatieff writes, "Democracies live by free markets, but a free market in everything—enriched uranium, ricin, anthrax—will mean the death of democracy. Armageddon is being privatized, and unless we shut down these markets, doomsday will be for sale."[11]

★   ★   ★

THE DANGER FROM TERRORISM will continue until Islamic fundamentalist cells are destroyed. There is no hope that fundamentalists will turn away from their goal to drive the West and Israel from the Middle East. There is some hope that the secular governments of the region will turn on the terrorists, since these governments are as much an enemy to the fundamentalists as are the West and Israel. But it is idle to expect a great campaign against terrorism to emanate from these secular dictatorships. Mostly they will operate like Saudi Arabia—trying to stop terrorist attacks but refusing to alienate the fundamentalist elements in their societies by declaring open war on them. Likewise it is idle to expect a democratic transformation in the Middle East that will bring peace and tranquility in its wake. Our experience with Iraq and Afghanistan should show us that the road to democracy will be long and hard. The way must be carved out by leaders who themselves have no experience in democracy, compromise, or the rule of law and who will be under tremendous pressure to revert to the traditional authoritarian methods that have ruled in the Middle East for centuries.

This leaves the United States—and the other democratic nations of the world—with a clear mandate: we must root out and destroy terrorist cells, both in the Middle East and elsewhere. That is why we must adapt our intelligence services and our military to the tasks of finding terrorists and going anywhere at any time to destroy any terrorist group that is found.

We can no longer emphasize, as the key to our strategy, creating replicas of Western democracies in the Middle East, with the hope that these new governments will quell terrorism. Given the sobering results in Iraq and in Afghanistan, we probably will not attempt a democratic revolution in another Middle Eastern state. For this reason, we can expect more cooperation from Western Europe than we received in our attack against Iraq. A new awareness of European vulnerability arose on November 2, 2004, when a Muslim extremist murdered Dutch filmmaker Theo van Gogh because of van Gogh's film criticizing Islamic violence against women. Indeed, just over a week later, on November 11, former Dutch foreign minister Jaap de Hoop Scheffer, the new head of NATO, said that Europeans must move closer to the American view of the urgency of the terrorist threat.

But Western Europe is coming to the fight against terrorists and tyrants reluctantly at best. This reluctance deepened after Islamic terrorists killed 191 and injured 1,400 persons in ten bomb attacks on Madrid commuter trains on March 11, 2004. The attacks led three days later to the election of Socialist José Luis Rodríguez Zapatero, who repudiated the partnership with the United States, claimed that Iraq was an "unjust war," withdrew Spain's 1,300 troops from Iraq, and aligned Spain with France and Germany.[12]

The terrorists who attacked Madrid knew exactly what they were doing. Their ultimate target was not Spain but the United States. That is, they wanted to isolate America in the war on terror. They knew that once in office, Zapatero would pull Spain out of Iraq, and that other leftist Europeans would become even less willing to cooperate with the United States in the Iraq effort, for fear of prompting similar attacks. The terrorists clearly saw ending the U.S.-Spanish alliance as a way to drive a wedge between Europe and the United States. Indeed, on April 14, just a month after the Madrid bombings, an audiotape from Osama bin Laden surfaced in which the al Qaeda leader offered a "truce": he would stop terrorist actions in European states if they ended military action in Muslim countries. Fortunately, European foreign ministers rejected bin Laden's offer, but al Qaeda had made its point blatantly.

Zapatero argued that the Iraq takeover had nothing to do with the war on terror. This was foolish. *Terrorists* killed 191 Spaniards. Their objective was obvious: to turn the Spanish government over to a pacifist who would pull Spain's troops out of Iraq. Terrorists comprehend, un-like Zapatero and some leftists, that whether democracy takes a hold in Iraq or not, Iraqis may at least establish a stable, equitable government in the heart of the Arab world. Terrorists want instability and chaos in Iraq in hopes of installing a theocratic tyranny there. That is why they so clearly tried to scare European governments into pulling out of Iraq.

Skeptics of the U.S. efforts in the Middle East say that the difficul-ties encountered in trying to set up democracies in Afghanistan and Iraq—along with Somalia's inability to create even a functioning gov-ernment, much less a democracy—show that equitable societies cannot exist in Muslim lands. George W. Bush believes just the opposite, that democracy *is* possible throughout the Middle East. But even if true democracy fails, we will still be partially successful if we create govern-ments that are merely less oppressive. Such governments are unlikely to harbor terrorists. And eliminating terrorism is our principal goal.[13]

Iraq has of course become a divisive issue. And the divisions—both within the United States and among our natural allies—only compli-cate our efforts to eliminate terrorism. We must concentrate on that goal above all else. To achieve it we have to cooperate with Europe, though in the end the responsibility for ending terrorism will fall pri-marily on American shoulders. We must therefore be willing to go after terrorists wherever they exist. In all likelihood we will have to enter renegade states that don't want us there or failed states, like So-malia, that cannot prevent terrorist cells from locating there. This may inspire qualms and misgivings among some of our Western European allies. But the emphasis in the future will probably be on rooting out terrorists rather than on overthrowing tyrants like Saddam Hussein. Consequently, the grounds for dispute between America and Europe should lessen dramatically in the years ahead.[14]

In addition to Western Europe, we are going to need the United Nations. It can be of great assistance in giving international sanction to restoring failed states and rogue nations *after* peace has been achieved. But we cannot rely on the United Nations to command missions to pacify these countries, or to lead the war against terror. The United Nations is not structured for leadership. Its Security Council can be nullified by a single permanent member's veto, and its General Assembly is only a talking club, not a body where issues can be resolved.

Stated plainly, the task is ours. And we will not shirk our duty.

★   ★   ★

MANY CRITICS OF American foreign policy—both abroad and at home—assert that the United States has overextended itself by unnecessarily intervening in other nations' affairs. Some liberal critics even chastise the United States for becoming an "imperial power." But these criticisms are completely off the mark. Those who worry about America's projection of power are overlooking how America got to the position it occupies at this moment in history: the world's dominant political force and military power, the only nation that will actually go into the world and strike down evil. We were not always in this position—as this book has shown, for the first century and a quarter of our existence, we essentially turned our back on Europe. But it is the position we have been naturally and logically building to throughout our existence.

From the beginning, even when we had no military force to speak of, Americans expanded our holdings on the North American continent at the expense of Europe's colonial powers. Then in 1823, still a new and tiny nation compared to the European powers, the United States boldly proclaimed that the Western Hemisphere was cut off from European colonization and interference; with the Monroe Doctrine, America announced that no world power could challenge us. Later, when Britain could no longer provide the military protection on which we had depended for much of our early history, the United States was obliged to build the largest and most powerful navy in the world, and then an army and air force able to defeat any provocation anywhere on earth. We went out into the world in World War I and again in World War II, methodically destroying the enemies endangering us. We were willing to risk nuclear war when the Soviet Union placed missiles in Cuba in 1962, which jeopardized not only the United States but the safety of the entire hemisphere.

Ultimately, the tasks awaiting the United States do not differ much from the tasks we faced earlier in our history. Today we are doing much the same as we did in World War II: going wherever we have to in the world to destroy the threats to our safety and our freedom. The threats then were tyrants and ruthless, aggressive regimes; today, terrorists and rogue states pose the greatest dangers to our national security. The terrorists struck directly at our homeland, proving definitively that, though we may nourish a nostalgic longing to do so, we can no longer hide behind our oceans, as we did early in our history. We can and must defeat these threats.

Indeed, it is inconceivable that the United States, after having conquered Afghanistan and Iraq and driven al Qaeda into hiding, will give up with the job half done. In Afghanistan we must establish order. In Iraq we must prevent the Shiites from setting up an Iranian-style tyranny, the Sunnis from reimposing a dictatorship, and both from oppressing the Kurds.[15] Beyond Iraq, we must track down and kill terrorists wherever they exist. We must keep Iran from building an atomic bomb. We must force North Korea to give up its nuclear program. We must stop these and any other rogue states from selling weapons of mass destruction to terrorists.

These are black-and-white issues for the vast majority of Americans, notwithstanding complaints from the Far Left. Just as America has gotten it right throughout our history, our government is getting it right today. The leftist critics have got it wrong—because what they are hoping for, peace without a price, will never come to pass on this earth.

NOTES

Note: Single names refer to authors whose volumes are cited in full in the Bibliography; other sources are given in full in the notes.

INTRODUCTION

1. Hamilton favored a strong central government and banking system and believed the country should be governed by a monopoly of the educated and privileged. "The people," he once said, "is a great beast." In his biography of Alexander Hamilton, Ron Chernow writes, "Too often, his political vision harked back to a past in which well-bred elites made decisions for less-educated citizens." See Chernow, 234. Hamilton wanted subsidies and tariffs to protect emerging industries, and he believed that America should look to England as its model—embracing urbanization, modern industries, and rule by a few over the many. His party became the Federalists. Thomas Jefferson believed the opposite. He distrusted strong federal institutions and elite and wealthy leaders, and he believed that the federal government should have limited powers, leaving day-to-day governance to the common people. His party, the Democratic Republicans, represented small farmers and craftsmen. See Kupchan, 168; Hicks, 218.

2. Thomas L. Friedman, "Because We Could," *New York Times,* June 4, 2003.

3. Kagan, 3.

CHAPTER ONE

1. In his book *Colossus* (page 34), Niall Ferguson writes that the United States, like Rome, expanded from a small core to become an inclusive empire because it was relatively promiscuous in conferring citizenship. Throughout

the American advance westward, however, the United States never, with the exception of the Native American tribes, aimed at conquering other peoples, as was the Roman practice for half a millennium. Americans never accepted the idea of holding other peoples in subjection, as the Romans did, and then allowing them, over the process of centuries in some cases, to become Roman. From the outset the United States sought one people, one society, and one government in which all shared equally. The exception of the American Indians was based on a firm American belief that tribal communities could not exist side by side with Western European civilization, of which the United States was a part. When most Indians refused to assimilate into this civilization, Americans either eliminated them or drove them beyond the frontier. As the frontier was closing down, Americans pushed Indians into reservations to keep them separate.

2. David Hackett Fischer in *Albion's Seed* traces four large waves of English-speaking immigrants who became the cornerstones of American society: (1) Puritans from the east of England to Massachusetts from 1629 to 1640; (2) a small Royalist elite and large numbers of indentured servants from the south of England to Virginia from around 1640 to 1675; (3) a movement ("the Quaker migration") from the north Midlands of England and Wales to the Delaware Valley from around 1675 to 1725; and (4) people from Scotland, northern Ireland, and the north of England to the Appalachian back country or frontier beginning before 1700, but concentrated in the period 1718–75. Fischer writes that "the legacy of four British folkways in early America remains the most powerful determinant of a voluntary society in the United States today." See Fischer, 7. A fifth movement of vital importance was that of the Germans. The original migration of Germans, before 1717, consisted mostly of Pietists—especially the Amish and the Mennonites—from the Rhineland and regions nearby, who settled mostly in southeastern Pennsylvania, becoming known as the "Pennsylvania Dutch." After 1717 a broader migration from many parts of Germany commenced, and most of these Germans went to the frontier. Yet these Germans, consisting mainly of farmers, tended to settle down and create permanent communities once they found fertile soil. (As a result, only about 5 percent of the population in North and South Carolina, Georgia, Tennessee, and Kentucky was German in 1790.) See Fischer, 635.

By far the most important settlers in breaking the frontier were those from the fourth group Fischer identifies, the immigrants from Scotland, northern Ireland, and the north of England. The vast majority of these immigrants were from Ulster, and they have gone down in American history as the "Scotch-Irish," although very few were Irish. Their forebears were Scottish Presbyterians who had been recruited to colonize Ulster in the seventeenth century. They had driven out the Irish and created a thriving country based on sheep and woolen cloth manufacture. But as soon as they got successful, the English

Parliament prohibited export of their cloth and ousted their Presbyterian pastors, while the English landlords began charging rents far higher than the land could support. The Scotch-Irish carried with them to America not only a powerful anger against Britain, but also their traditional, ingrained Scottish sense of freedom. In defense of freedom, they were willing to give up everything. The migration became a flood after 1717. The overwhelming bulk of it went through Pennsylvania, southwest through the Cumberland Valley to the Potomac, thence into the Shenandoah Valley of Virginia, and finally into the Piedmont uplands of North and South Carolina. The Scotch-Irish were an extreme distillation of all of the elements that produced the pioneer: They were restless, adventurous, easily aroused to violence, and saw the undeveloped lands to the west as theirs to claim without cost or hindrance. This was why the Scotch-Irish were America's great frontier breakers.

The Scotch-Irish and the Germans settled in separate groups. The Scotch-Irish went to one part of a river valley, the Germans to another. Next year's arrivals advanced beyond and repeated the process. These separate communities can be traced to this day. In Pennsylvania, Maryland, and the Shenandoah Valley of Virginia especially, one county will have a predominance of German names and Lutheran or Reformed churches, while its neighbor will show a large number of Scotch-Irish names and Presbyterian churches. See Leyburn, 190–91, 200–202; A. B. Faust, *The German Element in the United States* (New York: 1927), I, chapters 1–3.

3. Turner, 4.

4. Adam Smith gives a full discourse of this concept in the third part of Chapter 7 in Book IV of *The Wealth of Nations*.

5. While George Washington famously used his farewell address of 1796 to caution the United States against entering into "permanent alliances" with other nations, it was actually Jefferson who used the term "entangling alliances." Washington's address has become the great symbol of America's determination to detach itself from Europe's struggles, for in it the first president declared, "Why, by interweaving our destiny with that of any part of Europe, entangle our peace and prosperity in the toils of European ambition, rivalship, interest, humor or caprice? *It is our true policy to steer clear of permanent alliances with any portion of the foreign world.* . . . Taking care always to keep ourselves by suitable establishments on a respectable defensive posture, we may safely trust to temporary alliances for extraordinary emergencies [emphasis added]." But in his inaugural address of 1801, Thomas Jefferson told his "fellow citizens" he thought it "proper you should understand what I deem the essential principles of our government," among these, "peace, commerce, and honest friendship with all nations, *entangling alliances with none* [emphasis added]."

6. The Articles of Confederation went into effect on March 1, 1781, nearly seven months before the surrender of Lord Cornwallis at Yorktown. They were originally proposed on November 15, 1777.

CHAPTER TWO

1. After the war, Spain laid claim to the southern United States from the Tennessee and Ohio rivers on the north to the Flint River of Georgia on the east. It denied use of the Mississippi except as a privilege granted by Spain. When the United States refused to entertain these claims, the Spanish backed down, permitting traffic on the river and right of shipment at New Orleans upon payment of a moderate duty. The British were even more contentious. They decided to keep the Northwest, treaty or no treaty, refusing to abandon military posts throughout the region, and encouraging the Indians to defy American authority. In 1792 Britain proposed that virtually the entire Northwest be set aside as an "Indian barrier state," where no white man could acquire land. The British also proposed that this barrier be extended along the southern shores of Lake Ontario and the St. Lawrence River, that the frontier around Lake Champlain be "rectified" in Britain's favor, and that the United States cede territory down to present-day Minneapolis, Minnesota, to give Britain access to navigation on the Mississippi. John Jay, sent as an envoy to London, refused all British territorial demands and secured a promise that the British would abandon their posts in the Northwest by June 1, 1796. Britain probably would not have made these concessions except that it was involved in the European wars brought on by the French Revolution of 1789 and didn't want to take on any more opponents.

2. Pratt, 89.

3. Gilbert Chinard, ed., *The Correspondence of Jefferson and DuPont de Nemours* (Baltimore: Johns Hopkins Press, 1931), xxvii–xliv, 48–54.

4. This equity was a mark of the speed at which democracy took hold in the United States—much against the wishes of the propertied elements. They wanted a Constitution to *restrict* freedom, not promote it. All the delegates to the Philadelphia Convention of 1787 were of the conservative upper class. They sought a strong central government to protect their class. The well-to-do were afraid that small farmers, artisans, and other lower elements would secure control of state governments and confiscate their property. Their aim was a government democratic enough to be adopted but not so democratic as to menace upper-class control. The Constitution as adopted in 1789 reflected much of what they desired. It prohibited the states from making any laws (on contracts, credit, payment of debts, and issuance of paper money) hostile to the interests of the propertied classes. Powers were largely handed over to persons once or twice removed from the populace: the president was chosen by electors; judges were chosen by the president; the Senate was chosen by state legislatures (direct elections came only in 1913). The sole directly elected body was the House of Representatives. The Constitution possessed no Bill of Rights. Nevertheless, it contained some radical popular features. It affirmed the doctrine of popular sovereignty. It provided a strictly republican government. These elements quickly led to democratic practices that minimized the

undemocratic aspects of the Constitution. Part of the reason was that, by establishing two entirely separate agencies of government, federal and state, each operating on the same individuals, citizen participation received a powerful boost from the local to the national levels. The people also refused to accept a basic law without a Bill of Rights. A movement to add it commenced at once, and North Carolina postponed ratification until positive steps were under way to create it; the Bill of Rights would be embodied in the first ten amendments to the Constitution. In the election of 1800, the Federalist Party, which represented the commercial and wealthy elite, ended its brief ascendancy, going down in defeat because it refused to recognize the opinions of the masses. Thomas Jefferson's Democratic Republican Party, representing small farmers, artisans, and workers, won. From that point on, democracy ruled in America. See Hicks, 197–212, 255–56.

5. He mentioned only that he was the author of the Declaration of Independence and of the Virginia Statute for Religious Freedom, and father of the University of Virginia. Jefferson's grave is on his estate at Monticello, near Charlottesville, Virginia.

CHAPTER THREE

1. Tocqueville, 267–69.

2. The *Oxford Dictionary of Quotations* (New York: Oxford University Press, 2001), 778. The *Economist* in its November 8, 2003, issue devotes a special section to the United States, "A Nation Apart." The section quotes Thomas Jefferson that the principles of the United States "are perhaps more peculiar than those of any other in the universe." Other thinkers also noted America's unique origins and unusual politics. The section listed some of the present-day differences between the United States and other countries: it is the wealthiest nation; it is the most religious; it is highly decentralized with federal, state, and local governments all collecting their own taxes; it has the most elective offices of any country; it has never had a socialist or a fascist movement of any size; its conservative parties have no aristocratic roots; it has one of the lowest tax rates and the least generous public services of any rich country; it has the highest military spending; it has the highest proportion of young people at universities; and it has the most persistent work ethic. The section records Tocqueville's observations of why America is exceptional—its emphasis on democracy, which changes how people think and act; its great size; the institutions it inherited from England; and its decentralized administration.

3. By 1802 the United States had surmounted the most dangerous attempt in its history to destroy democracy and create an authoritarian society. The attempt came in 1798 when the ruling Federalist Party of President John Adams and Alexander Hamilton—the party of property, commerce, and rule by an elite minority—was unhappy with the immigration of many French, Irish, and English radicals inspired by the theories of liberty and equality spawned by

the French Revolution of 1789. These immigrants drifted to the democratic, freedom-loving Democratic Republican Party of Thomas Jefferson. Many were highly educated men who, as editors or pamphleteers, criticized the Federalists severely. To combat them, the Federalists passed laws extending naturalization from five to fourteen years and authorizing the president to order any alien he regarded as dangerous to leave the country. The Alien Acts were never applied, but they intimidated many pro-Republican immigrants. The Federalists then passed the Sedition Act to prohibit all criticism of Adams's administration, and making it a crime to oppose publicly any act of Congress. Only a few persons were tried, but the laws accomplished much by threat. The laws were a clear violation of the First Amendment to the Constitution, which protects freedom of speech. Since this was before the time (1803) when the Supreme Court took on the task of determining the constitutionality of a law, Jefferson and James Madison put forward their famous Kentucky and Virginia Resolutions, which proposed that the states should decide when Congress had exceeded its powers under the Constitution. The Kentucky Resolution, written secretly by Jefferson, called on other states to join Kentucky in declaring the Alien and Sedition Acts "void and of no force, and in requesting their repeal in the next session of Congress." Jefferson expected no such action by other states. Rather, the resolutions provided him with a platform—the dangers of Federalist rule—to run on for the presidency in 1800. If the Federalists would violate the Constitution in one way, he said, they would soon obliterate the rights of states and individuals. Jefferson won a clear victory. The acts either expired or were repealed between 1800 and 1802. Because of the decisive actions of Jefferson, Madison, and their followers, no American government henceforth dared to pass such totalitarian laws.

4. Turner, 30.

5. This book concentrates primarily on the American expansion westward and on American foreign policy. It therefore does not deal with a domestic issue raised by the eminent Harvard political scientist Samuel P. Huntington in his 2004 book *Who Are We?: The Challenge to America's National Identity.* Huntington maintains that heads of transnational corporations, members of the liberal elite, holders of dual citizenship, cosmopolitans, and Hispanics are eroding national identity. He describes America's core culture as "the Christian religion, Protestant values and moralism, a work ethic, the English language, British traditions of law, justice, and the limits of government power, and a legacy of European art, literature, philosophy, and music." In addition, he lists "the American creed with its principles of liberty, equality, individualism, representative government, and private property." Yet there is little evidence that these core elements are declining in strength. Besides, American culture has always accommodated social and cultural change. American culture is an amalgam of all the elements that have domesticated in America, not just the original ones from Britain. Huntington complains that "over 50 per-

cent of the immigrants coming into the country are Hispanic, from Mexico and elsewhere in Latin America. And about half of the people coming into the country speak a single, non-English language. That is totally unprecedented." Despite Huntington's fears, the likelihood is great that Latinos will assimilate in the tradition of the American melting pot. In California, with the highest proportion of the population (39 percent) speaking other than English at home, the tendency toward English as the primary language is great — not only because becoming American is easier and more profitable than remaining Spanish-speaking, but also because California referendum Proposition 227 in 1998 got rid of bilingual education in the public schools. Statistics show that by the third generation, two-thirds of Latinos in California speak only English. See Deborah Solomon, "Three Cheers for Assimilation," *New York Times Magazine,* May 2, 2004; "A Survey of California," *Economist,* May 1, 2004, 12; Louis Menand, "Patriot Games," *New Yorker,* May 17, 2004, 92–98.

6. Robert U. Johnson and C. C. Buel, eds., *Battles and Leaders of the Civil War,* 4 vols. (New York: Century Magazine, 1887–88), reprint, Secaucus, N.J., no date, vol. 4, 745.

7. Much of a Southern planter's capital was tied up in the ownership of labor, whereas a Northern industrialist, when business fell off, discharged excess workers and took no responsibility for them. Likewise the Southern planter had much more capital invested in land than a factory owner did. Land values could rarely be transformed into ready money in time of need. Also, large plantation owners bid up the prices of good cotton land, thereby requiring even more capital to be tied up in a comparatively unproductive economic factor. Finally, factory workers tended machines, which produced far more goods per person than did slaves, who performed nearly all cotton, rice, and sugarcane cultivation by hand. Only the deceptive profits of a few large planters disguised the economic fallacy behind slavery.

8. A major influence in extending democracy throughout the country was the growth of popular sovereignty, epitomized by Andrew Jackson, president from 1829 to 1837. Jackson struck a deep reservoir in the American population that was committed to preserving the liberties of ordinary citizens and profoundly suspicious of elites. These civil libertarians not only insisted on universal manhood suffrage in the western states, but they also pressured the legislatures of eastern states to remove high property qualifications for voting. Virginia and North Carolina were the last to yield, waiting until the 1850s before giving up a requirement that only landowners could vote. Democracy also took hold in selecting members of the electoral college that chooses the president and vice president. The Constitution left to the states how to designate electors. Most states at first allowed the legislatures to select them. By 1828, however, only two states, Delaware and South Carolina, retained this method, the rest choosing by popular vote. A few states chose electors by districts. But this was awkward, and, by splitting the state's vote, it reduced the state's

importance. Ultimately all states adhered to the choosing of electors on a statewide ticket.

9. Mead, 218–35. He cites Fanny Trollope, *Domestic Manners of the Americans* (London: Penguin Books, 1997), 95–96.

10. Tocqueville, 483–89.

CHAPTER FIVE

1. Tocqueville, 392–94.

2. Nicholas P. Trist paid for his insubordination. He lost his job, and Polk would not give him salary and expenses after November 16, 1847, when he received his letter of recall. Twenty years later a more impartial administration awarded him compensation for his services and expenses in negotiating the treaty.

CHAPTER SIX

1. Claudia Goldin and Frank Lewis, "The Post-bellum Recovery of the South and the Cost of the Civil War: Comment," *Journal of Economic History* 38, no. 2 (June 1978): 487–92.

2. Lincoln opposed any agreement of any kind regarding slavery, even a strategic move to avoid war and give time for a compromise to be worked out. When Crittenden's proposal was being circulated, Lincoln wrote a colleague, "Have none of it. Stand firm." See Eliot A. Cohen, *Supreme Command* (New York: Free Press, 2002), 30.

3. In his first inaugural address, Lincoln declared: "[N]o State upon its own mere motion can lawfully get out of the Union; . . . *resolves* and *ordinances* to that effect are legally void, and . . . acts of violence within any State or States against the authority of the United States are insurrectionary or revolutionary, according to circumstances. I therefore consider that in view of the Constitution and the laws the Union is unbroken, and to the extent of my ability, I shall take care, as the Constitution itself expressly enjoins upon me, that the laws of the Union be faithfully executed in all the States. Doing this I deem to be only a simple duty on my part, and I shall perform it so far as practicable unless my rightful masters, the American people, shall withhold the requisite means or in some authoritative manner direct the contrary. I trust this will not be regarded as a menace, but only as the declared purpose of the Union that it will constitutionally defend and maintain itself. . . . Plainly the central idea of secession is the essence of anarchy. . . . Physically speaking, we can not separate. We can not remove our respective sections from each other nor build an impassable wall between them. . . . In *your* hands, my dissatisfied fellow-countrymen, and not in *mine,* is the momentous issue of civil war. The Government will not assail *you.* You can have no conflict without being yourselves the aggressors. *You* have no oath registered in heaven to destroy the Government, while I shall have the most solemn one to 'preserve, protect, and defend

it.'" Abraham Lincoln, First Inaugural Address, March 4, 1861 (available at www.bartleby.com/124/pres31.html).

4. David Halberstam wrote that "racism remains the darkest stain on us." He added that "America was the only one of the developed nations that . . . experienced its colonial era on native soil. When the age of empire was finally over in the middle of the twentieth century, all the other colonial powers could pull back, announce they were out of business of empire, and cut, as it were, the umbilical cord that bound colony to mother country. In America that, of course, was impossible, and the implications of it are overwhelming to this day: it means our evolution in the postcolonial era into one America is nothing less than the ultimate test of us as a democracy." See David Halberstam, ed., *Defining a Nation* (Washington, D.C.: National Geographic, 2003), 20.

5. This was especially so because the North's railroad and telegraph system was far more extensive than the South's (10,048 miles versus 20,578 miles). During the war the North actually increased its rail and telegraph systems tremendously, while the South, lacking industries, was unable to sustain and repair its rail and telegraph lines. This fatally weakened the South's ability to move armies quickly to meet crises.

6. Bevin Alexander, *Robert E. Lee's Civil War* (Holbrook, Mass.: Adams Media, 1998), 171n.

7. The French, at least, seemed to recognize the Americans' newfound military might well before the twentieth century began. In December 1861 Napoleon III of France engineered a joint intervention by France, Britain, and Spain against Mexico, using the excuse of Mexico's failure to pay foreign debts. Britain and Spain quickly withdrew when it became clear that Napoleon III was intent on setting up a French-dominated monarchy under the Archduke Maximilian, brother of Emperor Francis Joseph of Austria. Popular support for Maximilian was nonexistent, and ousted Mexican president Benito Juarez led a guerrilla war that kept French forces confined to Mexico City. The United States was unable to act until the Civil War ended, but when it did, U.S. Army generals were eager to drive the French army out of Mexico by force. Secretary of State William H. Seward, sure that France would withdraw merely with the *threat* of war, informed Napoleon III in November 1865 that French intervention could not be allowed. France got the message and withdrew all its troops by spring 1867. Maximilian, now abandoned, was captured by forces of Juarez and shot. European nations recognized that the United States would evict their forces if they attempted such an adventure anywhere in Latin America, and none ever tried it again. In American eyes, the Mexican experience elevated the Monroe Doctrine into a national principle.

8. The first measure to break up monopolies, the Sherman Antitrust Act of 1890, failed because the courts refused to uphold it. Around the turn of the twentieth century, however, a group of energetic journalists — "muckrakers" — detailed the abuses of business. One of them, Lincoln Steffens, writing for

McClure's magazine, exposed corrupt alliances between business and politics in nearly every American metropolis. President Theodore Roosevelt saw an opportunity and attacked the Northern Securities Company, which in 1901, by means of a holding company, took control of three competing northwestern railroads, the Great Northern, the Northern Pacific, and the Chicago, Burlington, and Quincy. In 1904 the Supreme Court reversed earlier decisions and held that Northern Securities violated free competition and must be dissolved. Roosevelt scored a few more victories, but the solution was the better regulation of business rather than the disassembling of large business enterprises. The first effective move in this direction was the Hepburn Act of 1906, which gave the Interstate Commerce Commission the authority to set rates for railroads, express companies, and pipelines. The same year a federal law required the inspection of meats, and the Pure Food and Drug Act placed some restrictions on prepared foods and patent medicines. An advance for labor came out of a strike by anthracite coal miners in eastern Pennsylvania in 1902. As coal became scarce and cities like New York began to suffer from cold, a letter from a mine operator, George F. Baer, surfaced: "The rights and interests of the laboring man will be protected and cared for—not by the labor agitators, but by the Christian men to whom God in His infinite wisdom has given the control of the property interests of the country." Roosevelt, incensed at such arrogance, worked out a deal for the governor of Pennsylvania to request federal troops to keep order. An army general then would dispossess the owners and run the mines. This threat brought the owners to heel and produced better conditions for the miners.

9. Kennedy, 149, 202, 242–43; O'Brien and Clesse (Angus Maddison essay), 183–91. More growth would come in the twentieth century as a result of another acquisition the United States made in the nineteenth. In 1867 the United States bought Alaska from Russia for $7,200,000. At the time, most Americans saw little use for the remote region, thinking it largely barren and ice-covered. Only later did they learn that Alaska contained vast resources in minerals, forests, and oil.

10. Turner, 1.

CHAPTER SEVEN

1. Darwin published *The Origin of Species* in 1859 and *The Descent of Man* twelve years later. The leading Social Darwinist was British philosopher Herbert Spencer (1820–1903).

2. The United States had already acquired two other stepping-stones to the Philippines: Wake Island, 2,130 miles west of Hawaii, and Midway Island, about a thousand miles northwest of Hawaii. Unpopulated Wake had been claimed by an American explorer, Commander Charles Wilkes, in 1841, and the United States took possession of tiny Midway in 1867. The United States also acquired Tutuila in the Samoan Islands, northeast of New Zealand.

It had possessed rights to a coaling station at Pago Pago harbor there since 1878.

3. Japan seized these German islands in the early stages of World War I and kept them after the war. Some of them became famous in the campaigns of World War II: Kwajalein and Eniwetok in the Marshalls, Truk in the Carolines, and Saipan and Tinian in the Marianas.

4. Britain abetted Japan in this endeavor. Since Russia was Britain's chief rival in Persia (Iran) and Afghanistan, Britain drew toward Russia's chief rival in the Far East. In 1902 Britain and Japan signed an alliance declaring that each would remain neutral if the other became involved in war with a third power, and that each would come to the support of the other if it were attacked by two or more enemies. This treaty gave Japan a free hand against Russia. The Anglo-Japanese alliance was renewed in 1905 and again for a ten-year period in 1911.

CHAPTER EIGHT

1. Fromkin, 153–67, 203.

2. *The Economist,* January 10, 2004, 73, citing Robert K. Massie, *Castles of Steel: Britain, Germany, and the Winning of the Great War at Sea* (New York: Random House; London, Jonathan Cape, 2003). In 1914 Berlin stockyards were slaughtering 25,000 pigs a week; by September 1916, only 350 a week.

3. Tuchman, 122.

4. Howard, 86.

5. Kennedy, 202, 280.

6. These, presented before Congress in January 1918, were (1) open covenants openly arrived at; (2) freedom of navigation on the seas in peace and war; (3) equality of trade among all nations; (4) reduction of national armaments; (5) adjustment of colonial claims in the interests of the people concerned; (6) evacuation of all Russian territory; (7) evacuation of Belgium; (8) restoration of French-occupied territory and return of Alsace-Lorraine; (9) additions to Italy of Italian-speaking peoples; (10) autonomy for the peoples of Austria-Hungary; (11) evacuation of Romania, Serbia, and Montenegro and access to the sea for Serbia; (12) Turks in the Ottoman Empire assured of sovereignty, but other peoples given autonomy; (13) an independent Poland with secure access to the sea; (14) and "a general association of nations for mutual guarantees of political independence and territorial integrity."

7. Allen, 22.

8. The Treaty of Saint-Germain, signed September 10, 1919, left Austria only a small rump state, which was prohibited from joining Germany. The Treaty of Trianon, signed on November 27, 1919, cut down the Magyar state to an irreducible minimum, leaving many Hungarians under different flags. New states appeared: Finland, Estonia, Latvia, Lithuania, Poland, Czechoslovakia, Yugoslavia (including Serbia, Montenegro, Bosnia-Herzegovina, Slovenia,

and Croatia), and Albania. Romania gained Transylvania from Hungary and Bessarabia (present-day Moldova) from Russia.

9. Pratt, 504–5.

10. Article 10 reads as follows: "The members of the league undertake to respect and preserve as against external aggression the territorial integrity and existing political independence of all members of the league. In case of any such aggression or in case of any threat or danger of such aggression, the council shall advise upon the means by which this obligation shall be fulfilled."

11. Mead, 51–52.

12. On the advice of American leaders, Wilson added to the covenant a declaration safeguarding "regional understandings like the Monroe Doctrine." Opponents felt this was not a sufficient guarantee, while the Japanese saw in it the authority to dominate Manchuria and China. After all, they said, didn't they have "regional understandings" in those lands? Later, opponents in the Senate proposed an amendment asserting that only the United States could interpret the Monroe Doctrine and that it was "wholly outside the jurisdiction" of the League.

13. Allen, 25.

14. Ibid., 24.

CHAPTER NINE

1. The German ships were later moved to Scapa Flow in the Orkney Islands, north of Scotland.

2. At first Lloyd George demanded that the United States give up its naval building program in exchange for the declaration Wilson added to the covenant safeguarding "regional understandings like the Monroe Doctrine." Ultimately he accepted Wilson's promise not to pursue the buildup.

3. Battleships in the post–World War I era were the main striking force for the world's navies. They developed from the British navy's *Dreadnought* of 1906. Battleships possessed central batteries of large guns (14- to 16-inch caliber) that could severely damage or destroy even well-armored warships at long ranges of a dozen or more miles. Heavy armor was mounted to protect battleships from gunfire and a newly emerging threat, bomber aircraft. Naval architects also were developing methods of armoring battleships under the waterline against mines and torpedoes fired by submarines, fast surface craft, or airplanes. Battleships became much faster with the use of turbine engines fired by oil, more efficient than coal. The U.S. Navy's *New York* and *Texas* (27,000 tons each), commissioned in 1914, mounted 14-inch guns. The Royal Navy's *Queen Elizabeth* class (27,500 tons), put into service 1915–16, mounted 15-inch guns and reached speeds of 25 knots. Battleships under construction at the end of the war were designed for 16-inch guns. Battle cruisers were capital ships with battleship-sized guns. They were originally able to move several

knots faster than battleships because they carried less armor. But improvements in battleship design and engines had virtually eliminated battle cruisers' speed advantage by the end of World War I. Battle cruisers' major purpose was to run down and destroy hostile armored cruisers. Cruisers were fast warships, usually displacing fewer than 10,000 tons, and carrying 6- and 8-inch guns. They were designed principally for commerce protection and raiding. The cruiser was dangerous because it could destroy any vessel except a battleship and could outrun a battleship. Hence, the battle cruiser to run after and catch it.

4. Hirsh, 82.

5. A. Whitney Griswold, *The Far Eastern Policy of the United States* (New York: Harcourt, Brace, 1938), 311.

6. Hugh Borton, *Japan's Modern Century* (New York: Ronald Press, 1955), 298.

CHAPTER TEN

1. Joel, 2:25; Churchill, *Gathering Storm,* 66.

2. Leuchtenburg, 6, 41.

3. Hicks et al., 489.

4. Allen, 27.

5. Leuchtenburg, 143–44, 154–56.

6. Ibid., 178–202.

7. Ibid., 111.

8. Kennedy, 282–83, 327–28.

9. By the summer of 1932 industrial production in many countries was only half that of 1928. Causes of the Depression included overexpansion of agriculture, leading to crop surpluses and lower prices; overexpansion of industry, leading to too much production; increasing use of labor-saving machines, which allowed fewer workers to produce more goods; the practice of many businesses of keeping profits and reinvesting them in more production instead of paying them out in higher wages; overuse of credit (especially the new "installment plan") by both business and consumers, due to low interest rates, leading to much speculation in stocks; an extraordinarily large number of independent banks, with few reserves, leading to a run on banks in a given region in the event of a crop failure or other local loss; dependence of European nations on loans from American investors to pay for imports, and the inability of these nations to repay by shipping goods into the United States because of high tariffs. See Hicks et al., *American Nation,* 543–45. While the United States possessed 43.3 percent of the world's manufacturing output in 1929, it had only 28.7 percent in 1938. Immense portions of the nation's industrial plant lay idle. See Kennedy, 330. Contributing greatly to the disintegration of world trade was Britain's decision to go off the gold standard in September 1931. The pound's value fell by 30 percent, shattering the global financial system.

Japan then left the gold standard later in 1931, and the United States followed suit in 1933. This left the international economy without any guiding hand. See Kupchan, 80–81.

10. Frank B. Kellogg was U.S. secretary of state from 1925 to 1929. Aristide Briand was the French premier at the time.

11. Pratt, 539.

12. The chairman was Earl Victor Alexander George Robert Bulwer-Lytton of Britain, son of the viceroy of India and himself a former governor of Bengal. Other members were from France, Germany, Italy, and the United States.

13. Churchill, *Gathering Storm,* 52–53.

14. Pratt, 597.

15. Mead, 316.

16. The other base sites were Bermuda, the Bahamas, Jamaica, Antigua, St. Lucia, and Trinidad.

17. Kennedy, 325–33.

CHAPTER ELEVEN

1. Klaus Fuchs, a German-born naturalized Briton, worked in Britain on nuclear research, then went to the United States in mid-1944 to work on the atomic bomb. When arrested after the war in England, he admitted passing information to the Soviet Union since 1943. He drew a fourteen-year prison term but was released in 1959 and went to East Germany. Julius and Ethel Rosenberg were executed in 1953 in the United States after being convicted of passing atomic secrets to the Russians; those secrets were secured by Ethel's brother, Sergeant David Greenglass, who was assigned to the atomic-bomb project at Los Alamos, New Mexico. See *Encyclopedia Britannica,* 15th edition, vol. iv, 341; vol. viii, 674; Halberstam, 40–47.

2. In a meeting with Stalin in Moscow in October 1944, Churchill believed Stalin's intent was mainly to restore order and prevent civil war in the countries under his influence. He said trustingly to the Soviet leader, "We are very glad that you have declared yourselves against trying to change by force or by Communist propaganda the established systems in the various Balkan countries." See Churchill, *Triumph and Tragedy,* 227, 232.

3. Ibid., 639.

CHAPTER TWELVE

1. Horowitz and Carroll, 294.

2. Mead, 39, citing Ralph Waldo Emerson, "Essay VII: Politics" in *Essays* (New York: Thomas Y. Crowell Company, 1926), 412.

3. Mead, 85. Mead perceives four "schools," or approaches, to foreign policy that are deeply rooted in American society. He says U.S. policies generally are a compromise of one or more of them. The schools are (1) Hamiltonian (after

Alexander Hamilton), aimed at promoting American economic enterprise at home and abroad by means of an alliance between government and big business; (2) Wilsonian (after Woodrow Wilson), which has a vision of a universal moral order on earth and believes we have the duty to change the world's behavior and spread American values, including the rule of law, through the world; (3) Jeffersonian (after Thomas Jefferson), which holds that the United States should be less concerned about spreading democracy abroad than safeguarding it at home and is skeptical of unsavory allies abroad and seeks to avoid war; and (4) Jacksonian (after Andrew Jackson), which holds that the security and economic well-being of Americans is the most important goal of government, seeks to avoid war but win those we're forced to fight, and represents the American populist and popular culture of honor, independence, courage, and military pride. Mead holds that Jacksonians are instinctively democratic and populist. Hamiltonians mistrust democracy. Wilsonians don't approve of the political rough-and-tumble. Jeffersonians support democracy in principle but fear that tyrannical majorities can overrule minority rights. Mead summarizes: "The representative nature of American political society means that there is at least a rough equivalence between the political strength of the given schools and their weight in the nation." See ibid., xvii, 88–95, 138, 238.

4. Halberstam, 262.

5. The decision to create this world required the United States to abandon the protection of its industries from foreign competition. High tariffs in the nineteenth century kept lower-priced foreign, mostly British, manufactured goods out of the American market and permitted the creation of a huge American industrial plant to satisfy the domestic market. The high Smoot-Hawley Tariff of 1930 likewise protected American industry, but retaliation by other countries shattered our export trade and added greatly to the depth of the 1930s Depression. In 1945, however, American industry no longer needed protection. Rather, other countries needed to run trade surpluses with the United States to acquire dollars to pay for food and reconstruction.

6. At the end of World War II, British troops occupied French Indochina south of the sixteenth parallel and the Nationalist Chinese that part north of the line. The Nationalists, angry at French collaboration with the Japanese during the war, allowed Ho Chi Minh, leader of the small Communist Party, and other Vietnamese nationalists, to create the Democratic Republic of Vietnam on September 2, 1945. Although a Communist, Ho Chi Minh was concerned first with Vietnamese nationalism. To hasten Chinese evacuation, France on February 28, 1946, agreed to give up its extraterritorial rights within China. The British and Americans had relinquished similar rights during World War II. On December 19, 1946, the French formally disbanded the new republic's militia (the Vietminh or Vietnamese Independence League) in Hanoi. This set off war. Although the French were successful in controlling the cities, the Vietminh resorted to guerrilla warfare and controlled most of the countryside. In

1949 Ho Chi Minh accepted support from China and Russia, leading the United States to increase aid to France. In 1947 the "falling dominos" theory had surfaced in connection with the Truman Doctrine and containment. Secretary of State Marshall said then that if Greece fell to the Communists, Turkey might follow, and "Soviet domination might thus extend over the entire Middle East and Asia." In 1951 the domino theory was applied to Southeast Asia. A State Department official said, "If Indochina went, the fall of Burma and the fall of Thailand would be absolutely inevitable." These would be followed by Communist victories in Malaysia and India.

7. In the late nineteenth century, an organized movement known as Zionism arose in Europe with the aim of reconstituting a Jewish state in Palestine. In November 1917, seeking the support of Jews in the United States in financing its war against Germany, Britain issued a statement through the foreign secretary, Arthur James Balfour. This "Balfour Declaration" proposed two mutually exclusive goals: "His Majesty's government views with favor the establishment in Palestine of a national home for the Jewish people, it being clearly understood that nothing shall be done which may prejudice the civil and religious rights of existing non-Jewish communities." Arabs violently opposed the immigration of Jews, but a limited number settled in Palestine under British protection. This small migration increased greatly after Adolf Hitler took over Germany in 1933. The Jewish population rose from 84,000 in 1922 to 445,000 in 1939 (30 percent of the population). The British adopted a policy in 1939 to limit Jewish immigration, and only a few European Jews found circuitous ways to escape to Palestine during World War II. In May 1942 a Zionist conference at the Biltmore Hotel in New York City called for unrestricted Jewish immigration into Palestine and the establishment of a Jewish commonwealth. By the end of the war Zionist political activity had won U.S. government support, and the Truman administration put pressure on Britain. Thus, the success of the Zionist effort rested to a considerable degree on the backing of the United States. The great upheaval that followed displaced many Arabs, creating a tremendous and enduring problem because the neighboring Arab states refused to absorb the refugees into their populations. The Greeks and Turks handled in a far wiser manner a somewhat parallel upheaval of populations after Turkey rebuffed a Greek attempt to annex much of western Turkey following World War I. To reduce further conflicts, the Turks and Greeks agreed to a compulsory exchange of populations in 1923—1,300,000 Greeks in Turkey were moved into Greece, and 400,000 Turks in Greece were moved into Turkey. In like manner, the expulsion of 12 million Germans from Eastern Germany, Czechoslovakia, and Hungary after World War II caused much pain and resentment, but the displaced Germans were absorbed in the overall German population and the issue was solved.

8. Even today no Arab country except Jordan allows Palestinians to become citizens, hold passports, own land, or send their children to local schools.

Lebanon forbids most Palestinians to enter seventy-two professions, including law and medicine, and denies them access to the public health system. In 1991 Kuwait expelled 300,000 Palestinians for collaborating with the Iraqi invasion. See Frum and Perle, 184.

9. Kennan explained the new program in an article he wrote anonymously in *Foreign Affairs* magazine in July 1947.

10. Henry A. Wallace, Roosevelt's liberal third-term vice president and Truman's secretary of commerce, made a speech in Madison Square Garden, New York, in September 1946 in which he said the United States had "no more business in the political affairs of eastern Europe than Russia had in the political affairs of Latin America." Truman fired Wallace. When the president announced aid to Greece and Turkey, both of which had authoritarian governments, Wallace said "there is no regime too reactionary" to receive U.S. aid, "provided it stands in Russia's expansionist path." Wallace put his finger on a dilemma the United States was to face on a number of occasions in the decades ahead: whether to back repressive non-Communist governments in order to block Soviet aggression. Although leaders knew full well that morally the United States should spurn such governments, to do so politically would lead into a minefield. In most cases the United States decided that the threat of Communism, which, if not stopped, could result in worldwide repression, was a greater danger than a government that repressed only its own people. Because of a sense of overriding danger from Communism, American leaders sometimes did not examine sufficiently the governments they were supporting, and thus they suffered greatly in world opinion.

11. The NSC's membership includes the president, vice president, and secretaries of state and defense. The CIA replaced the Office of Strategic Services (OSS), which had operated during World War II.

12. The Soviets exploded their first A-bomb in late August 1949. Thereafter it was becoming clear that reliance on the A-bomb was insufficient to stop the Soviet advance—since local wars and insurrections might be started that would not merit an atomic attack. The National Security Council produced a new plan, NSC-68, developed by Paul Nitze, that called for the United States to be prepared to halt Communist expansion of any type throughout the world. It made no distinction between the Soviets, the Chinese Communists, the Communists in Vietnam, or third world Communist movements. All had to be kept from advancing. NSC-68 held that the Soviets and Chinese were working together "to eliminate all Western influence from the Asiatic mainland." It adopted the falling-domino theory for Southeast Asia, holding that "loss of any one of the countries to the enemy would almost certainly result in the loss of all the other countries." In addition to the development of hydrogen bombs, NSC-68 advocated the expansion of conventional military forces. Although the plan was implemented, little progress had been made before the Korean War broke out. This commenced an immediate buildup of

conventional forces along with nuclear weapons. See Kupchan, 38–41; Ferguson, *Colossus,* 77–78.

13. At the Bretton Woods Conference in New Hampshire in July 1944, the International Monetary Fund and the World Bank had been created. These were designed to stabilize international currency and trade for economic expansion and included a system of exchange rates of currencies. The Roosevelt administration sought to build a new economic order that would dissolve prewar blocs and assure growth. It imposed a global system of regulated open markets, with all currencies at fixed rates to the dollar. The United States pledged to redeem American paper dollars in gold at a fixed price of thirty-five dollars an ounce. This made the dollar the world's reserve currency, because it could always be exchanged for gold. As Walter Russell Mead writes, "The U.S. Federal Reserve System was the de facto central bank for all the market economies; the United States could effectively control the monetary policies of all its allies, and it generally did so in the interest of the domestic American economy." See Mead, 73.

14. Integration began first in 1951 with the European Coal and Steel Community (France, West Germany, Benelux), followed by the European Economic Community in 1957 (including Italy), a move that eliminated internal tariffs and set up a common external tariff. Other countries joined, and the European Economic Community graduated to the European Union in 1993. This brought in a common currency, the euro, in January 2002, adopted by twelve of the EU states.

15. The B-29 was eventually superseded by the B-36, a propeller-driven aircraft with six engines, a range of 7,500 miles, and a top speed of 430 miles per hour. In 1951 the jet-engine B-47 came on line, with a speed of 600 miles an hour and a range of 6,000 miles (if refueled by the new KC-97 tanker); it could reach an altitude of 45,000 feet. The Air Force's Strategic Air Command (SAC) chose these bombers to deliver nuclear bombs before intercontinental ballistic missiles (ICBMs) were developed in the late 1950s and early 1960s.

16. Despite unanimous objections by scientists and civilians on the Atomic Energy Commission's advisory council, the commission's chief, Lewis Strauss, backed by physicist Edward Teller, urged the development of the hydrogen bomb, with a force thousands of times greater than the atomic bomb. In January 1950 Truman ordered work on the H-bomb to proceed. By the fall of 1952 the United States had successfully tested this new weapon, and less than a year later, on August 12, 1953, the Soviet Union did the same.

17. The American fear of Communism dramatically affected domestic affairs, not just foreign policy. The nation's attention was riveted when Alger Hiss, a former State Department official, was accused of being a Communist spy. In January 1950 Hiss was convicted of perjury for denying that he had passed classified documents in the 1930s to a former Communist, Whittaker

Chambers. A month later, Senator Joseph McCarthy of Wisconsin launched a long campaign against Communist infiltration of the government when he claimed he had "a list of 205 [government employees] that were made known to the secretary of state as being members of the Communist party" but were still working in the State Department. McCarthy later changed the numbers of alleged party members. Although a Senate investigation in 1950 concluded that McCarthy's allegations were "a fraud and a hoax," McCarthy set off a witch hunt for Communists that continued until 1954. David Halberstam writes, "McCarthyism crystallized and politicized the anxieties of a nation living in a dangerous new era. He took people who were at worst guilty of naiveté and accused them of treason." Halberstam quotes George Reedy, a United Press reporter, regarding McCarthy: "Joe couldn't find a Communist in Red Square — he didn't know Karl Marx from Groucho." Beginning in March 1954 the three major networks—at the insistence of Senate Minority Leader Lyndon B. Johnson—televised the Army-McCarthy hearings. Viewers witnessed McCarthy attacking colleagues, threatening witnesses, and ignoring legal procedures. His favorable ratings fell to 34 percent. When McCarthy amended his denunciation of "twenty years of treason" to "twenty-*one* years," thereby implicating President Eisenhower in a cover-up of Communism, he finally went too far. In July 1954 the Senate voted 67–22 to censure McCarthy for tending "to bring the Senate into dishonor and disrepute." With that McCarthy lost his power. An alcoholic, he died in 1957. See Horowitz and Carroll, 375–76; Halberstam, 52, 55.

18. The story of American involvement in China is told in Alexander, *Strange Connection*. The Communist victory in China, plus the news that the Russians had exploded the A-bomb, accelerated a fear within the United States of Communist subversion.

19. On August 5, 1949, the State Department issued a white paper stating that the Nationalists had allowed much U.S. military equipment to fall into the hands of the Communists and that even more aid would not have saved Chiang Kai-shek's regime. "The unfortunate but inescapable fact is that the ominous result of the civil war in China was beyond the control of the government of the United States. Nothing that this country did or could have done within the reasonable limit of its capabilities could have changed that result. It was a product of internal Chinese forces which this country tried to influence but could not." See Foster Rhea Dulles, *American Policy toward Communist China, 1949–1969* (New York: Thomas Y. Crowell, 1972), 42–44.

20. This defensive line was not new. In 1949 a National Security Council study outlined the identical line, and nearly a year before Acheson spoke, General Douglas MacArthur had laid out the same line in an interview with a British journalist.

21. Because the Russians at the moment were boycotting the U.N. Security Council, the United States was able to get U.N. approval for the war in Korea,

and to have General MacArthur designated as U.N. commander. By far the majority of forces used in the war, however, came from the United States and South Korea.

22. Soviet pilots did take part in aerial dogfights along the Yalu River in the later stages of the war. The purpose was not to affect the outcome of the war, however; it was to train Soviet pilots in jet fighter tactics.

23. This implies that the Chinese were not trying to stop the reunion of the Korean Peninsula, since the North Korean army had virtually ceased to exist and the South Korean army could have conquered North Korea with relative ease. Beijing's aim was to prevent *American* forces on the Yalu River.

24. Alexander, *Korea,* 452–53, 471–82.

25. See Ferguson, *Colossus,* 93; Henry Kissinger, "Reflections on American Diplomacy," *Foreign Affairs,* October 1956, 37–57.

CHAPTER THIRTEEN

1. Some persons claimed that Red China's occupation of Tibet in 1950 was evidence of aggression. But Tibet had been a historical part of China for centuries and was detached by the British after the ouster of the last Chinese emperor in 1912 when China was unable to respond. It remained a British protectorate until India got independence in 1947. India stepped into Britain's shoes as de facto sovereign and sought to foster Tibetan independence as a cover for Indian influence. The Chinese Reds ignored New Delhi's efforts and occupied eastern Tibet in October 1950. In May 1951 Beijing signed a treaty with Tibet granting it political, economic, and religious privileges. But the Reds feared the United States might be trying to arouse support for an independent Tibetan regime. In September 1951 Chinese troops occupied Lhasa, the capital, and largely disregarded the May 1951 agreement.

2. The ironic proof that the domino theory was hopelessly wrong emerged when Vietnam was at last reunited in April 1975. The Vietnamese quickly fell out with China, which was a historic enemy and nearby, but kept ties with the Soviet Union, which was nonthreatening and distant. Vietnam expelled Chinese merchants and opened Cam Ranh Bay to the Soviet navy. When Vietnamese troops invaded Cambodia to oust the Khmer Rouge, China decided to "punish" the Vietnamese. Chinese forces invaded in February 1979 but got nowhere and withdrew after three weeks.

3. Although there was a lot of talk about the military importance of the offshore islands, the claims never had any validity. For a 1961 analysis showing their unimportance, see the John F. Kennedy Presidential Library, Boston, NSF file, Box 21–23, Memorandum of Mr. McGeorge Bundy, the White House, "The Offshore Islands—Alternative Courses and Probable Consequences," August 25, 1961.

4. For the full story of the crises over Quemoy and Matsu, see Alexander, *Strange Connection,* 147–63, 174–77.

5. The Civil Rights Act of 1964 gave the federal government the power to sue to desegregate public accommodations and schools, prohibited the denial of equal job opportunities in all but the smallest businesses, and created the Equal Employment Opportunity Commission (EEOC) to sue for compliance. The Voting Rights Act of 1965 abolished voter literacy tests and empowered the U.S. attorney general to assign federal examiners to register voters in states practicing discrimination.

6. Peters, 10.

7. Horowitz and Carroll, 366.

8. The United States took in most of the 150,000 Hungarians who fled to Austria during the revolt.

9. On July 1, 1968, the United States, Britain, the Soviet Union, and fifty-nine other countries signed the Nuclear Nonproliferation Treaty, in which signatories agreed not to assist states that didn't possess nuclear explosives in obtaining them. In 1992 France and China signed, and in 1995 the treaty was extended indefinitely by a vote of 174 nations in the United Nations.

10. Gordon H. Chang, "JFK, China, and the Bomb," *The Journal of American History,* 74, no. 4 (March 1988): 1287–1310.

11. As early as the summer of 1949, before the establishment of the People's Republic of China in October 1949, the Communist leadership solicited a visit by the American ambassador to China, John Leighton Stuart, to seek a settlement with the United States. It took place before the Chinese Reds opened negotiations with Moscow and showed they were hunting for an alternative to embracing the Russian bear. President Truman, however, spurned the Red Chinese advance.

12. Charges implicating President Kennedy in the assassination of Diem surfaced on February 28, 2003, when the Lyndon B. Johnson Presidential Library in Austin, Texas, released thirty hours of recordings made surreptitiously by President Johnson in early 1966. On a call to Senator Eugene McCarthy on February 1, 1966, Johnson complained about the Kennedy administration and its left-wing allies in the Senate. Johnson said: "They started on me with Diem, you remember. 'He was corrupt and he ought to be killed.' So we killed him. We all got together and got a god-damn bunch of thugs and assassinated him. Now, we've really had no political stability [in South Vietnam] since then." A few minutes later he called General Maxwell B. Taylor, until recently the ambassador to South Vietnam. Johnson said (speaking of unnamed persons in the Kennedy administration): "They started out and said, 'We got to kill Diem, because he's no damn good. Let's, let's knock him off.' And we did." See James Rosen, "What's Hidden in the LBJ Tapes," *Weekly Standard,* September 29, 2003, 12–13.

13. Gabriel Kolko, *Anatomy of a War: Vietnam, the United States, and the Modern Historical Experience* (New York: Pantheon, 1985), 157. President Johnson's decision not to invade North Vietnam aroused tremendous disapproval among some military leaders then and later. Despite the outcome of the Korean War, a

strong element in the military believed that all wars should lead to the complete surrender of the enemy, as the United States had demanded of Germany and Japan in World War II. But military victory was out of the question in Vietnam. China, unwilling to allow an American army along its southern frontier, would have entered the war if the United States had occupied North Vietnam. If this had happened, it would have precipitated a much wider war that might have drawn in the Soviet Union. These factors exposed the fallacy of the argument that military victory is the only purpose of war. As the nineteenth-century Prussian strategist Karl von Clausewitz wrote, war is only an *extension* of politics, or a *means* for a nation's political purpose to be carried out when other means fail. Military victory is never an end in itself. A more perfect *peace* is the end of all warfare. In the case of Vietnam, this more perfect peace could be attained only by political agreement, not by military victory.

14. A February 1966 CIA appraisal of Beijing's view of the United States explicitly confirms this view. The CIA reported that a vital principle of Chinese policy was "to keep, at all costs, American troops from access to China's borders. Mao believes, and no one in his party disagrees, that if the United States were to place, as a result of requirements placed on her by the Vietnamese conflict, sizeable troop strength on the Vietnam/China border, America would, in turn, find the temptation to topple the Peking [Beijing] government irresistible and would join with Nationalist China to invade the mainland. There are no assurances which the United States could make to China to assuage this fear, and the United States can always accept as a premise that China will move with troops to keep American garrisons off her Vietnamese, Korean, Indian or other borders." See Johnson Presidential Library, Austin, Texas, National Security country file, Asia and Pacific, China, Box 239, China Cables, vol. VI 3/66–9/66, "Peking's View of the United States," February 10, 1966.

15. The American leadership curiously clung to the opinion that the Chinese were involved in aggression in Southeast Asia, although the Chinese messages to Washington clearly demonstrated that they were interested not in intervening but only in protecting Chinese frontiers. On November 11, 1964, Secretary of State Dean Rusk, appearing on a CBS television program, replied to a question as follows: "This [matter of whether the United States and Communist China are on a collision course regarding Vietnam] turns entirely on Peiping's [Beijing's] decision on that crucial question, about whether they are prepared to leave their neighbors alone. We've made it very clear that we are not going to pull away and leave southeast Asia to be overrun by these people from the north. Therefore, the answer to your question lies in Peiping. We feel that they must come to the decision to leave these people alone in southeast Asia." See Johnson Presidential Library, Austin, Texas, Office files of Harry McPherson: Vietnam 1967, part II, "Statements by President Johnson and Secretary of State Rusk on U.S. Policy toward the Republic of China and Communist China, 1964–1967.

16. The Vietnamese Communist method of waging war is described in detail in Bevin Alexander, *The Future of Warfare* (New York: W. W. Norton, 1995), 100–204.

17. The Khmer Rouge, under Pol Pot, took control of the capital Phnom Penh in mid-April 1975 and forced all urban dwellers, including hospital patients, to flee into the countryside. Pol Pot's idea was to build a new society of rural communes. He forbade sexual intercourse and abolished families. The communes were a disastrous failure. The process created terror and little else. The Khmer Rouge killed outright 100,000 people with any education, while 400,000 died from death marches into rural areas. In all, 1.2 million Cambodians, a fifth of the entire population, perished. The Khmer Rouge were not allies of Vietnam, however, and Vietnamese forces invaded Cambodia in 1979, ousted the Khmer Rouge, and installed a new regime.

18. The United States lost 90 of 659 helicopters used to airlift South Vietnamese soldiers, while 453 were damaged.

19. President Nixon's obsession with Vietnam caused him, in 1971, to dismantle the system of fixed exchange rates set up in 1944 under the Bretton Woods agreement. Bretton Woods had supported a liberal system of international trade, because it engendered financial stability among our allies' market economies. Since the 1950s military spending, foreign aid, and overseas investment had diverted capital from the U.S. domestic market. In the first half of 1971, the Organization of Petroleum Exporting Countries (OPEC) increased oil prices, causing the U.S. trade deficit to triple. The "dollar drain" reduced U.S. gold reserves and lowered the value of currency. Corporate debt and government budget deficits increased competition for credit, causing interest rates to rise and inflation to set in. The resulting drop in real wages brought labor unrest and strikes. Nixon cut government spending to reduce inflation and encouraged higher interest rates. The result was "stagflation"—rising prices and high unemployment. In an attempt to reverse the process, Nixon in 1971 took the United States off the gold standard—the promise to U.S. trading partners to redeem paper dollars in gold at a fixed rate of thirty-five dollars an ounce. Nixon also froze wages, prices, and rents, and imposed a 10 percent surtax on imports. This abruptly destroyed the Bretton Woods system and, in the words of Walter Russell Mead, "inflicted lasting damage on the American economy and on U.S. relations with both Western Europe and Japan. . . . The inflationary waves set off by the currency crash led to the oil price shocks and the economic stagflation of the 1970s." Since 1971 the world has relied on "fiat money," or money created by government fiat and backed only by the promises of central bankers to protect the value of their currencies. See Mead, 74; Horowitz and Carroll, 462–63; "Heading for a Fall, by Fiat?" *Economist*, February 28, 2004, 74.

20. Power, 122.

CHAPTER FOURTEEN

1. In theory Cuba, under dictator Fidel Castro, is also Stalinist. But Cuba depended on subsidies from the Soviet Union to survive. When these ended, Cuba was left with no viable economy; it is slowly collapsing. Castro exists only at the sufferance of the United States.

2. Alexander, *How Wars Are Won,* 357n.1.

3. By the early 1980s the Soviet Union was running an annual budget deficit of 7 to 8 percent of gross national product (GNP) and was suffering from extreme inflation. This inflation was masked by rigid price controls, which created a black-market economy for consumer goods and removed most of these goods from store counters. The Soviet Union was falling further and further behind the West in computers and other technologies. The Reagan administration put additional pressure on the Soviet economy by talking Saudi Arabia into keeping down the price of oil, thereby denying the Soviet Union higher prices for its oil. The United States also pressured its European allies to delay a huge natural gas pipeline project from Siberia. This prevented a boost to the Soviet economy. The totalitarian Soviet state, run by its rigid *nomenklatura,* or official bureaucracy or hierarchy, was incapable of change. Its only weapon was suppression. Soviet Communism stifled creativity or spontaneous production, bringing only terror, bureaucracy, the lack of a profit motive, the rejection of market forces, and a centralized decision-making process. In order to meet the challenges of microelectronics, computers, space technology, and worldwide communications, the Soviet Union had to jettison Communism.

4. The Communist inability to understand human nature led to one of the greatest catastrophes in history. In 1929–30 Joseph Stalin ordered Russia's peasants to surrender, without compensation, their farm animals and their land to collective farms (*kolkhoz*). The peasants were to be paid on the basis of the amount and the skill of their work. The state was to receive required deliveries of food at low prices. The farmers, told to give up their small amounts of wealth and get nothing in return, acted quite logically. They killed and ate great numbers of their farm animals rather than surrender them. This mass slaughter drastically reduced the animals available for farm traction and food production, creating a deficit that took many years to make up. The peasants, now working for a state-directed *kolkhoz,* often malingered or devoted their attention to the small garden plots permitted around their cottages. Farm production dropped severely. Stalin made the disaster worse by rounding up millions of persons who resisted, branding them *kulaks* (well-to-do farmers, though many were poor), and shipping them off to Siberia, where most died.

5. Halberstam, 322.

6. Chua, 83.

7. Frum and Perle, 203.

8. Because of Iranian ties to terrorists in Lebanon who were kidnapping Americans, Reagan allowed National Security Council officials in 1985 to ar-

range a secret exchange of U.S. weapons for hostages. The deal sent 2,000 anti-tank missiles to Iran. In return, Tehran agreed to arrange the release of U.S. captives in Lebanon. But as soon as two hostages were released, two other Americans were seized, showing that the Iranians were running a scam. When a Beirut newspaper leaked details of the deal in 1986, Reagan abruptly ended the relationship with Iran.

9. In raw economic terms, America's ascendancy has become overwhelming. In 1999 the U.S. gross domestic product (GDP) per person was $30,200; Japan's, $24,500; France's, $22,700; Canada's, $21,700; Italy's, $21,500; Britain's, $21,200; Germany's, $20,800; South Korea's, $13,700; Russia's, $4,700; China's, $3,460; and North Korea's, $900. See *National Geographic Atlas of the World,* seventh edition, 1999. In 2002 America's GDP was $10.5 trillion; Japan's, $4 trillion; Germany's, $2 trillion; Britain's, $1.6 trillion; France's, $1.4 trillion; China's, $1.2 trillion; Mexico's, $600 billion; India's, $500 billion; and Russia's, $340 billion. See *Economist,* May 1, 2004, Survey of California, 4.

10. Mead, 10.

CHAPTER FIFTEEN

1. Ralph Peters writes: "The stasis of Islamic civilization is the most colossal failure of our time, a situation without precedent. . . . A billion people, as proud as they are ill-governed and ill-prepared for modern life, have found they cannot compete with other civilizations on a single front. . . . A civilization that is anti-meritocratic, that oppresses and torments women, that mocks the rule of law, that neglects education and lacks a work ethic simply cannot prosper under modern conditions." See Peters, 6–7. David Frum and Richard Perle write that Arabs can see on television and through the Internet what life is like in Europe and America, but they live in polluted cities ruled by corrupt officials; are entangled in excessive regulations; are confronted with native elites who have seized most of the wealth; are taxed by governments that provide nothing and lose every war; have no forum for public discourse; see every dissident killed, jailed, corrupted, or driven into exile; possess no effective school system; and must allow children to be taught by clerics whose minds "contain nothing but medieval theology and a smattering of third world nationalist self-pity." See Frum and Perle, 160–61.

2. Lewis, 47; *Economist,* Survey of Islam and the West, September 13, 2003, 6. A 2002 U.N. report stated that the Arab nations, with 280 million people, annually translate about 330 books, one-fifth of the number translated by Greece, with a population of 11 million. One-third of students in Saudi universities are enrolled in Islamic studies. See Frum and Perle, 156. The 2003 Arab Human Development Report states that between 1980 and 1999 the nine leading Arab economies registered 370 patents (in the United States) for new inventions. During the same twenty-year period, South Korea alone registered 16,328 patents for inventions. See Thomas L. Friedman, "War of Ideas,

Part 6," *New York Times,* January 25, 2004. In 2004 the *Economist* showed that democratic institutions are gravely lacking in the eighteen major Arab countries. Out of a possible 60 points measuring political freedom, the rule of law, religious freedom, press freedom, economic openness, and women's rights, Morocco scored the highest at 35 points, while Saudi Arabia scored the lowest at 13 points. See "Freedom Calls, at Last?" *Economist,* April 3, 2004, 47–48.

3. Lewis, 159.

4. Ferguson, *Colossus,* 178–79.

5. In early 2003, journalist Raid Qusti wrote in the *Arab News,* an English-language daily in Jeddah, Saudi Arabia: "Women will always be the core issue that will hinder any social progress in Saudi Arabia. We limit their roles in public, ban them from public participation in decision making, we doubt them and confine them because we think they are the source of all seduction and evil in the world. And then we say proudly: 'We are Muslims.'" See Lawrence Wright, "The Kingdom of Silence," *New Yorker,* January 5, 2004, 59. Wright comments that "there are some parts of the country where a woman never unveils — her husband and children see her face only when she dies."

6. In early 2004 Crown Prince Abdullah inaugurated a "national dialogue" to suggest remedies to the Saudi educational system, in which students are taught that a good way to show love of God is to treat infidels with contempt. The effort was opposed by 160 academics, clerics, and judges, who charged that would-be reformers are "partisans of infidelity, polytheism, and delusion." The kingdom's top state-appointed religious authority, Sheikh Abdel Aziz Aal al-Sheikh, reproached an economic forum in Jeddah in 2004 because some women attended. "Mixing," the sheikh thundered, "is the root of all evil" and "the origin of vice and adultery." See "The Risks of Reform," *Economist,* January 24, 2004, 41–42.

7. The basis of the *sharia* is the Koran, but only 80 of the Koran's 6,000 verses lay down rules of public law. Much of what is called *sharia* derives from the *sunna,* or the teachings of the prophet; the *ijma,* or the consensus of religious scholars; and the *qiyas,* or legal reasoning.

8. Amir Taheri, "The Crackup of the Arab Tyrannies?" *Weekly Standard,* July 7–14, 2003, 28–31.

9. As a consequence of the war, the Suez Canal was closed from June 1967 to June 1975.

10. Although the United States had only 6 percent of the world's population in 1973, it consumed 30 percent of global energy production. Nearly 40 percent of our oil came from overseas.

11. In 1981 Khomeini wrote: "If laws are needed, Islam has established them all. There is no need after establishing a government to sit down and draw up laws." Khomeini imposed the doctrine of *wilayat al-faqih,* or rule by the jurist, under which the final arbiter of political power was the cleric best qualified to understand the true meaning of Islamic law and tradition. By happy

coincidence Khomeini found that he himself was just that best jurist, and he ruled Iran as an autocrat. After Khomeini's death in 1989, the constitution provided that all legislation must be passed through a mullah-dominated Council of Guardians to make sure it complies with Islamic law as they see it. Although the constitution allows for a president and a Consultative Assembly, they are powerless without the guardians' blessing. On January 11, 2004, the Council of Guardians barred 4,000 candidates from standing for parliamentary elections. The reasons most cited were the candidates' supposed "indifference to Islam and the constitution" and their questioning the almost limitless powers enjoyed by the supreme leader, Ayatollah Ali Khamenei, who assumed much of the power enjoyed by the late Ayatollah Khomeini. See "Their Last Chance?" *Economist*, January 17, 2004, 19–21.

12. The shah had not been a well-liked figure. The monarchy had been restored by a CIA-aided coup in 1953, and the shah used Iran's oil revenues to pay for American arms and to finance rapid modernization of the country. American intelligence services failed to pick up on the rising tide of Shiite fundamentalism that aroused great resentment of the shah's emphasis on material goods, emancipation of women, and a secular, nonreligious government.

13. The Iranians originally seized sixty-six American citizens, but granted fourteen early release. The remainder they kept as prisoners until January 20, 1981.

14. Israeli settlements in the West Bank and Gaza contributed to the difficulty of reaching an agreement. Menachem Begin became prime minister in May 1977, and, like many Israelis, he felt the West Bank was an inalienable part of Israel, the historic Samaria and Judea. He began a settlement program in the region, overseen by Ariel Sharon, minister of agriculture. When Yitzhak Shamir replaced Begin in September 1983, he continued Begin's settlement policy, hoping to isolate the Arab towns and villages that might form the basis for a Palestinian state. Few Israelis responded until Sharon began subsidizing communities within easy commuting distance of Jerusalem and Tel Aviv. By 1992 the Jewish population in the occupied territories was approaching 100,000. Yitzhak Rabin became prime minister in June 1992. To patch up relations with the United States, Rabin ordered a freeze on Israeli settlements. But in fact the settler population in the occupied territories grew from 100,000 to 135,000 during Rabin's term.

15. Ferguson, *Colossus*, 124. Months later another suicide bomber attacked the U.S. embassy in Kuwait, killing four.

16. Hezbollah (Arabic: *Hizb Allah*, or Party of God) was formed in 1982 by Shiite clerics with the goal of driving Israel from Lebanon and forming an Islamic state there. Hezbollah is based in Shiite areas of southern Lebanon and southern Beirut. It coordinates closely with Shiite Iran and gets much support from Iran. Hezbollah has engaged in many terrorist attacks, including kidnappings and car bombings, and emerged as a major political party in Lebanon at the end of the civil war in 1990.

17. In October 1985 Israeli aircraft bombed the PLO headquarters, now in Tunis. When Libyan-supported terrorists planted bombs in airports in Rome and Vienna in December 1985, the United States unleashed air and naval attacks against Libya in April 1986. Once U.S. intelligence linked Libyans to the bombing of a West German discotheque frequented by U.S. soldiers in April 1986, the administration launched a second attack that killed forty people and destroyed the family quarters of the Libyan dictator, Muammar al-Qaddafi. These attacks reduced the number of terrorist incidents over the following year.

18. In November 1988 the Palestine National Council meeting in Algiers voted to accept U.N. Resolutions 242 and 338, calling for Israel to evacuate the occupied territories and for all countries "to live in peace within secure and recognized boundaries." Yasser Arafat refused at first to say whether this meant the PLO recognized Israel's right to exist. The United States thereupon denied Arafat a visa to make a trip to the United Nations. He did speak to a reconvened United Nations in Geneva but again failed to be explicit about PLO policy. Just after the conference, however, Arafat in a press conference finally recognized Israel's right to exist and renounced terrorism as well. George Schultz, the U.S. secretary of state, at once announced that the United States would conduct "open dialogue" with the PLO. See "International Relations," *Encyclopaedia Britannica,* 2003. Encyclopaedia Britannica Premium Service, Available at www.britannica.com/eb/article?eu'108380.

19. In 1995 the PLO and Israel signed a follow-on interim agreement, known as Oslo II, which provided for Israeli withdrawal from seven Palestinian population centers in three phases over eighteen months. The Palestinians believed they had been promised all of the West Bank and Gaza except Jerusalem, settlements, and security outposts *before* final status talks began. The Israelis said the matter was entirely within their discretion and pointed out that Arafat had accepted the pact without any precise percentage. See Albright, 291.

20. Hamas is an acronym for *Harakat al-Muqawamah al-Islamiyyah* (Islamic Resistance Movement). It is dedicated to the destruction of Israel and to the creation of an Islamic state in Palestine. After the Six-Day War in 1967, the pan-Islamic Muslim Brotherhood set up charities, clinics, and schools in Gaza and the West Bank. The brotherhood's activities were nonviolent, but groups in the occupied territories began to call for a *jihad,* or holy war, against Israel. As a result, Hamas was formed by members of the brotherhood and factions of the PLO in December 1987. In its charter Hamas holds that Palestine is an Islamic homeland that can never be surrendered, and that waging holy war to wrest it from Israel is a religious duty for Muslims. Hamas denounced the 1993–94 peace agreement between the PLO and Israel. Along with another group, the Islamic Jihad, it intensified its suicide bombing campaign. Yasser

Arafat appointed Hamas members to important positions in the Palestinian Authority.

21. Arafat's duplicity was revealed after July 30, 1997, when two terrorist bombs exploded in the Mahane Yehuda market of Jerusalem, killing 14 Israelis and injuring 170 more. Madeleine Albright, U.S. secretary of state, demanded that Arafat arrest the extremists, confiscate arms, and ban groups that advocated violence. Arafat condemned the killings but said he could not crack down on extremists because the peace process was, in his view, stalled. In late August 1997 Arafat was photographed embracing a leader of Hamas. On September 4, 1997, three suicide bombers struck along Ben Yehuda promenade in West Jerusalem. See Albright, 293–94.

22. Instead of recognizing the Palestinian Authority's failure to rein in the terrorists as the root cause of the inability of both sides to reach an agreement, Europeans blamed the victim, Israel, rather than the criminal terrorist perpetrators. An opinion poll commissioned by the European Union in fall 2003 ranked Israel as the greatest threat to world peace, ahead of Iran and North Korea. See the *Economist,* November 8, 2003, 8.

23. Albright, 142–43.

24. In 1998 the FBI got information that implicated Iranian officials in directing the Khobar Towers attack, using Hezbollah to carry it out. See ibid., 324.

CHAPTER SIXTEEN

1. Power, 320. Samantha Power's *A Problem from Hell,* 247–327, 391–464, offers an astute and complete study of the wars in the former Yugoslavia, and I am indebted to her for much of the information in this chapter.

2. In the summer of 1995, after the Serbs had murdered 7,000 Muslim men and boys at Srebrenica, senior officials in London, Paris, and Bonn said nothing about their inaction for four years previously and complained of Washington's refusal to live up to its traditional role as leader of the Atlantic alliance.

3. The idea of making the rest of the world live up to higher moral standards has never been a major goal of Americans. In a February 2000 Pew poll, only 39 percent of Americans believed that defending human rights abroad should be a "very important" aim of the United States. See Mead, 288.

4. Powell was, in fact, following rules laid down in November 1984 by Secretary of Defense Caspar Weinberger. See Eliot A. Cohen, *Supreme Command* (New York: Free Press, 2002), 186–87.

5. Power, 259. Americans were repulsed by the atrocities reported out of Croatia and Bosnia, but for a long time this did not translate into the political will to put American troops into the region.

6. Albright, 176.

7. One-world "Wilsonian" liberal groups advocated an international police force, perhaps under U.N. control, to end human rights violations. The

United States would not have to supply troops to this force, only money. The liberal groups also called for international law courts and other instruments to punish wrongdoers wherever they lived. But these recommendations ran hard against powerful opposition to any institutions that could infringe on the sovereignty of the United States. Americans do not want to pool sovereignty with other countries, because it means a reduction of our own sovereignty. The key to the one-world approach of these liberal groups is the idea of a supranational authority that binds sovereign nations to accept its dictates. This idea inspires fanatical opposition from the vast majority of Americans. See Mead, 290–91.

8. See Hirsh, 30–31.

9. In 1994 the Western powers established a process for close air support if U.N. peacekeepers came under fire. Peacekeepers also could request air strikes against preselected targets if safe areas came under attack. It was a cumbersome arrangement. "Dual keys" had to be turned. The civilian head of the U.N. mission, Yasushi Akashi, had to turn the first key. If this happened, then NATO commanders would have to turn the second and send jets. Most requests were stalled at the Akashi level because U.N. civilians were skeptical of NATO bombing. They believed air strikes would cause Serbs to round up U.N. hostages. This actually happened in November 1994 and May 1995. See Power, 392.

10. Madeleine Albright, U.S. ambassador to the UN, described the box the Clinton administration had put itself into. "We labored to escape the basic dilemmas in our policy," she writes. "We couldn't lift the arms embargo because we didn't have the votes on the Security Council, and we could not achieve a permanent cease-fire because that was unacceptable to the Bosniaks and would reward ethnic cleansing. Nor could we use significant force to punish the Bosnian Serbs because U.N. peacekeepers might be taken hostage and the humanitarian missions derailed." See Albright, 184.

11. Power, 437.

12. Madeleine Albright, secretary of state in the second Clinton administration, made sure the Dayton accords were implemented and Bosnia did not fall back into a chaos of war and killings. She fought the policy outlined in March 1996 by National Security Adviser Anthony Lake of an "exit strategy" to remove American troops after one year. This was unrealistic, Albright said: "Of Bosnia's prewar population, one in ten had been wounded or killed during the conflict. Of the survivors, five in ten had lost homes; eight in ten were relying on the UN for food; nine in ten were unemployed. It would obviously take more than a year to recover." In November 1996 Clinton set up another NATO-led Stabilization Force, or SFOR, that was to depart by June 1998. In a speech on May 22, 1997, Albright asserted the need to keep troops in Bosnia until the nation was secure and peaceful, and she warned neighboring Croatia and Yugoslavia (Serbia and Montenegro) to support the Dayton accords or be

subject to severe sanctions. Her efforts led President Clinton, in December 1997, to drop any deadline for withdrawal of American troops. See Albright, 264–71.

CHAPTER SEVENTEEN

1. We felt great pride in the heroic attempt by the thirty-three passengers and seven crew members on United Airlines Flight 93 to recapture their aircraft from four terrorists who had hijacked the plane shortly after takeoff from Newark Airport. Their struggle caused the Boeing 757 to crash in a sparsely populated area near Shanksville, Pennsylvania, at 10:10 A.M. on September 11, 2001, possibly saving countless lives. It is widely presumed that the terrorists intended to use the aircraft to crash into the U.S. Capitol.

2. The American intelligence community's inability to find out what was happening in Iraq revealed a breakdown in the U.S. intelligence-gathering system. CIA director Tenet, before a Senate committee in February 2004, admitted that Germany had passed along, thirty months before 9/11, a tip on Marwan al-Shehhi, the pilot who crashed Flight 175 into the South Tower of the World Trade Center. But nothing was done about it. "The Germans gave us a name, Marwan—that's it—and a phone number," Tenet said. "They didn't give us a first and a last name until after 9/11, with then additional data." *New York Times* columnist Maureen Dowd wrote, "For crying out loud. As one guy I know put it: 'I've tracked down women across the country with a lot less information than that.'" See Maureen Dowd, "Sorry, Right Number," *New York Times,* February 29, 2004. President Bush appointed an independent commission to study the nation's intelligence apparatus. Tenet resigned in July 2004. An official British inquiry by Lord Butler concluded in July 2004 that British intelligence was likewise at fault in holding that Iraq possessed stocks of chemical and biological weapons. But it held that Tony Blair's government had not deliberately misled the public. Blair responded on July 14, 2004: "I cannot say that getting rid of Saddam was a mistake at all." If the United States and Britain had backed down on their threat to invade Iraq, he added, Saddam would have resumed programs to build the weapons, and that would have emboldened other dictators to follow suit.

The Bush administration also made a grievous mistake by failing to anticipate the breakdown of authority when Saddam fled, the looting of public buildings, the difficulty in getting power and other infrastructure restored, the problems of restarting the production and export of oil, and the guerrilla war that commenced almost at once. Most of the problems were predictable. The National Intelligence Council, made up of academics and intelligence professionals, estimated in January 2003 that an invasion of Iraq would result in a deeply divided Iraqi society prone to internal conflict. A senior Bush administration official said that the need to overthrow Saddam overrode the danger because "we couldn't live with the status quo" in the Middle East. See Douglas

Jehl and David E. Sanger, "Prewar Assessment on Iraq Saw Chance of Strong Divisions," *New York Times,* September 28, 2004. Part of the problem was a quarter century of mismanagement by Saddam Hussein, an antiquated and ill-maintained infrastructure, sneak attacks on the electric power grid and oil pipelines, and the smuggling of fuel, since gasoline in neighboring lands cost twenty times what it did in Iraq. But there were other problems. The original plan was for the U.S. administrator, retired general Jay Garner, to transfer power to an interim government made up mostly of returned Iraqi exiles by June 2003. But we found that the proposed leadership had no real following among Iraqis. At this point former ambassador L. Paul Bremer III took over and established the Coalition Provisional Authority, and the United States became an occupying power instead of being liberators.

3. William Safire, "Sixteen Truthful Words," *New York Times,* July 19, 2004; on Duelfer, see Douglas Jehl, "Iraq Study Finds Desire for Arms, but Not Capacity," *New York Times,* September 17, 2004.

4. Columnist Maureen Dowd forcefully stated this liberal view in the *New York Times:* "It was clear at the time that going after Saddam to punish Osama made no sense, that Cheney & Co. were going to use Saddam as a lab rat for all their neocon agendas. It was clear, as the fleet sailed toward Iraq, that the Bush crew had no interest in diplomacy — that it wanted to castrate the flaccid UN, the flower child Colin Powell and his pinstriped State Department, snotty Old Europe, and the despised Saddam to show that America is a hyperpower that is not to be messed with." See "The Prince of Tides, Tacking and Attacking," *New York Times,* September 23, 2004.

5. John Lewis Gaddis, "Kill the Empire! (Or Not)," *New York Times,* July 25, 2004.

6. "Tape Opposing Vote Attributed to bin Laden," *New York Times,* December 28, 2004.

7. In public hearings in March and April 2004, the U.S. commission investigating the attacks on the World Trade Center and the Pentagon provided information pointing, over nearly a five-year period prior to 9/11, to failures by both the Clinton and the George W. Bush administrations to address the danger. The Clinton administration did not create and carry out an effective strategy to deal with al Qaeda, and it failed to educate the American public. The issue was clouded by the testimony of Richard A. Clarke, former counterterrorism expert in the Clinton and Bush administrations and author of a book released at the same time as the hearings. Clarke claimed that the Bush administration largely ignored the al Qaeda threat prior to 9/11, and that after 9/11 President Bush seemed preoccupied with finding a link between the attacks and Iraq. The war in Iraq, Clarke charged, "greatly undermined the war on terrorism." Then National Security Adviser Condoleezza Rice rejected Clarke's argument, testifying that Clarke had defended the administration's counterterrorism policies in past statements. Her most telling argument was

that the country did not have the political will to organize against terrorism until blood was shed on American soil.

8. Robert Kagan, "America's Crisis of Legitimacy," *Foreign Affairs*, March/April 2004, 71.

9. Dominique Moïsi, "Reinventing the West," *Foreign Affairs*, November/December 2003, 67–73.

10. Kagan, 3–5.

11. Thomas L. Friedman, "The End of the West?" *New York Times*, November 3, 2003.

12. During the cold war, "preemption" meant taking military action against a state about to launch an attack. "Prevention" meant beginning a war against a state that might pose such a risk in the future. The Bush administration actually planned a "preventive" war against Iraq, reasoning that the United States could not wait until a terrorist attack had become a clear and present danger, but had to go after a state that might be harboring terrorist cells. Bush's logic aroused the opposition of several other countries, who feared that the United States would unilaterally violate the sovereignty of any state it suspected of gross wrongdoing. See John Lewis Gaddis, "Grand Strategy in the Second Term," *Foreign Affairs*, January/February 2005, 3–7.

13. Samuel R. Berger, "Foreign Policy for a Democratic President," *Foreign Affairs*, May/June 2004, 47–63. Berger also writes: "When our goals are embodied in binding agreements, we can gain international support by enforcing them when they are violated." Yet our allies were *not* willing to enforce numerous violations of U.N. Security Council resolutions by Saddam Hussein going back to 1991. Thus it is doubtful whether we can rely on our allies joining us to enforce future "binding agreements."

14. Kupchan, xiii–xvii, 28–29, 41. The French essayist Emmanuel Todd in *After the Empire: The Breakdown of the American Order* (New York: Columbia University Press, 2003) also takes this view.

15. John Lewis Gaddis, "Grand Strategy in the Second Term," *Foreign Affairs*, January/February 2005, 6.

16. Ferguson, *Empire*, 370; Chalmers Johnson, *The Sorrows of Empire: Militarism, Secrecy, and the End of the Republic* (New York: Metropolitan Books, 2004). Ferguson in his *Colossus* makes much the same argument.

17. In the 1991 Gulf War, only 10 percent of ordnance consisted of "smart" bombs. In 2003, some 90 percent of all bombs that dropped on Iraq were guided by inerrant means, especially by the satellite-directed global positioning system (GPS), which can deliver a bomb with great precision to virtually any point on earth. Targets now can be destroyed with almost pinpoint certainty. This means each bomb is more effective, and far fewer are needed to destroy a target. Although the United States in 2003 had only a few more aircraft than it did in 1991, accuracy multiplied the effectiveness of air power tenfold over what it was then. With air supremacy, American unmanned aerial

vehicles (UAVs), plus satellites, helicopters, and other detection devices, were able to spot any Iraqi force or military element that showed itself—even single tanks, vehicles, and small units of men. These targets could be destroyed quickly by bombs or missiles guided by GPS, laser, radar, infrared, and other homing devices. The only way enemy forces can survive is by hiding and by wide distribution over the landscape. Not being able to concentrate or to attack in force, the Iraqi army was impotent. Although a few individuals and units delivered blows against isolated American detachments, the Iraqi military had no hope of affecting the outcome of the war. Nowhere did the Iraqis dare to bring attack units together for fear they would be destroyed in place. This paralyzed operations. The Iraqi army simply melted away.

18. The CIA downplayed the possibility of a guerrilla uprising in Iraq and believed the Iraqis would welcome the Americans. The National Intelligence Council, senior experts from the intelligence community, discussed the risk of insurgency only in the last paragraph of a thirty-eight-page assessment in January 2003. Said General Tommy R. Franks, head of the U.S. Central Command during the attack on Iraq: "There was never a buildup of intelligence that says: 'It's coming. It's coming. It's coming.'" See Michael R. Gordon, "Poor Intelligence Misled Troops About Risk of Drawn-Out War," *New York Times,* October 20, 2004.

19. Ansar al-Islam's doctrines have much in common with the ultraorthodox Wahhabi movement from Saudi Arabia. Among its aims are the introduction of *sharia* law and "the propagation of virtue and the prevention of vice." Its operatives have killed women without burqas and prohibited females from being educated. Ansar's operatives come from Iraq, Jordan, Morocco, Palestine, Syria, and Afghanistan. See FoxNews.com, October 23, 2003; Catherine Taylor, "Taliban-style Group Grows in Iraq," *Christian Science Monitor,* March 15, 2002.

20. The al Aqsa Martyrs Brigades are West Bank militias affiliated with Yasser Arafat's al Fatah faction and were one of the driving forces behind the Palestinian *intifada*. In March 2002, after deadly suicide bombings in Jerusalem, the State Department added the groups to the list of foreign terrorist organizations. One of al Aqsa's leaders, Naser Badawi, told the *New York Times* in March 2002 that Arafat had never asked the group to stop its suicide bombings. See Council on Foreign Relations, Terrorism: Q&A, available at www.terrorismanswers.com/groups/alaqsa.

21. Sun Tzu, *Art of War,* translation by Samuel B. Griffin (London/New York: Oxford University Press, 1963, 1971), 77–78. Sun Tzu's text is as follows: "For to win one hundred victories in one hundred battles is not the acme of skill. To subdue the enemy without fighting is the acme of skill. Thus, what is of supreme importance in war is to attack the enemy's strategy. Next best is to disrupt his alliances. The next best is to attack his army."

22. Afghanistan's first election, held on October 9, 2004, was a substantial

success, primarily because Afghans wanted to choose the country's leaders through a peaceful, democratic process. But the Taliban kept turnout down in two provinces where they have a strong presence, and they have vowed to continue fighting democracy. See Carlotta Gall and David Rohde, "Assessing the Afghan Election," *New York Times,* October 20, 2004.

23. Niall Ferguson reminds us that Americans are not much interested in peacekeeping. The U.S. electorate will not tolerate prolonged exposure of our troops to suicide bombers, snipers, and rocket-propelled grenades fired at convoys. "The obvious solution," Ferguson writes, "is to continue the now well-established practice of sharing the burdens of peacekeeping with other United Nations members — in particular America's European allies, with their relatively generous aid budgets and their large conscript armies. If they are not used for peacekeeping, it is hard to see what these soldiers are for, in a Europe that has declared perpetual peace within its own borders and is no longer menaced by Russia." See Ferguson, *Colossus,* 297.

24. While democracy is an ideal, the actual goal of the United States is to ensure that governments and societies pose no threat to others. The real dispute is about how to achieve this goal. The conservatives say it can be gained only by a military campaign to root out all terrorist cells wherever they exist. The liberals say peace can be achieved by a multinational, law-enforcement-like approach. Richard Holbrooke, a Clinton-era diplomat, claims there is no war on terror. The term, he says, is "just a metaphor," like saying "the war on poverty." In the 2004 presidential campaign, Democratic candidate John Kerry said, "We have to get back to the place we were [before 9/11], where terrorists are not the focus of our lives, but they're a nuisance." Kerry likened terrorism to prostitution and illegal gambling, which we can never end but can be reduced to a level "where it isn't on the rise." Kerry sees terrorists as nonstate actors, resembling criminal syndicates. He believes terrorists do not depend on states and that only a unified community of nations, using primarily law-enforcement tools, can reduce terror to a "nuisance" level. Furthermore, Kerry said the United States should pass a "global test" of legitimacy before taking action against terrorists or states. This implies that the United States cannot do as it pleases, but must work with other countries to establish norms and provide security. Kerry's view fits in nicely with that of French president Jacques Chirac, who said in 2004 that France seeks a multilateral world in which the United Nations sets the laws by which all nations abide — code words for limiting American power. In contrast, conservatives see a world in which individuals and nations are self-reliant and free to form voluntary associations. George W. Bush sees a struggle between states promoting terror and those trying to exterminate terror, and he holds that terrorism cannot survive independently of states. In summary, Kerry regards terror as a police problem requiring the United States to cooperate closely with other nations, while Bush sees it as a war led by the United States, a vast struggle against both

terrorists and rogue regimes. See Matt Bai, "Kerry's Undeclared War," *New York Times Magazine,* October 10, 2004; Roger Cohen, David E. Sanger, and Steven R. Weisman, "Challenging Rest of the World with a New Order," *New York Times,* October 12, 2004; David Brooks, "Not Just a Personality Clash, a Conflict of Visions," *New York Times,* October 12, 2004; Adam Wolfson, "The Two Faces of Liberalism," *Weekly Standard,* October 18, 2004, 21–23.

25. Chua, 123–24, 261–63, 277.

26. A four-member panel headed by James M. Schlesinger, a former defense secretary, reported on August 24, 2004, that Secretary of Defense Donald H. Rumsfeld and his aides did not anticipate or respond swiftly to the insurgency that commenced in Iraq shortly after military victory in April 2003. This set the stage for abuses, the panel reported. Tillie K. Fowler, a member of the group and a former Republican congresswoman from Florida, said: "We found a string of failures that go well beyond an isolated cellblock in Iraq." The next day an internal army investigation confirmed that American military intelligence officers were directly involved in the abuses. The report implicated twenty-seven military intelligence personnel and civilian contractors in forty-four cases of prisoner abuse, while eight others witnessed and did not report what they had seen. Classified sections of this report leaked to the *New York Times* said that Lieutenant General Ricardo S. Sanchez, the top commander in Iraq, approved severe interrogation practices intended only for captives held in Guantánamo Bay, Cuba, and in Afghanistan. Sanchez initially authorized the use of stress positions on prisoners during harsh interrogation procedures, the use of dogs, yelling, loud music, light control, and isolation. Sanchez revoked the policy a month later, but Abu Ghraib interrogators did not fully understand the changes and believed, for example, that dogs could be used in interrogations without General Sanchez's approval. See Douglas Jehl, "A Trail of 'Major Failures' Leads to Defense Secretary's Office," *New York Times,* August 25, 2004; Thomas Crampton, "Inquiry Faults Intelligence Unit for Abuses at Iraqi Prison," *New York Times,* August 25, 2004; Douglas Jehl and Eric Schmitt, "Army's Report Faults General in Prison Abuse," *New York Times,* August 27, 2004.

27. Columnist David Brooks writes that many people refuse to face the monstrous fact that terrorists experience sheer pleasure in slaughtering innocents. After terrorists killed more than 300 people, most of them children, in Beslan, Russia, in early September 2004, Dutch foreign minister Bernard Bot, speaking on behalf of the European Union, declared: "All countries in the world need to work together to prevent tragedies like this. But we also would like to know from the Russian authorities how this tragedy could have happened." Brooks responded: "It wasn't a tragedy. It was a carefully planned mass murder operation. And it wasn't Russian authorities who stuffed basketball nets with explosives and shot children in the back as they tried to run away." See David Brooks, "Cult of Death," *New York Times,* September 7, 2004.

28. Edward Luttwak, senior fellow at the Center for Strategic and International Studies, writes: "The plain fact is that there are not enough aspiring democrats in Iraq to sustain democratic institutions." He notes that the majority Shiites have expressed preference for clerical leadership, that the minority Sunnis reject democracy because they refuse to accept a subordinate status, and that the Kurds prefer clan and tribal loyalties in the place of representative democracy. See Edward N. Luttwak, "Iraq: The Logic of Disengagement," *Foreign Affairs*, January/February 2005, 26–36.

29. U.S. Army intelligence agents used astute detective work to track down Saddam Hussein on December 13, 2003. Troops of the U.S. 4th Infantry Division pulled him out of a coffinlike bunker at a decrepit farmhouse at Ad Dwar on the Tigris River near Tikrit. After meticulous investigation, intelligence officers located a former member of Saddam's security organization who tipped Americans off to Saddam's whereabouts. Agents had built a map or chart of five extended families related to Saddam and used it to identify five key "enablers" or lieutenants who had specific jobs—logistics, planning, operations, and financing. The tipster himself was Saddam's chief of staff. When captured, Saddam had with him a briefcase with the names of hundreds of Baathist operatives, most of whom the U.S. military hunted down and captured.

30. The security line would postpone indefinitely the "road map" designed to arrive at a negotiated settlement between the Palestinians and Israelis. The plan calls for an electronic chain-link fence, concrete walls, trenches, and other obstacles to create a fortified frontier between the Israelis and the Palestinians, making it difficult for terrorists to infiltrate into Israel. The barrier would place 8 percent of the West Bank on the Israeli side and would take in most of the 150 formal settlements in the West Bank where 230,000 Jewish settlers live. But it would require dismantling small settlements in the Gaza Strip as well as outposts that have gone up in the West Bank. The occupants of these dismantled settlements would be moved back into Israel. Sharon maintained that "the security line will not be the final border of the state of Israel. But until the implementation of the road map, that is where" the military would be deployed. On May 3, 2004, Sharon's rightist Likud Party rejected the pullout plan 60–40 in a nonbinding vote. But Sharon's proposal is the only viable solution, because Palestinian militants are almost certain to derail any effort by Arab moderates to construct a reasonable peace accord with Israel. Sharon's plan is all the more logical since two-thirds of the Israeli population support it.

31. In February 2004 U.S. forces captured an appeal from Zarqawi to senior al Qaeda leaders, asking for help in instigating a civil war between Sunni and Shiite Iraqis. Zarqawi held that this was the only way to rescue the terrorist movement in Iraq. He reported that extremists were gaining little support among Iraqis and had been unable to scare the Americans into leaving. Instead, Americans were growing stronger every day. "By God, this is suffocation!"

Zarqawi exclaimed in frustration. See Dexter Filkins, "U.S. Says Files Seek Qaeda Aid in Iraq Conflict," *New York Times,* February 9, 2004; Douglas Jehl, "Al Qaeda Rebuffs Iraqi Terror Group, U.S. Officials Say," *New York Times,* February 21, 2004.

32. At Saudi Arabian housing compounds for foreign oil workers in Yanbu, on May 1, 2004, and in Khobar, on May 29–31, 2004, Islamic terrorists killed a total of twenty-nine people—eleven Westerners, eight Indians, two Sri Lankans, three Filipinos, one Egyptian, and four Saudis. They were attempting to interrupt oil production and destabilize the country. At Khobar, the terrorists killed non-Muslims and let Muslims go. They also took a number of foreigners hostage and slit the throats of nine of them. Saudi security forces stormed the building where the four terrorists were holed up with their captives. But three of the four got away, raising suspicion that the Saudi security forces were complicit in their escape.

CONCLUSION

1. The U.S. Army demonstrated elements of this new system when it combined seventy-ton Abrams tanks and twenty-five-ton Bradley fighting vehicles with artillery, ordinary infantry, and AC-130 gunships to demolish Moqtada al-Sadr's militia fighting in the closely built urban environment of Najaf, Iraq, in August 2004. The army pushed to the gates of the Iman Ali shrine at the center of the old city, inflicting huge casualties on Sadr's insurgents, while suffering almost none itself. See Alex Berenson, "Fighting the Old-Fashioned Way in Najaf," *New York Times,* August 29, 2004.

2. Personal message from John Arquilla, author, with David Ronfeldt, of *Swarming and the Future of Conflict* (Santa Monica, Calif.: Rand Corporation, 2000). Arquilla and Ronfeldt are also authors of "Networks, Netwars and the Fight for the Future," on *First Monday, Peer-Reviewed Journal on the Internet,* October 2001, firstmonday.org. Dr. Arquilla is professor of defense analysis at the U.S. Naval Postgraduate School, Monterey, California.

3. The bipartisan 9/11 commission recommended that the military's Special Operations Command (Socom) take over from the CIA authority for all paramilitary operations, whether clandestine or covert. The CIA has resisted surrendering its paramilitary missions, but the 9/11 commission concluded that "the United States cannot afford to build two separate capabilities for carrying out secret military operations, secretly operating standoff missiles, and secretly training foreign military or paramilitary forces." The Special Operations Command, created in 1978, operates like a miniature armed service that organizes, trains, and equips the nation's premier warriors. In 2004 there were just under 50,000 personnel in Special Operations, but only one-third were "trigger pullers" or operators. Under Socom are the Army Special Operations Command, Fort Bragg, North Carolina; the Naval Special Warfare Command, Coronado, California; and the Air Force Special Operations Command,

Hurlburt Field, Florida. See Eric Schmitt and Thom Shanker, "Special Warriors Have Growing Ranks and Growing Pains in Taking Key Antiterror Role," *New York Times,* August 2, 2004. For an astute and comprehensive analysis of the Army's Special Forces, see Linda Robinson, *Masters of Chaos* (New York: Public Affairs, 2004).

4. On November 14, 2004, Iran promised Britain, France, and Germany that it would suspend its enrichment of uranium, but it did not agree to give up its program indefinitely. The key agreement with the European powers was to cease, at least temporarily, its insistence on processing uranium into a precursor of uranium hexafluoride. A fast-spinning centrifuge can separate this gas into its two isotopes, the rare U-235, which splits easily to fuel a nuclear bomb, and the more abundant U-238, which is much more stable. See "Iran Agrees to Suspend Uranium Enrichment," *New York Times,* November 14, 2004.

5. The United States is finally getting assistance from China with regard to North Korea. Ever since the Korean War, Beijing had left to the United States the job of keeping North Korea from embarking on new aggressions. But by 2003 it had become alarmed about a collapsing but nuclear-armed state on its border, especially as more and more refugees were fleeing across the frontier along the Yalu and Tumen rivers to escape hunger. In 2003 China moved 150,000 troops to the frontier to take over security from the ordinary border guard. This action appeared to signal that China will not tolerate a nuclear North Korea.

6. William J. Broad, David E. Sanger, and Raymond Bonner, "A Tale of Nuclear Proliferation: How Pakistani Built His Network," *New York Times,* February 12, 2004.

7. The centrifuges were made in a Malaysian factory. There a Swiss engineer, one of Khan's operatives, watched over the production of the delicate parts, which are advanced, highly sophisticated hollow tubes made of a superhard steel alloy. The tubes, with steel rotors attached, spin near the speed of sound to separate the rare U-235 isotope from natural uranium. This isotope is fuel for a nuclear bomb. A cascade, made up of thousands of centrifuges, concentrates this isotope. See William J. Broad, "Slender and Elegant, It Fuels the Bomb," *New York Times,* March 23, 2004.

8. Four million tons of exploitable uranium are available in North Korean mines. North Korea may have a secret facility to turn raw uranium into uranium hexafluoride, though it's possible the processing was done outside North Korea. When heated uranium hexafluoride turns into a gas, ideal for processing with centrifuges to recover uranium's rare U-235 isotope. Bomb fuel is about 90 percent U-235. See David E. Sanger and William J. Broad, "Evidence Is Cited Linking Koreans to Libya Uranium," *New York Times,* May 23, 2004.

9. Seymour M. Hersh holds that Qaddafi had been seeking reconciliation with the West for years, and had been talking with American and British

intelligence agents for nine months prior to the seizure of the *BBC China*. He writes that Qaddafi tipped off U.S. and British agents that the centrifuge delivery was under way. "It was, in essence, a sting," Hersh writes. See Seymour M. Hersh, "The Deal," *New Yorker,* March 8, 2004, 32–37. On October 6, 2003, American officials presented evidence to Pakistan that between 1989 and 2003 a group led by Abdul Qadeer Khan provided crucial technology to enrich uranium to Iran, North Korea, and Libya, and that he also approached Iraq, Syria, and possibly other nations. In November 2003 the IAEA informed Pakistan of illicit technology transfers to Iran. On February 5, 2004, Pakistani president Pervez Musharraf granted a full pardon to Khan, who, in an appearance on Pakistani television the day before, admitted sharing nuclear technology with other countries. Musharraf, who depends on the army to stay in power, pardoned Khan to prevent an investigation of the army's role in the operation. Military experts said it was virtually impossible that Khan could have carried out his work without the tacit support of the army. Pakistan received missile parts from North Korea—believed to be the quid pro quo for nuclear aid. Musharraf conceded that he had suspected for three years that Khan was selling nuclear technology to other countries, but he claimed that he was not sure until the United States supplied proof. CIA Director George J. Tenet said in a speech on February 5, 2004, that the CIA had penetrated Khan's network some time before October 6, 2003, and a senior Bush administration official said that the United States conveyed warnings about Dr. Khan's activities to Musharraf in 2001. This led Musharraf to retire Khan in March 2001 with the aim of preventing the transfer of any more nuclear secrets. But Khan's black market continued to operate until the fall of 2003.

10. "A World Wide Web of Nuclear Danger," *Economist,* February 28, 2004, 26.

11. Michael Ignatieff, "Lesser Evils," *New York Times Magazine,* May 2, 2004.

12. Europe is slowly waking to the danger that Princeton Islamic historian Bernard Lewis highlighted on July 28, 2004. Lewis told the German newspaper *Die Welt* that Europe would be Islamic by the end of the century "at the very latest." Europe had no hope of becoming a global counterweight to the United States, Lewis argued. "Europe will be part of the Arabic west, of the Maghreb," he said. Historically, Maghreb refers to the coastlands and the Atlas Mountains of northwestern Africa (Morocco, Algeria, and Tunisia), a region conquered by the Arabs in the early centuries of Islamic expansion. Muslims are coming into Europe now from North Africa, the Middle East, and Pakistan. But Islam is a major political issue, since Turkey, with over 70 million people, mostly Muslims, wants to enter the European Union. The kind of society an Islamic majority might impose on Europe was hinted at in late summer 2004, when Turkish prime minister Recep Tayyip Erdogan planned to revive criminal penalties for adultery. In response to a storm of protest in Europe, Erdogan withdrew the proposal. But Turkey still discriminates against

non-Muslim minorities and bans theological training for Orthodox Christians. See Christopher Caldwell, "Islamic Europe?" *Weekly Standard,* October 4, 2004, 15–16; "Will Turkey Accept Europe?" *Economist,* September 25, 2004, 64–65; David L. Phillips, "Turkey's Dreams of Accession," *Foreign Affairs,* September/October 2004, 86–97.

13. *New York Times* columnist David Brooks has great hope for democracy in the Middle East. "Elections suck the oxygen from a rebel army," he writes. "They refute the claim that violence is the best way to change things. Moreover, they produce democratic leaders who are much better equipped to win an insurgency war. . . . It's simply astonishing that in the United States, the home of the greatest and most effective democratic revolution, so many people have come to regard democracy as a luxury-brand vehicle, suited only for the culturally upscale, when it's really a sturdy truck, effective in conditions both rough and smooth." See David Brooks, "The Insurgency Buster," *New York Times,* September 28, 2004.

14. Europe, for example, wants Washington to abandon its requirement for a regime change in Tehran as a price for Iran's readmission to international political commerce. As Rand Corporation senior adviser Robert E. Hunter writes, "It is one thing, in the European view, to want Iran to give up its pursuit of nuclear weapons and support for terrorism; it is another to try to eliminate Iran as an independent actor in the Middle East. Virtually all Europeans would argue that the balance of costs and benefits argues persuasively against the latter." See Robert E. Hunter, "A Forward-Looking Partnership," *Foreign Affairs,* September/October 2004, 16.

15. James Dobbins, director of the International Security and Defense Center at the Rand Corporation, writes that the United States has "a clear desire to leave Iraq and an equally clear willingness to stay until the Iraqi government . . . proves capable of securing its territory and protecting its citizens." See James Dobbins, "Iraq: Winning the Unwinnable War," *Foreign Affairs,* January/February 2005, 18–19. A democratic society is *not* a precondition for evacuating the country.

BIBLIOGRAPHY

Albright, Madeleine. *Madam Secretary. A Memoir.* New York: Hyperion, 2003.

Alexander, Bevin. *Korea: The First War We Lost.* New York: Hippocrene Books, 1986, 2000, 2004.

————. *Robert E. Lee's Civil War.* Holbrook, Mass.: Adams Media, 1998.

————. *The Strange Connection. U.S. Intervention in China, 1944–1972.* Westport, Conn.: Greenwood Press, 1992.

————. *How Wars Are Won. The 13 Rules of War—From Ancient Greece to the War on Terror.* New York: Crown, 2002.

Allen, Frederick Lewis. *Only Yesterday. An Informal History of the 1920's.* New York: Harper & Row, 1931; New York: Perennial Classics, 2000.

Ash, Timothy Garton. *Free World. America, Europe, and the Surprising Future of the West.* New York: Random House, 2004.

Beard, Charles A., Mary R. Beard, and William Beard. *New Basic History of the United States.* Garden City, N.Y.: Doubleday, 1960.

Berkowitz, Bruce. *The New Face of War. How War Will Be Fought in the 21st Century.* New York: The Free Press, 2003.

Boot, Max. *The Savage Wars of Peace. Small Wars and the Rise of American Power.* New York: Basic Books, 2002.

Chernow, Ron. *Alexander Hamilton.* New York: Penguin Press, 2004.

Chua, Amy. *World on Fire. How Exporting Free Market Democracy Breeds Ethnic Hatred and Global Instability.* New York: Doubleday, 2003.

Churchill, Winston. *The Second World War.* 6 vols. *The Gathering Storm. Their*

Finest Hour. The Grand Alliance. Closing the Ring. The Hinge of Fate. Triumph and Tragedy. Boston: Houghton Mifflin Co., 1948–53.

Cohen, Eliot A. *Supreme Command.* New York: Free Press, 2002.

Ferguson, Niall. *Empire. The Rise and Demise of the British World Order and the Lessons for Global Power.* New York: Basic Books, 2002.

————. *Colossus: The Price of America's Empire.* New York: Penguin Press, 2004.

Fischer, David Hackett. *Albion's Seed. Four British Folkways in America.* New York: Oxford University Press, 1989.

Fromkin, David. *Europe's Last Summer. Who Started the Great War in 1914?* New York: Alfred A. Knopf, 2004.

Frum, David, and Richard Perle. *An End to Evil. How to Win the War on Terror.* New York: Random House, 2003.

Gaddis, John Lewis. *Surprise, Security, and the American Experience.* Cambridge, Mass.: Harvard University Press, 2004.

Halberstam, David. *The Fifties.* New York: Villard Books, 1993.

Herman, Arthur. *How the Scots Invented the Modern World.* New York: Crown, 2001.

Hicks, John D. *The Federal Union. A History of the United States to 1865.* Boston: Houghton Mifflin, 1937.

Hicks, John D., George E. Mowry, and Robert E. Burke. *The American Nation. A History of the United States from 1865 to the Present.* Boston: Houghton Mifflin, 1965.

Hirsh, Michael. *At War with Ourselves. Why America Is Squandering Its Chance to Build a Better World.* New York: Oxford University Press, 2003.

Horowitz, David A., and Peter N. Carroll. *On the Edge. The U.S. in the 20th Century.* Belmont, Calif.: Wadsworth, 1998.

Howard, Michael. *The First World War.* New York: Oxford University Press, 2002.

Huntington, Samuel P. *Who Are We? The Challenges to America's National Identity.* New York: Simon & Schuster, 2004.

James, Lawrence. *The Rise and Fall of the British Empire.* New York: St. Martin's Griffin, 1995.

Kagan, Robert. *Of Paradise and Power. America and Europe in the New World Order.* New York: Alfred A. Knopf, 2003.

Kennedy, Paul. *The Rise and Fall of the Great Powers. Economic Change and Military Conflict from 1500 to 2000.* New York: Random House, 1987.

Kupchan, Charles A. *The End of the American Era. U.S. Foreign Policy and the Geopolitics of the Twenty-first Century.* New York: Alfred A. Knopf, 2003.

Leuchtenburg, William E. *The Perils of Prosperity 1914–1932.* Chicago: University of Chicago Press, 1958, 1993.

Lewis, Bernard. *What Went Wrong? The Clash Between Islam and Modernity in the Middle East.* New York: Oxford University Press, 2002; New York: HarperCollins, 2003.

Leyburn, James G. *The Scotch-Irish.* Chapel Hill: University of North Carolina Press, 1962.

McInerney, Thomas, and Paul Vallely. *Endgame. The Blueprint for Victory in the War on Terror.* Washington, D.C.: Regnery, 2004.

Mead, Walter Russell. *Special Providence. American Foreign Policy and How It Changed the World.* New York: Routledge, 2002.

O'Brien, Patrick Karl, and Armand Clesse, editors. *Two Hegemonies. Britain 1846–1914 and the United States 1941–2001.* Aldershot, England: Ashgate, 2002.

Peters, Ralph. *Beyond Terror.* Mechanicsburg, Pa.: Stackpole Books, 2002.

Power, Samantha. *A Problem from Hell: America and the Age of Genocide.* New York: Basic Books, 2002.

Pratt, Julius W. *A History of United States Foreign Policy.* New York: Prentice-Hall, 1955.

Prestowitz, Clyde. *Rogue Nation. American Unilateralism and the Failure of Good Intentions.* New York: Basic Books, 2003.

Priest, Dana. *The Mission. Waging War and Keeping Peace with America's Military.* New York: W.W. Norton, 2003.

Rabkin, Jeremy. *Why Sovereignty Matters.* Washington, D.C.: AEI Press, 1998.

Ross, Dennis. *The Missing Peace. The Inside Story of the Fight for Middle East Peace.* New York: Farrar, Strauss & Giroux, 2004.

Said, Edward W. *From Oslo to Iraq and the Road Map.* New York: Pantheon, 2004.

Smith, Adam. *The Wealth of Nations.* 2 vols. New York: Penguin Books, 1997, 1999.

Timmerman, Kenneth R. *Preachers of Hate. Islam and the War on America.* New York: Crown Forum, 2003.

Tocqueville, Alexis de. *Democracy in America.* Translated, edited, and with an introduction by Harvey C. Mansfield and Delba Winthrop. Chicago: University of Chicago Press, 2000.

Tuchman, Barbara W. *The Zimmermann Telegram.* New York: Ballantine Books, 1966.

Turner, Frederick Jackson. *The Frontier in American History.* New York: Henry Holt, 1921.

Ullman, Harlan. *Unfinished Business. Afghanistan, the Middle East, and Beyond—Diffusing the Dangers that Threaten America's Security.* New York: Citadel Press, 2002.

ACKNOWLEDGMENTS

I am most grateful to my editor, Jed Donahue, senior editor at Crown Forum, for his wise advice and tremendous contributions in bringing order, clarity, and coherence to this book. I especially want to thank him for suggesting the codas that sum up a number of the chapters.

In addition, I want to thank the rest of the team at Crown Forum for working so hard to see this book into final form, especially production editor Jim Walsh and production manager Jie Yang.

Finally, I wish to thank my wonderful agent, Agnes Birnbaum, for her friendship, her faith in me, and her sage counsel.

INDEX

ABOUT THE AUTHOR

BEVIN ALEXANDER is the author of eight books of military history, including *How Wars Are Won, How Hitler Could Have Won World War II,* and *Lost Victories,* which was named by the *Civil War Book Review* as one of the seventeen books that have most transformed Civil War scholarship. He was an adviser to the Rand Corporation for a recent study on future warfare and was a participant in a recent war game simulation run by the Training and Doctrine Command of the U.S. Army. His battle studies of the Korean War, written during his decorated service as a combat historian, are stored in the National Archives in Washington, D.C. He lives in Bremo Bluff, Virginia.